KYLIE

SONG BY SONG

KYLIE

SONG BY SONG

THE STORIES BEHIND EVERY SONG BY KYLIE MINOGUE, THE PRINCESS OF POP

MARC ANDREWS

FONTHILL

Fonthill Media Language Policy

Fonthill Media publishes in the international English language market. One language edition is published worldwide. As there are minor differences in spelling and presentation, especially with regard to American English and British English, a policy is necessary to define which form of English to use. The Fonthill Policy is to use the form of English native to the author. Marc Andrews was born and educated in Australia; therefore Australian English has been adopted in this publication.

Fonthill Media Limited
Fonthill Media LLC
www.fonthillmedia.com
office@fonthillmedia.com

First published in the United Kingdom and the United States of America 2022

British Library Cataloguing in Publication Data:
A catalogue record for this book is available from the British Library

ISBN 978-1-78155-870-6

Typeset in 10pt on13pt Sabon
Printed and bound in England

Acknowledgements

'Come into My World'

This book has been written to remind the world what a unique, varied, and remarkable back catalogue of music Kylie Minogue has crafted across five decades.

Long after the press prattle about her TV soapie start, love life, and cancer battle have faded, it will be Kylie's songs that endure, having consistently delivered some of the finest pop music of all time. From her early days as the 'Diana Ross' in Stock Aitken Waterman's aptly-named 'hit factory', Kylie's musical odyssey of fifteen studio albums has taken her from 'Princess of Pop' to 'Glastonbury Goddess'. Through acclaimed collaborations with artists as diverse as Nick Cave, Pet Shop Boys, Robbie Williams, Scissor Sisters, Coldplay, Sia, Giorgio Moroder, Dua Lipa, Years & Years, Gloria Gaynor, and London's Royal Philharmonic Orchestra, Kylie has repeatedly proven why she is one of the true global superstars of all time.

To back up that lofty claim, this book details Kylie's complete back catalogue of over 300 songs for all her 'lovers' aka fans.

Thanks to Ian Cole—from 'You Owe Me One' to 'Two for the Price of One'!

Thanks to Daniel Orszewski, Niko Martikas, Michael Wilton, Nic Kat, Trent Titmarsh, Andy 'Kyles' Purcell, and 'the other' Kylie (Martin).

This book is dedicated to Kylie Minogue. The first thing I ever wrote for *Smash Hits Australia* magazine in 1988 was a competition to win one of twenty-five 'I Should Be So Lucky' videos, shoppers. We have never been far apart since. How lucky, lucky, lucky can you get, eh?!

About the Author

'Better the Devil You Know'

Marc Andrews, like Kylie Minogue, was born in Melbourne in the late 1960s. He worked as a journalist at 'pop Bible' *Smash Hits* in Australia (1988–1990), UK *Smash Hits* (1990–1992), and was then editor of the Australian edition (1992–1995).

He is the author of four books: 2022's *Madonna: Song by Song* (Fonthill Media), 2012's *We Need to Talk: My Life as a Doggone Celebrity Journalist* as a Kindle exclusive for Amazon, 2011's *Pop Life: Inside Smash Hits Australia 1984–2007* with David Nichols and Claire Isaac (Affirm Press), and 2010's self-published novel *Revelations: 2 Weeks in Tel Aviv*.

His articles, interviews, and reviews have appeared in numerous magazines around the world over the last four decades, with stints working for 'industry Bible' *Mediaweek*, *The Daily Mail's* MailOnline, and gay glossy *DNA*, where he is currently entertainment editor. He has additionally contributed to *Classic Pop* magazine.

He is also the author of two Australian fanzines—1989's *Madonna: The Unofficial Story* and 1993's *Madonna: The Material Girlie Down Under*.

Based in London, Andrews resides there with his husband, dogs, and poptastic memorabilia. His favourite Kylie song is a tie between 'Better the Devil You Know' and 'Miss a Thing'.

CONTENTS

'Say Something'

Introduction

To know the purest love, the deepest pain
To be lost and found again, and again, and again
These are the dreams of an impossible princess

Dreams (1997)

The media-crowned Princess of Pop and self-styled Impossible Princess, also the name of her deeply intimate and personal 1997 album, Kylie Minogue is now in her fifth decade as a global superstar. Not bad going for someone who got their big break in show business playing a mechanic in an Aussie TV soap opera. Yet while her TV/movie career, her rollercoaster love life, her cancer battle, and even her posterior have kept her in the tabloids and gossip columns, much of this attention has often detracted from the thing she does best—making marvellous pop music. It took years, if not decades, before Kylie finally began to win any kind of critical acclaim for her records, especially having earned her chart stripes as the biggest cog in the Stock Aitken Waterman hit factory at the tail end of the 1980s.

In 1985, Kylie scored a lead role on *The Henderson Kids* series and later with her wages recorded her first demos (see Appendix I). A year later, she took on the role of tomboy mechanic Charlene in another Australian TV series, *Neighbours*, quickly becoming a major ratings draw, especially when romantically paired on-screen with her real-life, yet secret boyfriend Jason Donovan. In 1987, Kylie got up on stage at an Aussie Rules football club charity event to perform Sonny & Cher's 'I Got You Babe' with actor John Waters before returning for an encore of Little Eva's 'The Loco-Motion'. After passing on her two years earlier, Mushroom Records signed Kylie for her first single: a no-brainer—'Locomotion'—which became the biggest Australian hit of 1987. Mushroom also distributed the bulk of the PWL releases down under and as a favour to Kylie's Aussie record company, and boss Michael Gudinski (who sadly died in 2021), she was allotted studio time with hit makers Stock Aitken Waterman during a London visit later that year to promote *Neighbours*, now a British TV ratings sensation. Released in late 1987, 'I Should Be So Lucky' became Kylie's first UK chart-topper and set her music career as a global pop star in motion. She became so big so quickly she soon had to choose between TV fame and pop stardom, wisely opting for the later.

Her first album, *Kylie*, released in 1988, became a multi-million seller. Written and produced by SAW, the trio made writing big boisterous pop hits almost too easy, especially when sung by 'Smiley' Minogue, as the pop press christened her. The album spawned three more smash hits—'Got to Be Certain', 'Je ne sais pas pourquoi', and a re-recorded version of 'The Loco-Motion'—but Kylie's biggest hit of that year would be a Christmas #1 duet with Jason Donovan (who had subsequently joined the SAW stable) on loved-up ballad 'Especially for You'. Kylie also scored major chart successes in the US, Japan, Europe, and continued to be a big seller at home in Australia, despite no radio airplay and plenty of tall poppy syndrome.

Her second album, *Enjoy Yourself*, came just over a year after her first, and by the time of its release in October 1989, already boasted two more hits—'Hand on Your Heart' and 'Wouldn't Change a Thing'. Kylie undertook not only her first major tour, in Japan and the UK, but her first major movie role in *The Delinquents*. *Enjoy Yourself*, which became another million-selling album, spawned two more singles—'Never Too Late' and a cover of the 1958 weepie 'Tears on My Pillow', included in *The Delinquents*. Although the movie did well in Australia and the UK, it failed to get a US release and Kylie's music career subsequently stalled there.

Not that Kylie was probably too concerned, she was in love! Having moved on from Jason Donovan, Kylie was now embroiled in a heady romance with one of the biggest rock stars of the 1980s, Michael Hutchence, lead singer of Australian band INXS. When it came time for a new Kylie single in 1990, a conspicuous transformation had taken place. Just as SAW shifted their signature sound from pop-hi-NRG to pop-house, Kylie seized control of her image, and on 'Better the Devil You Know', her transition from pop star to pop artist commenced. Her third album, *Rhythm of Love*, released in November 1990, contained four of SAW's finest pop songs—'Better the Devil You Know', 'Step Back in Time', 'What Do I Have to Do', and 'Shocked'—and all became massive hits. Kylie, meanwhile, nursed a broken heart after splitting with Hutchence and threw herself into her work, including co-writing songs, albeit not with SAW initially.

Her fourth album, *Let's Get to It*, was released less than a year after her third, but with SAW now just reduced to Stock Waterman and Kylie clearly wanting more control, not just over her image but her music too. The album's biggest hit, third single 'Give Me Just a Little More Time' in January 1992, was a breezy '60s cover, but the more interesting moments on the album touched on rave culture, pushing SW, and thus Kylie, into sonically more adventurous arenas. Although her tours were sell-outs both in Europe and at home in Australia, Kylie wanted more. She terminated her contract with Pete Waterman's PWL label with a *Greatest Hits* album, spawning two more smaller hits.

In a bold move, Kylie signed to trendy dance label deConstruction. After two years of trying, discarding, and retrying styles, her fifth album, *Kylie Minogue*, was released in 1994. Launched with the stunning, career-defining 'Confide in Me', Kylie blasted to the top of the charts on her own terms. After second single, 'Put Yourself in My Place' peaked at #11 in both the UK and Australia, however, her new label panicked. A third single, a re-recorded version of 'Where Is the Feeling?', arrived seven months later and made less of an impact than it should have. In her personal life, after a reported dalliance with Lenny Kravitz, Kylie, now in her mid-twenties, became attached to French artist Stéphane Sednaoui, while her blossoming relationship with 'gay husband' William Baker led to him becoming her creative director and helping evolve her style.

It took three more years until Kylie released her next album, *Impossible Princess*. Despite critical acclaim and fan love, 'IndieKylie' failed to fly in the charts with lead single 'Some Kind of Bliss' missing the Top 20 in both the UK and Australia. Yet with all of the album's songs co-written by Kylie, it signified she not only deserved to be taken seriously as a songwriter, but was now taking this part of her job seriously too. After deConstruction dropped her after just two albums, Kylie went out on the road in Australia, reinventing herself as a top-line touring drawcard, and releasing the *Intimate & Live* album on her Oz label Mushroom.

Signing a new deal in 1999 for territories outside Australia with Parlophone, the brief was to bring Kylie back to pop. She began the new millennium with a first-rate #1 single, 'Spinning Around', followed by a slew of hits ('On a Night Like This', 'Kids' with Robbie Williams, and 'Please Stay') from her seventh studio album, *Light Years*. Of the fourteen tracks, Kylie co-wrote ten, providing the perfect launch pad for what would become the most successful period of her career and give her a second slice of American success.

Released in September 2001, 'Can't Get You Out of My Head', changed Kylie's career forever. A signature song and an instant classic pop tune, it also became one of the biggest-selling singles of all time. It granted Kylie her first US Top 10 hit in over a decade, helping the accompanying *Fever* album sell over 6 million copies globally. Three more hits followed—'In Your Eyes', 'Love at First Sight', and 'Come into My World'—as did the mammoth KylieFever2002 tour.

Just over two years later, *Body Language*, which bent the boundaries of pop, not to mention PopKylie, was unveiled via sexy lead single 'Slow' pushing plenty of buttons with its racy video. A year later in November 2004, *Ultimate Kylie*, a huge selling compilation of tracks across her three UK labels was issued, spearheaded by the Scissor Sisters co-write 'I Believe in You'. A mammoth tour, Showgirl: The Greatest Hits Tour, commenced the following year.

Tragedy struck midway through the concert series, however, when Kylie was diagnosed with cancer. Her career was put on hold for eighteen months before thankfully resuming after she went into remission and got the all-clear. Kylie celebrated her recovery with the newly-renamed Showgirl: The Homecoming Tour in late 2006.

Her tenth album, the aptly-titled *X*, was not, as many expected, Kylie's big statement album about her life-changing battle, but edgy, almost *avant-garde* pop/dance. Although first single '2 Hearts' did well, the rest of the singles suffered, especially in light of a leak of much of the album's material, including forty-plus demos. Before she got to her next album, Kylie toured extensively with the KylieX2008 concert and the following year hit North America for the very first time on the nine-date For You, for Me tour.

Produced by Stuart Price, Kylie's eleventh album, *Aphrodite*, was released in 2010 a few weeks after another career-defining hit, 'All the Lovers'. The following year's Aphrodite: Les Folies Tour marked another high point creatively for Team Kylie. A year later in 2012, celebrating her twenty-five years in the music business, Kylie put on her Anti Tour—only B-sides, album tracks, and unreleased tracks—as a valentine to her fans in a year she christened K25.

It would be four years between albums of new material, though 2012's *The Abbey Road Sessions*, which revamped songs from her back catalogue as jazz/big band numbers, was a critical and commercial success. The patchy 'Kiss Me Once' (2014), executive produced by Sia, was Kylie's first without long-time manager Terry Blamey as she focused on restarting her acting career. Kylie also seemed perpetually trapped in a loop of short-lived romantic affairs that inevitably ended in tears, if not tabloid prattle.

Shoring up her fan base, Kylie released the well-received *Kylie Christmas* album in 2015, repackaging it a year later as *Kylie Christmas: Snow Queen Edition*. Leaving Parlophone, and without a major label, Kylie tried out a number of different styles, including her experimental 'Kylie + Garibay' EPs, soundtrack work, and more club-based recordings with the likes of Giorgio Moroder, Jake Shears, and a briefly returning Stuart Price.

With a new major label in BMG under her own Darenote imprint, Kylie debuted *Golden* at #1 in the UK and Australia in 2018, a month before her fiftieth birthday. It was so titled because, as Kylie was keen to point out, 'we're not young, we're not old, we're golden'. After almost two decades of albums with reduced songwriting input, the country-tinged *Golden* was completely co-written by 'Min' (her nickname). Taking to the legends stage of Glastonbury the following year to promote her #1 compilation *Step Back in Time: The Definitive Collection*, fourteen years after cancelling her appearance due to her cancer diagnosis, Kylie was a solid gold triumph. She made history as the most viewed TV performance ever from the most revered festival. A year later 2020's dancefloor darling *Disco* followed, again totally co-written (not to mention self-engineered during lockdown) and boasting the best reviews of Kylie's career. Beating first week sales by younger rivals Lady Gaga and Dua Lipa, and becoming her seventh Australian #1 album, *Disco* also made history by affording Kylie the honour of being the first female artist in the UK to own a #1 album (her eighth) in five decades.

I once asked her many years ago if she ever saw an end in sight to making music: 'Not as yet,' Kylie replied. 'I always say I'm not going to be doing this when I'm 50, 60, whatever, but I also can't imagine not having music in my life.' And that is why this book is a celebration of our very possible Princess of Pop's music, songs, career, and artistry and why we still cannot get Kylie out of our heads. 1-2-3 now … la la la, la-la-la-la-la, la la la …

About Kylie's Recordings 'Sweet Music'

From the time of her first Australian release on Festival Mushroom Records and UK release on PWL Records, both in 1987, Kylie has recorded and officially released over 300 songs. They are spread across fifteen studio albums *(Kylie, Enjoy Yourself, Rhythm of Love, Let's Get to It, Kylie Minogue, Impossible Princess, Light Years, Fever, Body Language, X, Aphrodite, Kiss Me Once, Kylie Christmas/Snow Queen Edition, Golden,* and *Disco/Guest List Edition)*, thirteen compilations (*Greatest Hits* (PWL), *Hits+, Confide in Me, Greatest Hits* (BMG), *Greatest Hits 87–99, Artists Collection, Ultimate Kylie, Confide in Me: The Irresistible Kylie, Hits, The Best of Kylie Minogue, The Abbey Road Sessions, Confide in Me* (repackaged double album), and *Step Back in Time: The Definitive Collection*), eight live albums (*Intimate and Live, KylieFever2002, Showgirl, Showgirl: Homecoming Live, Live in New York, Aphrodite Les Folies: Live in London, Kiss Me Once Live at the SSE Hydro,* and *Golden Live in Concert*), twelve remix albums (*Kylie's Remixes, Kylie's Remixes: Vol. 2, Kylie's Non-Stop History 50+1, Mixes, Impossible Remixes, Greatest Remix Hits 1, Greatest Remix Hits 2, Greatest Remix Hits 3, Greatest Remix Hits 4, Boombox, Essential Mixes,* and *Disco: Extended Mixes*), two box sets (*Kylie: The Albums 2000–2010 and K25 Time Capsule*), nine EPs (*Live and Other Sides, Other Sides, Money Can't Buy, Darling, Pink Sparkle, A Kylie Christmas, Performance, Sleepwalker*, and *Kylie + Garibay*), and a number of non-album B-sides, soundtrack contributions, collaborations, charity tracks, and songs where she has received an artist credit.

All songs listed in this book are solo works by Kylie unless otherwise indicated. Because so many individual Kylie tracks have variations on their running length due to edits, radio edits, and various remix edits, the listings in this book generally refer to the standard album release duration/length, or their according single variation if applicable.

All songs have generally been listed chronologically in order of their release in each corresponding book chapter/era.

Only songs that have been officially released in some capacity by a *bona fide* record label (and on a few occasions on DVD) are considered part of the official *Kylie Song by Song* inventory, with the exception of the chapter on the *X* album leaks. Any unreleased, unofficial, widely reported/rumoured Kylie songs/demos of note are included in Appendix I. Any tracks only featured in her live concerts, or live albums/CDs, or TV performances, are included in Appendix II.

1

Glad to be 'Getting Closer' in Oz (1985–1987)

'A World Without Music' (Hearing Aid)

Festival Records: K-9868 **Single release:** October 1985 (Australia only)
Writers: Ricky May, Peter Sullivan, Jim Burnett
Producers: Greg Pethwig (sic), Peter Sullivan, Ricky May

Two years prior to 'Locomotion' and her role in *Neighbours*, this Australian charity single exists as Kylie's first musical recording. Credited to Hearing Aid, *à la* Band Aid, 'A World Without Music' was conceived by Kiwi entertainer May for Channel 10's Deafness Foundation telethon featuring local music and TV celebrities. Kylie, representing her then-TV show *The Henderson Kids*, scores a three-word solo. It is an inauspicious start, but she is certainly the standout.

Vid Bit!

A not-so-slick clip (director unknown) filmed during the recording session provides a fascinating, if slightly frightening, time capsule of mid-1980s Australasia. Fright wigs ahoy!

'Locomotion'

Mushroom Records: K319 **Single release:** July 1987 (Australia/NZ only)
Writers: Gerry Goffin, Carole King
Producer: Mike Duffy

Long before British hit makers Stock Aitken Waterman added Kylie to their poptastic roster, she had already topped the charts in her native Australia with a cover version of this music staple. Originally a #1 hit in 1962 for Little Eva (and again in the 1970s for Grand Funk Railroad), Kylie's 'Locomotion' chugged in after she warbled it in 1986 during a football charity event in her Melbourne hometown. PWL engineer Duffy, a Canadian on a working holiday in Oz, was given permission by Pete Waterman from the UK company HQ to produce the song in the style of SAW. Released two weeks after huge ratings for Charlene and Scott's wedding on *Neighbours*, 'Locomotion' topped the charts for months on end in Oz, becoming the biggest selling single of 1987. 'This song became my first single in Australia,' Kylie reminisced in 2020, 'and paved the way for a lifetime of music!'

Vid Bit!

Director: Chris Langman

The original Australian 'Locomotion' video finds Kylie blatantly engaging in product placement, swanning off on a private jet at Essendon airport, dancing like it is an '80s aerobics class and being her loveable sweet self. Her brother Brendan also has a brief cameo.

Remix Fix!

The Chugga-Motion Mix and Girl Meets Boy Mix were part of the Mushroom 12″ release.

'Glad to Be Alive'

Single release: July 1987 (Australian/NZ only B-side for 'Locomotion' single)
Writers: Claude Carranza, Craig Harnath
Producers: Craig Harnath, Mike Duffy

The original Aussie 'Locomotion' B-side was written by two members of local band and label mates Kids in the Kitchen. Considering 'Locomotion' was such a big Oz hit, there were some serious royalty cheques to be had for its B-side's composers. The perfunctory, if hastily hammered out, 'Glad to Be Alive' was later deemed a feel-good anthem by Myfizzypop blog who insisted 'there is some air guitar magnificence that let you get your stresses out and let your freak flag fly'. Gladly!

'Getting Closer'

PWL Empire: PWL6 **Single release:** November 1987 (B-side to 'Locomotion' in Sweden and Italy)
Writers: Stock Aitken Waterman
Producer: Mike Duffy

Originally planned as the follow-up to 'Locomotion' in 1987, and touted as such in *Smash Hits Australia* magazine, 'Getting Closer' was never to be, superseded by the pop behemoth to come that was 'I Should Be So Lucky'. Originally a minor UK hit in 1985, the soulful *Getting Closer* was—join the dots here—written by Stock Aitken Waterman for British female funk/pop artist Haywoode. How different would Kylie's career have been if 'Getting Closer' had been released as her second single? Not so lucky, lucky, lucky, perhaps.

2

Kylie Album/'Especially for You' Single (1988)

Kylie

Current Edition: PWL Records KYLIE 1
Originally released: July 1988
Side A

'I Should Be So Lucky'	3:25
'The Loco-Motion'	3:14
'Je ne sais pas pourquoi'	4:02
'It's No Secret'	3:58
'Got to Be Certain'	3:21

Side B

'Turn It into Love'	3:37
'I Miss You'	3:16
'I'll Still Be Loving You'	3:49
'Look My Way'	3:37
'Love at First Sight'	3:12

'I Should Be So Lucky'

PWL Records: PWL 8 **Single release:** December 1987 **Album:** *Kylie*
Writers/Producers: Stock Aitken Waterman

Kylie was lucky, lucky, lucky indeed with this, her first international, and second Australian single. Written by SAW as a favour to Kylie's Oz music label, 'I Should Be So Lucky' was assembled by the hit makers in under an hour at London's PWL Studios.

> 'I got a phone call from Mike Stock at the office who asked if there was something I had forgotten to tell him,' Waterman recounted. 'A small Antipodean called Kylie Minogue?' prompted Mike, 'Oh yes, I forgot, she's in town.' Mike said, 'No she's in reception!' I apologised for messing up and said we'll have to drop the whole project. Mike said, 'We can't, she's expecting to do something with us.' 'She should be so lucky,' I replied. 'Great,' Mike said, 'That'll do. 'I Should Be So Lucky'. Can we write some lyrics?'

'ISBSL' was an irresistible pop concoction, which Aitken conceded borrowed heavily from Madonna's 'Into the Groove'. 'Soap star in "quite good" single shock!' ran the headline in *Smash Hits*. A pop/hi-NRG hybrid it topped the UK, West German, and Australian charts, as well as reaching the US Top 40. In 2002, an unofficial musical, called *'ISBSL'*, featuring twenty-five Kylie hits, debuted briefly in Melbourne (though it is a likely, likely, likely title for an imminent official musical mooted by Team Kylie). That same year in 2002, Pete Waterman divulged 'ISBSL', was inspired by German composer Johann Pachelbel's 'Canon in D Major'. Classically lucky, indeed!

Vid Bit!

Director: Chris Langman

Filmed in Melbourne on a day off from *Neighbours*, Kylie is her fizzy tizzy self as she paces around a bedroom, giggles in a bubble bath, and pouts in front of a girlie chalkboard. A wildly windswept additional video, filmed for UK TV, had Kylie precariously crossing the Sydney Harbour Bridge in an open-top BMW. Unluckily for her perm, it was an awfully windy day!

Remix Fix!

In 2009, as part of the iTunes PWL archive release, seven mixes were released. The Fever2002 studio tour version of 'I Should Be So Lucky/Dreams' is also considered an official version.

'Got to Be Certain'

PWL Records: PWL 12 **Single release:** May 1988 **Album:** *Kylie*
Writers/Producers: Stock Aitken Waterman

Kylie's second international, and third Australian, single certainly had hit written all over it—#2 in the UK (held off the top spot by Wet Wet Wet's charity version of The Beatles' 'With a Little Help from My Friends') and #1 in Oz. The instantly appealing 'Got to Be Certain' had first been offered by SAW to English teen model, and Rolling Stones' Bill Wyman's teen wife, Mandy Smith, to record before being shelved due to her inability to get a leg up in the UK charts. When

'I Should Be So Lucky' became a runaway hit in early 1988 even the hit factory bosses themselves were unprepared. 'Someone said: "What's the follow-up?" We didn't have one,' Stock admitted, 'so I went out to Australia at the start of 1988 ... she would be working on *Neighbours* from 5am, then come to record with me at 6pm.' One of those songs was 'GTBC'.

Vid Bit!

Director: Chris Langman

Kylie's later complaints about her early career focused a lot on the 'Got to Be Certain' video—in particular sitting astride a merry-go-round that plainly hadn't been checked by OH&S in some time. There were a number of variations of the 'GTBC' video for different territories.

Remix Fix!

In 2009, as part of the iTunes PWL archive digital EP, five versions of 'GTBC' were released.

'The Loco-Motion'

PWL Records: PWLT 14 **Single release:** July 1988 **Album:** *Kylie*
Writers: Gerry Goffin, Carole King
Producers: Stock Aitken Waterman

If we chug-chug-chug our minds back a little, it is worth reiterating that it was Kylie herself who fast-tracked her recording career with 'The Loco-Motion'—not Pete Waterman, not SAW, and not any music company Svengali. For its UK debut, Kylie's Oz smash was reswizzled, proofed, and, importantly, made into a Waterman-friendly version, chugging up to #2 in the UK and #3 in the US. 'The Loco-Motion' still stands as Kylie's biggest single on American soil. With her third hit (and fourth in Australia) in a row, Kylie quickly became anointed the Princess of Pop. Her debut *Kylie* album, released the same month in July 1988, hit #1 in the UK, #2 Australia and #53 US, selling over 5 million copies worldwide, remaining her biggest-selling album until 2001.

Vid Bit!

Why fix something that ain't broken? Apart from a few re-edits, and excising the product placement, the new 'Loco-motion' video was not so dissimilar to the Oz original.

Remix Fix!

The 2009 iTunes PWL archive digital release rolled out eleven remix versions including Tony King's Oz Tour Mix ingeniously based around Lil Louis' throbbing and saucy 'French Kiss' hit.

'Je ne sais pas pourquoi'

PAWL Records: PWL21 **Single release:** October 1988 **Album:** *Kylie*
Writers/Producers: Stock Aitken Waterman

Kylie was on a roll hit-wise now as SAW entered their 'imperial phase'. Waterman much later acknowledged 'Je ne sais pas pourquoi' was inspired by some children from Wolverhampton and their fascination with language. It was also, pop kids, the fourth single from *Kylie* and another UK #2 hit, despite *Smash Hits* calling it a 'clumsy plodding ballad'. Kylie's Australian record company retitled it 'I Still Love You', but that love did not linger as it became the first Kylie single to miss the Top 10 there. It was also given a US single release, with the Australian title, but failed to chart. Because of doubts over whether 'Je ne sais pas pourquoi' was a strong enough single on its own in the UK, initially it was pushed as a double A-side alongside the more up-tempo 'Made in Heaven'. It was, *merci*.

Vid Bit!

Director: Chris Langman

Kylie speaks French (*mon dieu*!) and acts her way through some phony rain, a cashmere sweater, and static hair. 'Je ne sais pas pourquoi' is definitely a step up in sophistication in styling, set and special effects (colour with black and white) with a 1950s-era nod at her then upcoming role in *The Delinquents* movie.

Remix Fix!

Dave Ford contributed the Moi Non Plus Mix, while Phil Harding's much more hardcore The Revolutionary Mix might just qualify as Kylie's first true club/house remix. In the 2009 iTunes PWL Archive digital release ten versions of 'Je ne sais pas pourquoi' were unfurled.

'It's No Secret'

Mushroom Records: 9 27651-7 **Single release:** December 1988 (Australia/NZ/Japan/US) **Album:** *Kylie*
Writers/Producers: Stock Aitken Waterman

Recorded in Melbourne at the same time as 'Got to Be Certain' and 'Turn It into Love', 'It's No Secret' was Kylie's third American single and third Top 40 hit there, but only just. The loping melancholy ballad was presumably picked because it was not as 'euro-pop' sounding as everything else on *Kylie*. The US was the only territory where it was released (apart from Japan and a brief release before being withdraw in Australia/NZ), with the rest of the world scoring mega-duet 'Especially for You' instead.

Vid Bit!

Director: Chris Langman

Shot in the north of Australia at Port Douglas, Kylie ditches her pretty but lame acting (in all senses) boyfriend and heads to the ritzy Mirage resort before leaving for a long walk home with no train in sight. It's cheesy and clear product placement again, so hopefully Kylie got a free stay.

Remix Fix!

In 2009, as part of the iTunes PWL Archive digital release, seven versions were issued.

'Turn It into Love'

PWL Records/Alfa International: 07B7-2 **Single release:** December 1988 (Japan)
Album: *Kylie*
Writers/Producers: Stock Aitken Waterman

A firm fan favourite, one of Mike Stock's personal favourites and a somewhat forgotten classic from her debut album, the snappy 'Turn It into Love' earned a release as a single in Japan, topping the charts there for ten weeks. That allowed another SAW artist, the self-proclaimed 'Queen of Hi-NRG' Hazell Dean, to turn it into a Top 30 UK hit in 1988 as the lead single from her SAW-produced second album, *Always*. In Japan, a Japanese-language version of 'Turn It into Love' by female duo Wink also became a huge hit, much to Pete Waterman's later surprise.

Vid Bit!

Sequences from previous Kylie videos were origami-ed into a video for the Japanese market.

'I Miss You'

Release: July 1988 **Album:** *Kylie*
Writers/Producers: Stock Aitken Waterman

Despite PWL's avowed motto of 'all killer no fillers', this is SAW on autopilot, though Kylie gives a polished, professional vocal performance, better than the somewhat hackneyed lyrics, regulation key changes, and plodding tempo deserve. Little wonder she complained in an interview with the *LA Times* in 1988 'the album still isn't me'. In 2002, as well as revealing 'I Should Be So Lucky' was based on a classical work by Pachelbel, Waterman claimed the majority of the SAW catalogue was indebted to nineteenth-century German composer Richard Wagner. The 'brilliant' 'I Miss You' was, however, *Smash Hits*' preferred pick for the *Kylie* album's final UK single.

'I'll Still Be Loving You'

Release: July 1988 **Album:** *Kylie*
Writers/Producers: Stock Aitken Waterman

A welcome downtempo interlude that again scores a strong Kylie vocal, 'I'll Still Be Loving You' does indeed sound like it was written, and recorded, in a matter of minutes. 'Stock Aitken Waterman and the Hit Factory weren't so far removed from my role in *Neighbours*,' Kylie wrote in her 2002 book *La La La*. 'Learn your lines, red light on, perform lines, no time for questions, promote the product *et voila*!' In 2009 as part of the iTunes PWL Archive three versions of 'ISBLY' (original, instrumental, and backing track) were released with 'The Loco-Motion' package.

'Look My Way'

Release: July 1988 **Album:** *Kylie*
Writers/Producers: Stock Aitken Waterman

This sparkly pop number, originally written for SAW artist Haywoode, is widely recognised as one of Kylie's best early vocal performances. She herself noted that compared to the rest of her double-tracked voice on the *Kylie* album 'Look My Way' is where she convinced Pete Waterman to make it sound 'more like me than any song on the album'. To that end, Kylie performed it on Australian variety show *Hey Hey It's Saturday* to quell the 'singing budgie' criticism and prove she could cut it live. Luckily this way cool clip (including funny band hats!) is up on YouTube.

'Love at First Sight'

Release: July 1988 **Album:** *Kylie*
Writers/Producers: Stock Aitken Waterman

Not to be confused with her hit of the same name from the *Fever* era, the final track on the *Kylie* album was reportedly originally intended for SAW label mate Sinitta. Kylie nonetheless carries her version of 'Love at First Sight' off with cheery aplomb, irrepressible charm, and a throbbing bassline that rescues 'LAFS' from being forgotten about as the final song on side two of the album. For an interview with *Songwriter* magazine in 2015, Waterman admitted when it came to allowing their artists songwriting input, 'we didn't even have time to write our songs, let alone getting their opinions'. Kylie, incidentally, co-wrote 2001's 'Love at First Sight'.

'Made in Heaven'

Single release: July 1988 (B-side of 'Je ne sais pas pourquoi') **Album:** *Kylie*
Writers/Producers: Stock Aitken Waterman

Not included on *Kylie* and initially promoted as a double A-side with 'Je ne sais pas pourquoi', this was a much dancier knees-up than anything Kyle had tackled previously. although *Smash Hits* deemed it 'utterly average'. 'Made in Heaven' proved SAW were clearly trying to move with the times, leaning more heavily towards the emerging house music sound than the hi-NRG one of old. Pete Hammond's Maid In England Mix made a big heavenly stride to clubdom. After being forgotten about for decades, a ballad/film version of the divine 'MIH' materialised during Kylie's 2007 *White Diamond* documentary, before becoming the second song, and first big audience singalong, during 2012's Anti Tour.

Vid Bit!

Director: Chris Langman

Years before Madonna co-opted the cone bra Kylie wore a slightly less voluptuous version.

Remix Fix!

In 2009, for the iTunes PWL Archive digital release, six versions of 'MIH' were issued.

'Especially for You' (Kylie Minogue and Jason Donovan)

PWL Records: PWL 24 **Single release:** November 1988 **Album:** *Ten Good Reasons*
Writers/Producers: Stock Aitken Waterman

Every big artist needs at least one killer ballad early on and after getting close with 'Je ne sais pas pourquoi' Kylie and SAW finally nailed it on this big, shiny, gooey valentine of a duet. Originally asked mid-1988 about the possibility of a duet between Kylie and *Neighbours* co-star Jason by this author for *Smash Hits Australia*, Waterman laughed it off. He obviously had second thoughts, especially in light of Kylie and Jason's TV romance becoming a real-life, albeit unconfirmed, relationship. A UK #1 and Australian #2, 'Especially for You' remained Kylie's biggest-selling single in the UK until 'Can't Get You Out of My Head' some thirteen years later. Kylie and Jason have only performed 'Especially for You' twice since 1989 and both times in London—at 2012's celebratory *Hit Factory Live* concert (*The Guardian* wrote of Kylie 'it was like seeing the Queen turn up at your child's end of term school play') and in 2018 at her headline *Live in Hyde Park* show (though Jason was Kylie's dance partner not duet partner during this particular outing).

Vid Bit!

Director: Chris Langman

Will they, won't they? Spoiler alert: in the end Kylie and Jason do get to meet up. Filmed on the coldest November day in Sydney in over a century, Kylie and Jason also shot a short cameo which was used at the end of SAW's 1988 acid house 'SS Paparazzi' video. This would not be the last time Kylie and Jason would appear in a video together; in 1989, Kylie's legs and backside are featured (uncredited) at the end of Jason's 'Everyday (I Love You More)' video.

Remix Fix!

The extended version bumped up 'EFY' by almost a minute. The 2009 iTunes PWL Archive digital bundle featured five more versions (various extended, instrumental, and backing tracks).

'All I Wanna Do Is Make You Mine' (Kylie Minogue and Jason Donovan)

Single release: November 1988 (B-side of 'Especially for You')

Writers/Producers: Stock Aitken Waterman

Here SAW boldly borrow from 1978's Olivia Newton John/John Travolta duet 'You're the One I Want' from the *Grease* soundtrack. The B-side to the 'Especially for You' single bops along in a '50s skiffle-style compete with horns and a chorus that John Farrar, writer of 'You're the One I Want', could have sued for royalties from. Two new songs especially for Xmas? Nice work, SAW!

Remix Fix!

Too much of a good thing? Never, especially if it is Kylie and Jason together at last! Both 'Especially for You' and 'All I Wanna Do Is Make You Mine' were extended by SAW for a 12″ release. This would not be the last song K&J would sing on either, while the swansong of *Neighbours* occurred in 2022.

3

Enjoy Yourself Album (1989)

Enjoy Yourself

Current Edition: PWL Records KYLIE 2 T
Originally released: October 1989
Side A

'Hand on Your Heart'	3:51
'Wouldn't Change a Thing'	3:14
'Never Too Late'	3:22
'Nothing to Lose'	3:21
'Tell Tale Signs'	2:26
Side B	
'My Secret Heart'	2:41
'I'm Over Dreaming (Over You)'	3:23
'Tears on My Pillow'	2:30
'Heaven and Earth'	3:44
'Enjoy Yourself'	3:45

'Hand on Your Heart'

PWL Records: PWL 35 **Single release:** April 1989 **Album:** *Enjoy Yourself*
Writers/Producers: Stock Aitken Waterman

The lead single for Kylie's sophomore album was another brisk, perky pop tune that was pure teen trauma. Little wonder 'Hand on Your Heart' reached #1 in the UK and returned her to the Top 5 in her homeland. Stock revealed in 2020 that its R&B bassline was inspired by Ten City's glorious house anthem 'That's the Way

Love Is' that same year, although Aiken disputed this claiming it came from The Isley Brothers' 'This Old Heart of Mine' from 1966. In 2006, Swedish-Argentinian folkie José González released an acclaimed acoustic chill out version, which likely inspired Kylie's refashioned version for 2012's *Abbey Road Sessions* album.

Vid Bit!

Director: Chris Langman

This might just be the last dollop of teen Kylie, filmed in her hometown of Melbourne in March before her twentieth birthday in May, with her transformation to corrupted womanhood well under way courtesy of Michael Hutchence. If those heels Kylie stomps about here could talk!

Remix Fix!

Phil Harding's The Great Aorta Mix opens with a thirty-second Kylie acapella, while Dave Ford's Heartache Mix is heavily influenced by Shep Pettibone's mixes of the time for Janet Jackson, Duran Duran and Madonna. The 2009 iTunes PWL Archive digital bundles also included six versions by WIP (Steve Walker and Pete Waterman's son Paul who died in 2005).

'Just Wanna Love You'

Single release: April 1989 (B-side of 'Hand on Your Heart')
Writers/Producers: Stock Aitken Waterman

Here is another of Kylie's long-lost B-sides and in some ways a forerunner to 1991's 'Word is Out' in both style and lyrical substance. The fact the lyrics appeared to be a slightly sanitised, if still risqué, take on Kylie keen to enjoy anonymous sex ('There's nothing fatal in attraction/I'm just looking for some action') might have been the main contributing factor to it being hidden away. As part of the 2009 iTunes PWL Archive digital release three versions of 'Just Wanna Love You' (original, instrumental, and backing track) were included in the 'Hand on Your Heart' bundle.

'Wouldn't Change a Thing'

PWL Records: PWL 42 **Single release:** July 1989 **Album:** *Enjoy Yourself*
Writers/Producers: Stock Aitken Waterman

Recorded at the same time as 'Hand on Your Heart' and kept as its follow-up single, this big Northern Hemisphere summer hit (#2 UK) also went top ten at home (#6) and took that familiar 'funky drummer' drumbeat sample and turned it into one of Kylie's best, and best-remembered, singles of the era. 'The song says that even if no one else in the world can understand what you see in someone, who cares?' Kylie explained about 'Wouldn't Change a Thing'. 'It's what you believe in that really matters. You shouldn't have to change for anyone.' That said, Kylie was undergoing the biggest change of her career by dating Michael Hutchence, lead vox of Australia's biggest act, INXS. 'I'm not ashamed for the world to see' she sings. Quite.

Vid Bit!

Director: Pete Cornish

Yes, there is sunshine—even though it was filmed in London, her first video made outside of Australia—and Kylie in a frilly bra and denim shorts. There is definitely something else going on in the 'Wouldn't Change a Thing' video with more bellybutton, more confidence, and, most important of all, expensive hair. Kylie is also rubbish at putting deck chairs up, it's official!

Remix Fix!

The 2009 iTunes PWL Archive digital EP bundle for 'Wouldn't Change a Thing' included the percolating Your Thang, loved-up funky Espagna and Yoyo's house piano-driven 12″ mixes.

'Never Too Late'

PWL Records: PWL 45 **Single release:** October 1989 **Album:** *Enjoy Yourself*
Writers/Producers: Stock Aitken Waterman

As the third single from *Enjoy Yourself*, 'Never Too Late' completed the trifecta of pop bops fans had come to expect from the Aussie teen queen. Everything else that would come after this, even her next rash of SAW productions would be markedly different, if not more markedly mature. Chartwise 'NTL' proved something of a disappointment, peaking at #4 and ending her chart run of #1s and #2s in the UK. In her native Australia it missed the Top Ten altogether. The upside was Kylie's boyfriend Michael Hutchence declared it his favourite of her songs. Perhaps it was the song's opening line, 'Why can't you see that I'm still mad about you'? 'NTL' later attained immortal status after being uttered in a line of dialogue from the BBC's *Dr Who* in 2006.

Vid Bit!

Director: Pete Cornish

Winner of an Australian Logie Award for Most Popular Music Video, 'Never Too Late' is classic Kylie in goofy, if not overtly, campy mode hitting the dress-up box in serious fashion.

Remix Fix!

For the 2009 iTunes PWL Archive digital bundle five versions of 'Never Too Late' were included.

'I'm Over Dreaming (Over You)'

Release: October 1989 **Album:** *Enjoy Yourself*
Writers/Producers: Stock Aitken Waterman

'This song is a celebration,' Kylie told *Smash Hits*. 'This girl knows what she wants and has the courage to stand up and say so. It's about not being afraid and not clinging to old ways as a sense of security.' In 2012, the radiant 'I'm Over Dreaming (Over You)' finally got some love at last when Kylie performed it with gusto on her Anti Tour. On 2015's *Enjoy Yourself* Deluxe Edition Dave Ford's Mel & Kim-like Extended Version and house party 7" Remix were included.

'Nothing to Lose'

Release: October 1989 **Album:** *Enjoy Yourself*
Writers/Producers: Stock Aitken Waterman

Back on form with another house-inflected dance-pop track, 'Nothing to Lose' has a cosy familiarity to the superlative material SAW bestowed upon Donna Summer for her *Another Place Another Time* album released that same year. Kylie called 'Nothing to Lose' 'a great dance track, very strong, happy, real Stock Aitken & Waterman.' Should it have been the third single not 'Never Too Late'? 'NTL' is definitely one of the best non-singles from Kylie's early résumé.

'Tell Tale Signs'

Release: October 1989 **Album:** *Enjoy Yourself*
Writers/Producers: Stock Aitken Waterman

In 1989, Kylie performed 'Tell Tale Signs' live on Australia's *Hey Hey It's Saturday* again proving she was not merely an accomplished vocalist, but a great live performer (especially considering she had just jetted in). The song's 'bluesy feel', as Kylie called it, was one she recorded in the midst of her liaison with Michael Hutchence, filming *The Delinquents* and prepping for her first big tour the following year. Check YouTube for her 'nice song' recital.

'My Secret Heart'

Release: October 1989 **Album:** *Enjoy Yourself*
Writers/Producers: Stock Aitken Waterman

Kylie thought the music on this baroque-pop track would 'shock a few people' as the music was 'really different for me'. Settle down, Kyles! This is still pop music, despite the vaguely bombastic rococo flourishes demonstrating SAW were willing to tinkle slightly with their winning formula as long as they had a few definite hits pre-stocked in their pop cannon. In 2007, free jazz and contemporary classical guitarist Noël Akchoté covered 'My Secret Heart' on his twenty-track album of songs composed, performed, or inspired by Kylie called *So Lucky*.

'Tears on My Pillow'

PWL Records: PWL 47 **Single release:** January 1990 **Album:** *Enjoy Yourself*
Writers: Sylvester Bradford, Al Lewis
Producers: Stock Aitken Waterman

To promote Kylie's big movie debut in *The Delinquents*, Pete Waterman raked through his doo-wop faves deciding this 1954 hit from Little Anthony and The Imperials would befittingly capture the 1950s era in which the movie was set. 'Tears on My Pillow' topped the charts in the UK, though Australia was more resistant to its charms with a #20 chart placing, her lowest to date. It was released by Kylie's US label Geffen with a stark new cover, but missed the charts. Pete Waterman informed *Number One* magazine SAW were originally asked to do the entire soundtrack for *The Delinquents* but 'we just did the one track, "Tears on My Pillow", because Kylie wanted to do it.' This evergreen ditty proved a big singalong moment from 2012's Anti Tour.

Vid Bit!

Director: Chris Langman

Essentially a trailer for *The Delinquents*, which opened in Australia and the UK around Christmas that year to good box office, vampy Kylie channels '60s French sex symbol Brigitte Bardot as she bids a fond farewell to the first stage of her career. Just wait for what's to come, pop kids—SexKylie!

Remix Fix!

Pete Hammond's deft doo-wop No More Tears Mix almost doubled the original running time.

'Heaven and Earth'

Release: October 1989 **Album:** *Enjoy Yourself*
Writers/Producers: Stock Aitken Waterman

Years, if not decades, before it became hipster and then a necessity, Kylie was an eco-warrior and here is the proof on 'Heaven and Earth'. SAW's lyrics ('time is running out') were very close to her own views on the environment as she told *Smash Hits*, 'I feel the song has a valid message which is that no one can change the world overnight, but if we all out a little effort towards caring for our environment and stop taking it for granted, then we can keep this place beautiful.'

'Enjoy Yourself'

Release: October 1989 **Album:** *Enjoy Yourself*
Writers/Producers: Stock Aitken Waterman

The title track from Kylie's second album was, if nothing else, a pointer to where her music career was likely to go—down the disco with hands in the air like you just don't care. It was something else though as this irrepressible knees-up is the true predecessor to 1990's 'Better the Devil You Know' and one of Kylie's own personal favourites from her sophomore release. A long-time fan favourite (and highlight of 2012's Anti Tour) this uplifting, enjoyable upbeat track is one of the most underrated album tracks from the extensive SAW catalogue. In 2021, Mike Stock told *Billboard* the *Enjoy Yourself* album is his favourite SAW recording. Woo! In a huge 2022 online poll 'Enjoy Yourself' was voted #2 best SAW album track ever.

'Kylie's Smiley Mix'

Single release: October 1989 (B-side of 'Never Too Late')
Writers/Producers: Stock Aitken Waterman

No need to cut'n'paste your own mix of Kylie hits for your next cassette compilation—PWL were happy to do it for you, or at least the Hit Factory's Mixmaster Tony King was. Plonked on the B-side of the 'Never Too Late' single 'Kylie's Smiley Mix' arrived in two versions—the 7″ and 12″. The tracks that won smiley approval were 'I'll Still Be Loving You', 'It's No Secret', 'Je ne sais pas pourquoi', 'Turn It into Love', 'I Should Be So Lucky', and 'Got to Be Certain'. All aboard!

'We Know the Meaning of Love'

Single release: January 1990 (B-side of 'Tears on My Pillow')
Writers/Producers: Stock Aitken Waterman

As a sexier voiced Kylie ponders the future with a growl, 'We Know the Meaning of Love' is definitely one of the best of her Stock Aitken Waterman offcuts. Released as the B-side to 'Tears on My Pillow' (a by-the-numbers upbeat extra paired with a downtempo A-side), 'WKTMOL' found new appreciation in 7″ and 12″ mixes added to 2015's *Enjoy Yourself* re-release.

'Do They Know It's Christmas?' (Band Aid II)

PWL Records/Polydor: 873 646-2 **Single release:** December 1989
Writers: Midge Ure, Bob Geldof
Producers: Stock Aitken Waterman

The last #1 of the 1980s in the UK (and a Christmas #1 to boot) this was SAW's tarted up remake of the original 1984 global hit, featuring Kylie (who warbles first), Jason Donovan, Bros, Bananarama (phase II), Chris Rea, Jimmy Somerville, Sonia, Lisa Stansfield, Wet Wet Wet, Big Fun, Cathy Dennis, and more. 'DTKIC' languished almost forgotten until 2019 when devout SAW fans convinced Ure (and the Band Aid Trust) to release this version to streaming services. Phew.

Vid Bit!

Director: Kevin Godley

Paparazzi arrivals! Studio encounters! Group photos! Kylie and Jason duetting again (though split up and not recording together). This was also a first glimpse of Kylie after the devil inside himself, Michael Hutchence, began 'corrupting' her (i.e. fluffy perm gone, hot pants on).

4

Rhythm of Love Album (1990)

Rhythm of Love

Current Edition: PWL Records KYLIE 3 T
Originally released: November 1990

Side A	
'Better the Devil You Know'	3:52
'Step Back in Time'	3:05
'What Do I Have to Do'	3:44
'Secrets'	4:06
'Always Find the Time'	3:36
'The World Still Turns'	4:00
Side B	
'Shocked'	4:48
'One Boy Girl'	4:35
'Things Can Only Get Better'	3:57
'Count the Days'	4:23
'Rhythm of Love'	4:13

'Better the Devil You Know'

PWL Records: PWL 56 **Single release:** April 1990 **Album:** *Rhythm of Love*
Writers/Producers: Stock Aitken Waterman

The greatest Kylie song of all time? Maybe, but 'Better the Devil You Know' is undoubtedly the most beloved, danceable, and timeless from her SAW years, as the hit-making trio calculatingly gave this euphoric pop banger a ravey edge direct from 1989's 'summer of love'. The crowd-pleasing 'woah-oh-oh-oh' was nicked from D'Mob's 'C'mon and Get Your Love' featuring Cathy Dennis (later to play a major role in Kylie's millennial revival). A #2 UK hit (kept off by Adamski/Seal's 'Killer') and a platinum seller in Australia, 'BTDYK' failed to make a mark in the US despite its inclusion on the soundtrack of Hollywood movie *If Looks Could Kill*. In 2007, Kylie told me 'BTDYK' remains her favourite from her SAW years. Long considered a gay anthem, this was also Kylie's highest-rated entry in 2020 on *Classic Pop* magazine's rundown of the Top 40 SAW tunes—at #7. A year later, it ranked #2 (behind Donna Summer's 'This Time I Know It's for Real') in a fan vote of SAW tracks on Mike Stock's official site. At the same time in an extensive Facebook poll of Kylie fans, 'BTDYK' ranked as their #1 Kylie track of all time. In 2021, 'BTDYK' was also used for a bravura 'lip sync for your life' on *RuPaul's Drag Race Down Under*.

Vid Bit!

Director: Paul Goldman

With Michael Hutchence on board as Kylie 'confidante' (even if SAW wrote it about her staying with Jason!), the 'BTDYK' video heralded a new Kylie, a sexier Kylie, and a clubby Kylie. She herself pointed out that if you watched her videos in sequence with 'BTDYK' coming directly after 'Tears on My Pillow' 'it was like "Hang on, who's this? It's a completely different girl!"'

Remix Fix!

In 2009, the PWL archive store unloaded some fifteen devilishly angelic mixes of 'BTDYK', including nine ravey versions by Movers & Shakers and the less rave, more funk, yet slightly dull US Mix.

'Step Back in Time'

PWL Records: PWL 64 **Single release:** October 1989 **Album:** *Rhythm of Love*
Writers/Producers: Stock Aitken Waterman

After being switched with 'What Do I Have to Do', this non-stop disco bop became single #2 from SAW's golden Kylie era. 'Step Back in Time' romps through its yesteryear references and is, as *GQ* magazine observed: 'a taste of what Studio 54 might have been like if ABBA had been regulars'. The uncredited samples used in 'SBIT' are 1972's 'Hot Pants—I'm Coming I'm Coming I'm Coming' by Bobby Byrd and 1980's 'Give Up the Funk (Let's Dance)' by B. T. Express. While a #4 UK hit and #5 in Oz, the stature of 'SBIT' has grown immensely over the years. It has featured in at least nine of Kylie's various concert tours over the years and such is her continued affection for 'SBIT' her 2019 compilation was named *Step Back in Time: The Definitive Collection*.

Vid Bit!

Director: Nick Egan

Switching things up a notch again, Kylie shifted to LA for this sun-drenched Popsicle of a video paying loving homage to the decade that style forgot—the 1970s. Visual design legend Egan had worked extensively in video and album/single/merchandising design with INXS. And it shows.

Remix Fix!

The Digital EP (2009) included the Harding/Curnow Remix, the Tony King Remix and Original 12″ Mix. *Rhythm of Love* Deluxe Edition (2015) added The Big Shock remix by Steve Anderson for DMC (see Chapter 22). That means Kylie and Steve have now met on records and dance floors for 30-plus years!

'What Do I Have to Do'

PWL Records: PWL 72 **Single release:** January 1991 **Album:** *Rhythm of Love*
Writers/Producers: Stock Aitken Waterman

If 'Better the Devil You Know' was SAW's take on Kylie's love life, 'What Do I Have to Do' was unmistakably their interpretation of Kylie's sexual awakening via Michael Hutchence ('There ain't a single night that I haven't held you tight/But it's always inside my head and never inside my bed'). 'WDIHTD' is steamy, seductive, and came with a 'hardcore dance feel', according to Pete Waterman. It had the indignity of breaking her streak of Top 5 hits in the UK by stalling at #6, while it missed the Oz Top 10 at #11. Age-resistant, however, it continues doing what it has to do well.

Vid Bit!

Director: Dave Hogan

The first of Hogan's trifecta of Kylie videos and inspired by *Vogue Italia* movie pin-ups, 'WDIHTD' pushed Kylie further down the 'sex symbol' path than she had ever gone before. 'That's the video where my manager Terry was just flicking the pages of a magazine, not reading it, and he's like, "Are we finished with the lesbian scene yet Kylie?"' she told me in 1994, 'and I'm like, "Oh Terry, don't worry about it!" [giggles].' Sister Dannii also cameos. In 2021, for its thirtieth anniversary, Kylie posted she has 'so many memories of making this video … freezing cold in Covent Garden, the panther "tattoo", the pool scene, my sister, my FAVOURITE vintage leopard print coat and side-split dress and … ironing in Mugler!' Designer Thierry Mugler died in 2022.

Remix Fix!

Notable as the final Kylie single solely remixed in-house at PWL, the lives-up-to-its-name Pumpin' Mix includes samples of controversial US comedian Sam Kinison who died a year later.

'Secrets'

Release: November 1990 **Album:** *Rhythm of Love*
Writers/Producers: Stock Aitken Waterman

The strongest first four songs of a Kylie album? Check. SAW in their purple patch? Double check. 'Secrets' might have initially been a more obvious choice as fourth single from the album, but less likely as Kylie underwent a major transformation, not just via Michael Hutchence, but by growing into womanhood. 'Secrets' is up there with the best of Kylie's album tracks. In 1991 *EastEnders* actress Sophie Lawrence released her version, albeit with a surprise late key change.

'Always Find the Time'

Release: November 1990 **Album:** *Rhythm of Love*
Writers: Stock Aitken Waterman, Rick James
Producers: Stock Aitken Waterman

Funk 'superfreak' Rick James belatedly scored a songwriting credit on this track since 'Always Find the Time' sampled Mary Jane Girls' 1983 debut single 'Candy Man' (which missed the US Hot 100 but hit #60 in the UK that year). Bright, breezy, and with unexpectedly funky electro-touches, this is feel-good SAW killing it big time. 'Always Find the Time' is a true crowd-pleaser, sounding better than ever and barely dated, during 2012's Anti Tour. James's own time sadly came in 2004.

'The World Still Turns'

Release: November 1990 **Album:** *Rhythm of Love*
Writers: Kylie, Michael Jay, Mark Leggett
Producer: Michael Jay

Jay, the man behind Martika's 1988 hit 'Toy Soldiers' (later sampled by Eminem), wins the title of Kylie's first co-writer and producer, while co-writer Leggett is primarily a composer for TV. Lyrically the message of soul-lite but vocal heavyweight 'The World Still Turns', to move on from a broken romance, seemed to echo Kylie moving on from Jason Donovan to Michael Hutchence. In May 2020, Jay tweeted 'this week is 30yr anniversary of my 1st recording session with Kylie Minogue. Her label requested that she work with an American songwriter/producer. So Kylie came to my house and we wrote "The World Still Turns" for *Rhythm of Love* album'.

'Shocked'

PWL Records: PWL 81 **Single release:** May 1991 **Album:** *Rhythm of Love*
Writers/Producers: Stock Aitken Waterman

The fourth of the 'golden quartet' of singles released from *Rhythm of Love* in mid-1991, 'Shocked' marked the first time Kylie had been officially remixed outside the hit factory HQ. It was a real coup for Team Kylie to nab the DNA duo, then enjoying one of the year's biggest hits with their dance remake of Suzanne Vega's 'Tom's Diner'. DNA transformed 'Shocked' into a much cooler, clubbier, challenging song, and it was also—get out your hankies—Kylie's final single with SAW as a trio. Her thirteenth Top 10 hit in the UK, 'Shocked' also hit #7 in Australia. In 2020, PWL Archivist Mark Elliott divulged a thirteen-minute extended mix of the album version of 'Shocked' had been produced, then lost, while the same year Jazzi P revealed she earned a paltry £500 for her lightning rap on the DNA remake. Now that's truly shocking!

Vid Bit!

Director: David Hogan

Aiming for a 'strong and sexy' look in the video according to Kylie, once again her love interest was South African model Zane O'Donnell whom she was reportedly dating at the time—phew, if that sexual chemistry on screen could talk! Shot in Paris, 'Shocked' is a vague continuation of the 'What Do I Have to Do' video with Kylie rocked, if that's the right word, to her very foundations.

Remix Fix!

The, ahem, shockingly good DNA remake of 'Shocked' marked the first 'outside' commissioned Kylie remix (aside from the not-so-shockingly good US remix of 'Better the Devil You Know').

'One Boy Girl'

Release: November 1990 **Album:** *Rhythm of Love*
Writers: Kylie, John 'Willie' Wilcox
Producer: Keith 'K.C.' Cohen

Kylie's musical self-empowerment had begun and it must have been a true thrill for her to finally be singing her own monogamy-loving lyrics on 'One Boy Girl'. The middle rap section where she participates in a back-and-forth girl call deserves kudos for Kylie pushing herself to find a way forward as an artist. A much-improved 12" mix of *One Boy Girl* appeared on 2015's *Rhythm of Love* Deluxe Edition giving due credit for the rap to The Poetess (Felicia Morris).

'Things Can Only Get Better'

Release: November 1990 **Album:** *Rhythm of Love*
Writers/Producers: Stock Aitken Waterman

The year 1990 proved to be a turning point not just for Kylie but also SAW. This would be the last album the trio would work with Kylie on, as Aitken would leave the fold in 1991 citing 'stress'. 'Things Can Only Get Better' is a fitting finale to the brilliance of the trio. Their last work for Kylie together is a joy to listen to and even takes a few exciting chances—most notably with its 'ravey' pace, house piano and positive self-empowerment stance. More than merely 'Enjoy Yourself Part II', 'TCOGB' was proudly dusted off for 2012's Anti Tour. The 12″ mix only gets better too!

'Count the Days'

Release: November 1990 **Album:** *Rhythm of Love*
Writers: Kylie, Stephen Bray
Producer: Stephen Bray, Keith "K.C." Cohen

Kylie enlisted Bray, co-writer/producer of Madonna classics 'Express Yourself' and 'Into the Grove', for two tracks on *Rhythm of Love*. With four co-writes on the album, Kylie was abruptly taking control of her career and trying new collaborators, though the perky R&B of 'Count the Days' takes its obvious cues from Paula Abdul rather than Madonna. That probably has more to do with co-producer Cohen who worked his magic on Abdul's 1988 breakthrough *Forever Your Girl* album. Gleefully sung on 1991's Rhythm of Love tour Kylie had finally come into her own as an artist.

'Rhythm of Love'

Release: November 1990 **Album:** *Rhythm of Love*
Writers: Kylie, Stephen Bray
Producer: Stephen Bray, Keith 'K.C.' Cohen

Definitely the more successful of the two Minogue/Bray/Cohen collabs, this is a rhythm valentine to the nation of Janet Jackson/Jam & Lewis. While 'Rhythm of Love' provided a great album title, the song itself is more solid album material, when put shoulder to shoulder with the album's four outstanding SAW singles, or even next to the trio's *Rhythm of Love* killer filler. Speaking about the songs she had written for the *Rhythm of Love* album, Kylie told *Smash Hits*: 'I'm very proud of them. You know, it's so fantastic for me to have a piece of me in my work. I haven't had that before'. In 2021, SAW fans online voted *Rhythm of Love* the third best album produced by the trio (after Donna Summer's *Another Place and Time* and Bananarama's *Wow!*).

'I Am the One for You'

Single release: May 1991 (B-side of 'Shocked')
Writers: Kylie, Phil Harding, Ian Curnow
Producers: Phil Harding, Ian Curnow

Although heartily hi-NRG, high-spirited and with heaps of trendy-at-the-time house piano, 'I Am the One for You' is as if Farley 'Jackmaster' Funk's 1986 club classic 'Love Can't Turn Around' has been awkwardly shoved in a photocopier set at 'rave and repeat'. Hence 'IATOFY' only re-emerged years later on 1998's *Greatest Remix Hits 4* compilation, before reappearing on 2015's *Rhythm of Love* Deluxe Edition. 'IATOFY' is a fascinating, if flawed, PWL B-team curio.

5

Let's Get to It Album (1991)

Let's Get to It

Current Edition: PWL Records KYLIE 4 T
Originally released: October 1991
Original tracklist

'Word Is Out'	3:35
'Give Me Just a Little More Time'	3:08
'Too Much of a Good Thing'	4:24
'Finer Feelings'	3:54
'If You Were with Me Now'	3:11
'Let's Get to It'	4:49
'Right Here Right Now'	3:52
'Live and Learn'	3:15
'No World Without You'	2:46
'I Guess I Like It Like That'	6:00

'Word Is Out'

PWL Records: PWL 204 **Single release:** August (UK)/November (Australia) 1991
Album: *Let's Get to It*
Writers/Producers: Stock, Waterman

For the lead single from what would be Kylie's final PWL studio album, SAW had curtly downsized to just Stock Waterman. Repositioning her as a new jack/jill swingbeat singer, 'Word Is Out' was SW's knockoff riff on Bell Biv DeVoe's 1990 R&B hits 'Poison' and 'Do Me!'. '"Word Is Out" was great, but her image at the time didn't work with it,' Waterman later chimed in. 'Kylie dressed as a lady of the night down a dark alley just wasn't for her. That was Dannii's thing.' Languishing at a lowly #16 in the UK charts, 'WIO' broke Kylie's string of Top 10 hits, though Australia was kinder towards it with a #10 placing three months after its UK release. That was due to Mushroom wisely opting to issue the much more appealing 'Summer Breeze' mix.

Vid Bit!

Director: James Lebon

Filmed at London's Camden Markets and the alleyways behind PWL studios (the cheapskates!), featuring future TV presenter Davina McCall and photographer Mario Sorrenti, Kylie's hooker look in 'Word Is Out' is the textbook definition of a hot mess. 'WIO' director Lebon, a model/celeb hairstylist/artist whose father was Judy Garland's doctor, died in 2008.

Remix Fix!

PWL in-house mixmaster Tony King was called on to add some desperate groove magic and by golly earned his bonus that month! His Summer Breeze Mix rehabilitated a mediocre R&B wannabe into a glorious chilled-out beach anthem based on Drizabone's 'Real Love' Top 20 hit.

'Say the Word—I'll Be There'

Single release: August/November 1991 (B-side of 'Word Is Out')
Writers: Kylie, Stock, Aitken
Producers: Stock, Waterman

A heartfelt, blustery ballad to a dear friend that never found a home on the *Let's Get to It* album (best line: 'Kidnapped by anyone/I'll set you free'), 'Say the Word—I'll Be' has certainly aged more gracefully than the other 'word' song it was coupled with as a single. As a sturdy, earnest and charming ballad 'Say the Word', was Kylie's second co-written B-side, but first with Stock Waterman. In 2009, three versions (original, instrumental & backing track) got a digital release.

'If You Were with Me Now' (Kylie Minogue & Keith Washington)

PWL Records: PWL 208 **Single release:** October 1991 **Album:** *Let's Get to It*
Writers: Kylie, Keith Washington, Stock, Waterman
Producers: Stock, Waterman

With PWL in panic mode due to the chart disaster of 'Word Is Out' and low sales for 'Let's Get to It' (peaking at #15 in the UK and #13 in Australia), a week after the release of the album out sauntered 'If You Were with Me Now', a lush, if somewhat slushy, duet with then-up-and-coming R&B singer Keith Washington. While that in itself is remarkable—her first duet since her #1 with Jason Donovan—the song also holds a special place in music history as the first hit Kylie co-wrote. Although *Smash Hits* derided 'IYWWMN' as 'a drippy American-sounding ballad', it returned her to the UK Top 5 at #4. Washington released three LPs and dabbled in acting before becoming a radio DJ.

Vid Bit!

Director: Gregg Masuak

Romance is in the air and since Kylie is singing a 'serious' ballad that, of course, means it has to be in black and white. While she and Keith never actually meet in the video (a constant tale in her future videos), Kylie looks every inch the silver screen legend she promised to be.

Remix Fix!

While the original extended version is plush, the Orchestral Mix issued in 2015 is a must listen!

'I Guess I Like It Like That'

Single release: October 1991 (B-side of 'If You Were with Me Now') **Album:** *Let's Get to It*
Writers: Kylie, Stock, Waterman, Jean-Paul de Coster, Phil Wilde
Producers: Stock, Waterman

One of Pete Waterman's greatest gifts was his astute ability to spot a trend and jump on it, if not exploit it to the max, before everyone else. While the A-side singles from the *Let's Get to It* era suggested SW anticipating Kylie moving into a R&B-lite zone, the B-sides are where the really interesting stuff happened. Case in question, 'I Guess I Like It Like That'. Ruthlessly sampling Two Unlimited's #2 UK hit 'Get Ready for This' (de Coster and Wilde later credited as co-writers) 'IGILILT' was a proto techno-pop song. While still a shock evolution for the cooler club kids, 'IGILILT' added to her gay cachet, twirling her further away from teen fandom.

Remix Fix!

Dave Ford's Extended Version was just made for clubbing and—get mad, kids!—raving.

'Give Me Just a Little More Time'

PWL Records: PWL 212 **Single release:** January 1992 **Album:** *Let's Get to It*
Writers: Edythe Wayne, Ron Dunbar
Producers: Stock, Waterman

Waterman combed his chart history noggin for a suitable song for Kylie to cover with the main deviation from the original being her female voice (though US R&B singer Angela Clemmons covered it in 1982). Originally a #3 US/UK hit in 1970 for American soul act Chairmen of the Board, 'GMJALMT' was co-written by legendary Motown songwriting trio Holland Dozier Holland—the men behind most of Diana Ross & The Supremes' classics to name but a few. Due to a legal dispute, they were credited as 'Edythe Wayne'. The third single from *Let's Get to It* returned Kylie to #2 in the UK, though in Australia 'GMJALMT' failed to make the Top 20. From the *Let's Get to It* era, it was the only song on 2019's *Step Back in Time: The Definitive Collection.*

Vid Bit!

Director: Gregg Masuak

For the 'GMJALMT' video, Kylie was doused into sepia as if to convey she had once again 'stepped back in time'. Now no longer officially dating Michael Hutchence the saturated sunny clip also harked back to a more innocent Kylie era, which was presumably the timely idea.

Remix Fix!

There was a barely different Twelve Inch Version from Dave Ford, but who needed 'Give Me Just a Little More Time' for dancing when you had the ravetastic 'Do You Dare' on the B-side?

'Too Much of a Good Thing'

Release: October 1991 **Album:** *Let's Get to It*
Writers: Kylie, Stock, Waterman
Producers: Stock, Waterman

Stock Minogue Waterman took their starting template for 'Too Much of a Good Thing' from Lisa Lisa and Cult Jam's influential 'Let the Beat Hit 'Em' R&B/pop hit (#37 US and #17 UK) that same year, which forged a lucrative link between street hip-hop and club trax. Building on that base, Stock and Waterman proceed to plunder every clubbed out rave sample they legally can get away with before 'TMOAGT' settles down to a pleasant enough affair giving nods to Chic's 'Le Freak', plus fragments from The Emotions' 'Best of My Love' and Janet Jackson's 'Control'.

Remix Fix!

Phil Harding's 12″ mix of 'Too Much of a Good Thing' appeared on 1992's 'Celebration' single with Wild Cherry's disco classic 'Play that Funky Music' heavily sampled. Good choice!

'Finer Feelings'

PWL Records: PWL 227 **Single release:** April 1992 **Album:** *Let's Get to It*
Writers/Producers: Stock, Waterman

As a stepping off point for Kylie to the next stage in her career, 'Finer Feelings', as the fourth and final single from *Let's Get to It*, is one of the more fondly remembered songs from the album, even if it peaked outside the UK Top 10 at #11 and became her lowest-charting single (until 2010) in Australia at #60. Tapping into Kylie's newfound sexual awakening, SW encouraged her to share the grown-up revelation that without those finer feelings, 'it's just sex without the sexual healing'. Via its outsourced remix, 'Finer Feelings' also marked the official beginning of Kylie's illustrious working life with Brothers In Rhythm's Steve Anderson, her musical director and recurring co-composer/producer. Not simply a fine single, it is truly one of Kylie's finest.

Vid Bit!

Director: Dave Hogan

Filmed in Paris in sumptuous black and white, Kylie—dressed in a beret (well, it was France) and runway *haute couture*—had never looked more like a model, more glamorous, or more French. Oh yes, and there are fine cameos from two wayward baguettes too. Ooh la la!

Remix Fix!

While its album version was coyishly demure, the Brothers In Rhythm Mixes of 'Finer Feelings' showcase a clear link to their bravura future work for Kylie on 1994's 'Confide in Me'. For the 2009 iTunes PWL Archive digital release, seven versions (four of them from BIR) were included.

'Let's Get to It'

Release: October 1991 **Album:** *Let's Get to It*
Writers/Producers: Stock, Waterman

Mike Stock recalls Kylie being obsessed with Color Me Badd's chart-topper 'I Wanna Sex You Up' while he was writing tracks for her new album and asking for a song with the word sex in the title. What he did instead for the title track to her fourth album was literally rewrite 'I Wanna Sex You Up'. A badly colourless R&B clone, 'Let's Get to It', like its iffy, if not getting icky, album cover, reflected the then malaise in Kylie's career. Despite four UK Top 20 singles, *Let's Get to It* remains as the most unsuccessful album sales-wise and chart-wise of Kylie's recording history. Tony King's friskier 12″ version of 'LGTI' were bundled a year later as the 'Celebration' B-side.

'Right Here Right Now'

Release: October 1991 **Album:** *Let's Get to It*
Writers: Kylie, Stock, Waterman
Producers: Stock, Waterman

Not to be confused with a track of the same name Kylie recorded with legendary disco producer Giorgio Moroder in 2015, or the same named *X* demo in 2007, this 'Right Here Right Now' bears a strong passing resemblance to Kym Sims's 1991 soaring house classic 'Too Blind to See It', her solitary UK Top 10 hit. Kylie's 'RHRN' by contrast sags with too many strident background vocals and that little something special missing. For the 2009 iTunes PWL Archive, Tony King's more house-arresting 12″ mix was rightfully released.

'Live and Learn'

Release: October 1991 **Album:** *Let's Get to It*
Writers: Kylie, Stock, Waterman
Producers: Stock, Waterman

Here is yet another of *Let's Get to It's* genre-hopping tracks. Is 'Live and Learn' house, funk, soul, rave, or all of those in just one big not-so-hot muddle? Asked in 2015 if he and Stock knew *Let's Get to It* would be their final album with Kylie, Waterman replied: 'yes, I mean in hindsight, we should have actually sold that album before we made it ... Kylie had become such a big star she was overshadowing us and killing our creativity'. On 2015's *Let's Get to It* Deluxe Edition, a more pleasing rave soul 12″ mix of 'Live and Learn' was included.

'No World Without You'

Release: October 1991 **Album:** *Let's Get to It*
Writers: Kylie, Stock, Waterman
Producers: Stock, Waterman

The emotion-packed lyrics of 'No World Without You' ('I remember the day you went away/What was I to do') suggest Kylie was not a happy ex. Initially overlooked and ignored, like most of the *Let's Get to It* album at the time, 'No World Without You' is a valiant first stab by Kylie of writing her true feelings down, singing about them, and not being afraid to finally let the public into her private world. The final track on her final studio album with SAW, there was, happily, a world for Kylie without her hit-making team.

'Keep On Pumpin' It' (Vision Masters & Tony King Featuring Kylie Minogue)

PWL Records: PWL 207 **Single release:** November 1991 **Album:** *Let's Get to It*
Writers: Kylie, Stock, Waterman
Producers: Stock, Waterman, Vision Masters

'Keep On Pumpin' It' crept into the UK charts at #49 as part of PWL's masterplan to acquire Kylie the cool club cachet she desperately longed for. As with 'I Guess I Like It Like That', this pumping Italo-house dance floor burner complete with some wicked piano was originally sent out as a white label to DJs to keep Kylie's identity a secret. Vision Masters were Paul Taylor and Danny Hybrid together with PWL's own Tony King, with 'Keep On Pumpin' It' sampling Freestyle Orchestra's 'Keep On Pumping It Up' and 'IGILILT', hence the Kylie credit here.

Remix Fix!

Available in Angelic Remix (by Tony King), or Astral Flight versions (Phil Harding slyly referencing 2 Unlimited again). In 2009 for the iTunes PWL Archive digital release five versions of 'Keep On Pumpin' It' were issued.

'Do You Dare?'

Single release: January 1992 (B-side of 'Give Me Just a Little More Time')
Writers/Producers: Stock, Waterman

Continuing SW's cunning game plan to morph Kylie into the queen of rave-pop, 'Do You Dare?' was again sent out to DJs as a white label credited to 'Angel K'. 'Do You Dare?' is more of Kylie knocking on clubland's door and finding a welcome second home. In 2020, PWL Archivist Mark Elliott revealed an 'interesting' vocal of 'Do You Dare?' was 'kept back' from the 2015 PWL box sets, as were original demos of other Kylie classics. Daringly, Darenote Records decades later became the name of Kylie's own label imprint.

Remix Fix!

The NRG mix of 'Do You Dare?' plundered the house party era, while the New Rave Mix (also by Dave Ford) came directly from a rave somewhere in the middle of a cornfield. Possibly.

'Closer'

Single release: April 1992 (B-side of 'Finer Feelings')
Writers: Kylie, Stock, Waterman
Producers: Stock, Waterman

Not to be confused with the track of the same name from 2010's *Aphrodite* album, the B-side to 1992's 'Finer Feelings' single was the third in the series of Kylie 'rave-pop' tunes Stock and Waterman foisted on her single B-sides. They were infinitely more enjoyable, not to mention a true guilty pleasure for rave heads, than any of the more straight-laced A-sides. Once again, Pete Waterman was keeping his ear to the club floor with his team having signed Euro-technopop sensations 2 Unlimited on their way to selling millions of records.

Remix Fix!

The 2009 iTunes PWL Archive digital release included three mixes of 'Closer' by Dave Ford.

6

Greatest Hits Compilation (1992)

Greatest Hits

Original version: PWL International HFCD25
Originally released: August 1992
Tracklist

'I Should Be So Lucky'	3:23
'Got to Be Certain'	3:20
'The Loco-Motion'	3:14
'Je ne sais pas pourquoi'	4:01
'Especially for You'	3:58
'Turn It into Love'	3:36
'It's No Secret'	3:59
'Hand on Your Heart'	3:51
'Wouldn't Change a Thing'	3:14
'Never Too Late'	3:23
'Tears on My Pillow'	2:28
'Better the Devil You Know'	3:55
'Step Back in Time'	3:05
'What Do I Have to Do'	3:44
'Shocked' (DNA 7″ Mix)	3:10
'Word Is Out'	3:35
'If You Were with Me Now'	3:11
'Give Me Just a Little More Time'	3:07
'Finer Feelings'	3:53
'What Kind of Fool (Heard All That Before)'	3:41
'Where in the World?'	3:34
'Celebration'	3:57

'What Kind of Fool (Heard All That Before)'

PWL International: PWCD 241 **Single release:** August 1992 **Compilation:** *Greatest Hits*
Writers: Kylie, Stock, Waterman
Producers: Stock, Waterman

Kylie's last original single to be released on PWL truly marked the end of an era. 'What Kind of Fool' is like the less angelic cousin of 'Better the Devil You Know' with even Kylie later admitting she 'really didn't like' it. 'What Kind of Fool' barely managed to crack the Top 20 in both the UK and Australia, yet helped the *Greatest Hits* album hit #1 in the UK and #3 in Australia. Coupled with an infinitely better B-side, 1990's 'Things Can Only Get Better', 'What Kind of Fool', unexpectedly, found late critical love in 2020 when *Classic Pop* magazine compiled their Top 40 SAW tracks ranking it disputably highly at #25.

Vid Bit!

Director: Gregg Masuak

While sexpot Kylie is as ravishing as ever and as obsessed as ever with French cinema icon Brigitte Bardot, it could be argued the budget of the 'What Kind of Fool' video (based on Roger Vadim's 1956 Bardot classic *And God Created Woman*) was foolishly blown on hairspray!

Remix Fix!

The ravey house No Tech No Logical Mix came courtesy of Espaniola (an alias for PWL's Les Sharma), while the Tech No Logical Mix (by Dave Ford) is basically an Extended Mix. In 2009, for the iTunes PWL Archive release of 'What Kind of Fool', six versions were released.

'Where in the World?'

Release: August 1992 **Compilation:** *Greatest Hits*
Writers: Kylie, Stock, Waterman
Producers: Stock, Waterman

Sandwiched on 1992's *Greatest Hits* album between 'What Kind of Fool' and 'Celebration' was the third and final new song, and definitely the lesser of the three. 'Where in the World?' has a whiff of a Sonia B-side, though there is a decent tune, somewhere in its unexceptional world, struggling to be set free. Most likely it was actually a leftover from the 'Let's Get to It' album.

'Celebration'

PWL International: PWCD 257 **Single release:** November 1992 **Compilation:** *Greatest Hits*
Writers: Ronald Nathan Bell, James 'J.T.' Taylor, Claydes Charles Smith, George Melvin Brown, Robert Spike Mickens, Earl Eugene Toon Jr, Dennis Ronald Thomas, Robert Earl Bell, Eumir Deodato
Producers: Phil Harding, Ian Curnow **Additional Production:** Stock, Waterman

Kylie's final single with PWL is also one of her own personal favourites—the original 1980 Kool & The Gang 'Celebration' a US #1 and UK #7. Stock and Waterman handed Kylie's 'Celebration' over to henchman Harding and Curnow for her *Greatest Hits* album, but for its single release they received an additional production credit. Kylie's two best territories synced closely on 'Celebration'—#20 in the UK and #21 in Oz. Kylie later performed this discofest at Sydney's 2000 Paralympics opening ceremony, then tackled it during her *Kylie Christmas* shows in 2015 such is her affection for its celebratory mood. Kool & The Gang's Ronald Nathan Bell, who was inspired to write 'Celebration' after reading a passage in the Koran, died in 2020.

Vid Bit!

Director: Gregg Masuak

Filmed in Rio, Kylie's in Brazilian 'Carnival' mode basking in her newfound freedom—wahoo!

Remix Fix!

The Have A Party Mix from AKA (Tony King & Asha Elfenbein) is seven minutes of pure Kylie disco-pop joy. The Techno Rave Remix bonus track on 1993's *Kylie's Non-Stop History 50+1* album shifted 'Celebration' into a massive rave tune.

7

Kylie Minogue Album (1994)

Kylie Minogue

Current version: BMG 82876 510982
Originally released: September 1994
Original tracklist

'Confide in Me'	5:51
'Surrender'	4:25
'If I Was Your Lover'	4:45
'Where Is the Feeling?'	6:59
'Put Yourself in My Place'	4:54
'Dangerous Game'	5:30
'Automatic Love'	4:45
'Where Has the Love Gone?'	7:46
'Falling'	6:43
'Time Will Pass You By'	5:26
Japanese edition extra tracks	
'Love Is Waiting'	4:52
'Nothing Can Stop Us'	4:06
Canadian edition extra track	
'Confide in Me' (French version)	5:51

'Confide in Me'

deConstruction: 74321 227471 **Single release:** August 1994 **Album:** *Kylie Minogue*
Writers: Steve Anderson, Dave Seaman, Owain Barton
Producers: Brothers In Rhythm

'Confide in Me' needed to be the consummate single to launch Kylie's new post-SAW career on deConstruction Records in the UK (though she remained on Festival/Mushroom in Australia). Thankfully, it was. A bespoke song written specifically for her, 'Confide in Me' was not too much of a sonic leap from Brothers In Rhythm's 'Finer Feelings' remix from two years earlier. BIR were, however, a little too heavily influenced by Opus III's 'It's a Fine Day' (UK #5 in 1992) written by Barton, later added to its credits. Despite this and barely anyone noticing, 'CIM' re-established Kylie as a continuing force in pop music. Accordingly, her image shifted from the teen pop mags to the high gloss fashion mags—Kylie's rebirth was complete. 'Confide in Me' went to #2 in the UK (held off by Whigfield's 'Saturday Night'), #1 in Australia, and was also her only song to chart in the US in the 1990s (on the Dance Club Songs chart). Ranking Kylie's top singles in 2020, *Classic Pop* magazine placed 'Confide in Me' #1 calling it 'the opening gambit that closed out the PWL chapter for good and ushered in a new, more grown-up direction'.

Vid Fix!

Director: Paul Boyd

After working on videos for Lenny Kravitz, INXS, and Seal, Boyd's sole clip for Kylie did not disappoint. Gathering together an array of Kylie 'stereotypes', it tipped that concept on its head (and moved it around the screen) so viewers finally understood how multi-faceted Kylie was. Like the song itself, the 'Confide in Me' video remains a remarkable, sexy, affecting, and thought-provoking piece of pop art.

Remix Fix!

In 2020, Anderson revealed the inspiration for the BIR remix of 'CIM' came from Clivillés & Cole's remix of Michael Jackson's 1991 hit 'Black or White'. Justin Warfield, Diego Maradonna & Jonny Dollar and the disco-house Phillip Damien remixes (promoed for the US) were also part of the remix package. A *très* literal French version, 'Fie-toi à moi', was also recorded.

'Nothing Can Stop Us'

Single release: August 1994 (B-side of 'Confide in Me')
Writers/Producers: Bob Stanley, Pete Wiggs

At one early stage 'Nothing Can Stop Us', a sprightly retro '60s indie dance track, originally quirky British band Saint Etienne's third single in 1991, was in the running as Kylie's deConstruction debut single. Based on a groovy sample from Dusty Springfield's 'I Can't Wait Until I See My Baby's Face' from 1967, 'Nothing Can Stop Us' was played to UK magazine editors who were informed it would be her new single. Shortly after, however, deConstruction got cold feet and it ended up a B-side. 'It's a shame we didn't hear more of that record,' Sarah Cracknell from St Etienne later complained, 'but we were very flattered.' (See further entry in Appendix I.)

'If You Don't Love Me'

Single release: August 1994 (B-side of 'Confide in Me')
Writer: Paddy McAloon
Producers: Brothers In Rhythm

Piano-led ballads have always been Kylie's secret weapon, and this poignant and heartfelt track, a minor hit in 1992 by British act Prefab Sprout, delicately showcases her vocal abilities and range. Recorded in just one take by Kylie with Steve Anderson on the piano, 'If You Don't Love Me' was loved up again during 2011's Aphrodite Les Folies Tour. In 2013, Prefab Sprout leader McAloon (and writer of this powerful showstopper) twittered: 'Kylie Minogue really likes that track, doesn't she? She plays it everywhere, it's fantastic'.

'Surrender'

Release: September 1994 **Album:** *Kylie Minogue*
Writers: Gerry DeVeaux, Charlie Mole
Producers: Gerry DeVeaux, John Waddle, Tim Bran

Here's Kylie doing her seductive best to bring sexy back ('come to me'). DeVeaux is best known for his work with Lenny Kravitz and is actually Kravitz's cousin. A saucily cooed 'Talking Soul Mix' of 'Surrender' finally appeared on 2003's expanded *Kylie Minogue*. In 2004, DeVeaux told this author 'Surrender' was 'still the song most black people like most of Kylie's because I made her sing a little more black. She really sang her ass off.' Bottoms up, as it were!

'If I Was Your Lover'

Release: September 1994 **Album:** *Kylie Minogue*
Writer/Producer: Jimmy Harry

How do you follow writing 'Supermodel (You Better Work)' the signature hit for drag superstar RuPaul? By writing two tracks for by-now certifiable gay icon Kylie Minogue, naturally. 'If I Was Your Lover' was not the single, but the Jimmy Harry song where Kylie slinkily dips into Jackson-esque R&B terrain. Harry would work again with Kylie well over a decade later in her career and win a Golden Globe for co-writing 'Masterpiece' for Madonna's *W.E.* film.

'Put Yourself in My Place'

deConstruction: 7 4321 24657 2 **Single release:** November 1994 **Album:** *Kylie Minogue*
Writer/Producer: Jimmy Harry

Single #2 from the *Kylie Minogue* album was a masterful pop ballad and the only song on the album she did not record in the UK, flying to New York to sing it for producer/writer Harry. Peaking at #11 in both the UK and Australia 'Put Yourself in My Place' has grown in stature over the years and the 'think pink' space race video remains one of her best to date. The stunning sideways black and white single cover by Rankin, featuring Kylie with a set of headphones on, also deftly played into deConstruction's 'cool Kylie' remit. In 2020, *Classic Pop* magazine wrote perceptively about 'Put Yourself in My Place' that it 'saw its maker mastering the pop ballad'.

Vid Bit!

Director: Keir McFarlane

Inspired by Jane Fonda's 1960s sci-fi classic *Barbarella*, Kylie literally undresses before our very eyes with only gravity to hold her panties up, or not, as the case would be. 'Put Yourself in My Place' later won Best Video at the Australian ARIA Awards. In 2020, Kylie begrudgingly called it 'one of the more agonizing videos I've done'.

Remix Fix!

The Danny D remixes of 'Put Yourself in My Place' were a renewed attempt to steer Kylie into R&B turf, likewise the Drizabone and Allstar Mixes. The acoustic version of 'Put Yourself in My Place', an extra on 2003's expanded *Kylie Minogue*, might be her greatest lost musical moment.

'Where Is the Feeling?'

deConstruction: 74321 29361 2 **Single release:** July 1995 **Album:** *Kylie Minogue*
Writers: Wilf Smarties, Jayn Hanna
Producers: Brothers In Rhythm

This is where it all started going pear-shaped. The album's second single, 'Put Yourself in My Place', featured a terrific David Morales remix of 'Where is the Feeling?' abruptly dumped as its B-side. Rather than opt for massive crowd-pleasing M People track 'Time Will Pass You By' as third single, Kylie's deCon team curiously decided to have a second bash at 'Where is the Feeling?', originally an underground house hit *circa* 1993 for Within A Dream. After a delay due to Kylie filming the Pauly Shore comedy film *Bio-Dome* 9 (as Dr Petra Von Kant!), a new spoken word-style vocal was recorded. Yet after all that effort, 'Where is the Feeling?' could only muster #31 in Oz and a distressing #16 in the UK. 'I do have a lot of love for the album version,' Anderson said in 2020. 'It was our love letter to (house remixers/producers) David Morales and Frankie Knuckles.' The irony is Morales himself remixed 'Where Is the Feeling'. Lovingly too.

Vid Bit!

Director: Keir McFarlane

Cue arty black and white video where Kylie appears to be walking on water before someone—a handsome aquaman, no less—surfaces for a soggy snog. More importantly, where is the lifeboat?

Remix Fix!

'Where is the Feeling?' was re-recorded as a trip-hop anthem over three weeks for the BIR single/12″ versions. A funkier acoustic version (with live band) showed up on 2003's expanded *Kylie Minogue*. Feel around for Morales's mix for a true blast of 1990s house music at its best!

'Dangerous Game'

Release: September 1994 **Album:** *Kylie Minogue*
Writers: Steve Anderson, Dave Seaman
Producers: Brothers In Rhythm

Lovingly and lushly produced by Brothers in Rhythm, 'Dangerous Game' sounds like it fell off a Bond movie sometime in the 1980s. That said, it delivers one of Kylie's most powerhouse vocals to date. In 1996, two years after its release, 'Dangerous Game' was used on Aussie soapie *Home and Away* when Angel (Melissa George) scatters the ashes of her husband, Shane (Dieter Brummer), into the sea. Kylie and Melissa, two former teen Aussie TV queens, would eventually become BFFs. A relatively melodramatic, if not faintly, scary one-minute and twenty-second of swirling menacing strings and Kylie screaming was packed into the 'Dangerous Overture', released on a series of compilations and on the expanded *Kylie Minogue*.

'Automatic Love'

Release: September 1994 **Album:** *Kylie Minogue*
Writers: Kylie, Inga Humpe, The Rapino Brothers
Producers: Brothers In Rhythm

It's time to turn Kylie on, pop peeps, for the Euro-pop noir of 'Automatic Love', one of many tracks The Rapino Brothers crafted for *Kylie Minogue*, but the sole one to wind up on the album. To that end, 'Automatic Love' brings a true grandiose sensibility to the album missing elsewhere. 'It has one of the best vocals I've ever heard her do in my life,' Brothers in Rhythm's Anderson said later. 'It's mind blowing what she did on that.' Search out Kylie's sterling seated performance of 'Automatic Love' on *Parabens RTP* Portugal TV in 1996 as evidence, or the endearing acoustic version released years later on the *Hits+* compilation. The original less plush Rapino Brothers production of 'Automatic Love' leaked in 2020. (See entry in Appendix I.)

'Where Has the Love Gone?'

Release: September 1994 **Album:** *Kylie Minogue*
Writers: Alex Palmer, Julie Stapleton
Producers: Pete Heller, Terry Farley

'Where Has the Love Gone?' is the first of two 'beach house' productions on *Kylie Minogue* by Heller and Farley aka Fire Island. It was originally an underground deep house classic released in 1991 by co-writer Stapleton as her solo single called 'Where's Your Love Gone?' The Heller/Farley production for Kylie is pure unabashed mid-90s house music complete with prerequisite piano riffs, soulful backing vocals, and plaintive lyrics ('one sided love affair is no good to me/I'm a woman and I have my vanity'). It is hard to believe a song as good as this, featuring some of Kylie's most intense, if not most sensual vocals, was dismissed as a single.

'Falling'

Release: September 1994 **Album:** *Kylie Minogue*
Writers: Neil Tennant, Chris Lowe
Producers: Pete Heller, Terry Farley

Written by British pop duo Pet Shop Boys, the band's Neil Tennant later admitted they originally came up with a 'Stock Aitken Waterman Kylie' track and presumably that is why the Heller/Farley 'Falling' became instead a steamier affair drenched in dreamy sunsets, throbbing late night club nights and the after-party vibe of Ibiza. Originally conceived by Lowe for a remix of PSB's cover of the Village People's disco chestnut 'Go West', the backing track morphed into 'Falling', which Tennant considers among his worst lyrics. In 2001, PSB released their swirling demo of 'Falling' on *Very: Further Listening 1992–1994*. A throbbing retro-electro alternative mix of 'Falling' appeared on 2003's expanded *Kylie Minogue*.

'Time Will Pass You By'

Release: September 1994 **Album:** *Kylie Minogue*
Writers: Dino Fekaris, Nick Zesses, Jon Rhys
Producers: M People

What better way to end Kylie's radical dance album than with a song considered one of the greatest Northern Soul records of all time (by Tobi 'Legend' Lark). Kylie's moving and fairly faithful remake of 'Time Will Pass You By' was intended as the final single from the *Kylie Minogue* album, but cancelled due to her Nick Cave duet. With M People enjoying their hot mid-90s chart streak (band member Mike Pickering was also co-owner of deConstruction) and co-written by Fekaris, the man behind Gloria Gaynor's 1979 'I Will Survive' disco anthem, 'Time Will Pass You By' was a readymade hit-in-waiting for Kylie but it was not to be and did indeed pass her by. A fairly conventional mid-90s house remix by Paul Masterson showed up on 2003's expanded *Kylie Minogue*.

'Love Is Waiting'

Release: September 1994 (Japan only) **Album:** *Kylie Minogue*
Writers: Mike Percy, Tim Lever, Tracy Ackerman
Producers: Brothers In Rhythm

'Love Is Waiting' is dancefloor dynamite with Kylie reimaging herself as the new queen of disco. Co-writers Percy and Lever were members of '80s gender-bending act Dead or Alive, most famous for their 'You Spin Me Round' hit, with the inimitable Pete Burns (who died in 2016) out front, which is also important as the first #1 record SAW produced. The pair left DOA around 1986, producing Dannii Minogue's 'This Is It' single the year before they got studio time with Kylie. In 2020, Steve Anderson stated: '"Love Is Waiting" is one of my favourite things we've ever done and controversially I felt that could have gone where the M People song went'.

'Gotta Move On'

Arista: 74321 785342 **Release:** June 2000 **Compilation:** *Hits+*
Writers: Kylie, Marco Sabiu, Graziano 'Charlie' Mallozzi
Producers: The Rapino Brothers

In November 2000, Kylie's by then former label deConstruction (now part of BMG) released the *Hits+* compilation, less than two months after *Light Years* had returned Kylie to chart glory. While a cynical exercise in 'cashing in', the fact it included two unreleased tracks made it of interest, if not a must-have. The first of two Rapino Brothers efforts, 'Gotta Move On' is sophisticated Euro-pop with some rare xylophone work about 'brighter days' left off 1994's *Kylie Minogue* album. The *Hits+* album was a minor success peaking at #63 in Australia and #41 in the UK, where it was certified silver for sales of 60,000.

'Difficult By Design'

Release: June 2000 **Compilation:** *Hits+*
Writers: Kylie, Marco Sabiu, Graziano "Charlie" Mallozzi
Producers: The Rapino Brothers

The other *Hits+* track courtesy of Rapino Brothers is the more interesting of their two belatedly released 1994 offcuts. On this anthemic post-modern disco-house by design track Kylie muses the difficult issues of heartache, unhappiness, and how 'love is difficult sometimes'. Who could she be referring to? In 2020 in the midst of the first global lockdown, seven more Kylie/Rapino collabs (ten in total) miraculously appeared online (see Appendix I).

8

'Where the Wild Roses Grow' Single/*Impossible Princess* Album (1995–1997)

Impossible Princess (aka Kylie Minogue)

Current version: BMG 82876 511152
Originally released: October 1997
Original tracklist

'Too Far'	4:43
'Cowboy Style'	4:44
'Some Kind of Bliss'	4:14
'Did It Again'	4:21
'Breathe'	4:37
'Say Hey'	3:36
'Drunk'	3:58
'I Don't Need Anyone'	3:12
'Jump'	4:02
'Limbo'	4:05
'Through the Years'	4:19
'Dreams'	3:44
Japanese edition bonus track	
'Tears'	4:26

'Where the Wild Roses Grow' (Nick Cave and the Bad Seeds + Kylie Minogue)

Mute: 185 **Single release:** October 1995 **Album:** *Murder Ballads*
Writer: Nick Cave
Producers: Tony Cohen, Victor Van Vugt

After the middling success of her deConstruction debut, Kylie's long-term career prospects again appeared, momentarily at least, in jeopardy. To the rescue came Aussie indie-rocker Nick Cave with 'Where the Wild Roses Grow', a song about a dead woman called Elisa Day he had written to sing together with Kylie. 'I just recorded the song the day that I met him,' Kylie revealed later of their duet for Nick Cave and the Bad Seeds' *Murder Ballads* album, a prepping point for her artistic growth and the most intriguing, experimental, and commercially challenging period of Kylie's career to come. A global hit returning Kylie/Cave to #2 in their native Oz and peaking at #11 in the UK, it also won the coveted Song of the Year ARIA in Australia. The UK rock music press, previously resistant to Kylie's musical output, finally caved to her charms too. As Pete Waterman reflected in 2017: 'she couldn't have gone from us to "Can't Get You Out of My Head" the way she did. She had to get there via Nick Cave'.

Vid Bit!

Director: Rocky Schenck

Be prepared for a shock, viewers—Kylie is a ghost, she has been murdered and there is blood on her lips. As beautiful as a painting (inspired by John Everett Millais's *Ophelia* from 1851) flame-haired Kylie had never looked lovelier, sung better, or taken wilder chances.

'Death Is Not the End' (Nick Cave and the Bad Seeds Featuring Anita Lane, Shane MacGowan, PJ Harvey & Kylie Minogue)

Release: February 1996 **Album:** *Murder Ballads*
Writer: Bob Dylan
Producers: Victor Van Vugt, Tony Cohen, The Bad Seeds

Released in February 1996, this moody Dylan dirge was the second track featuring Kylie on Nick Cave & The Bad Seeds' *Murder Ballads* album, after 'Where the Wild Roses Grow' had been released as the album's first single. Besides Kylie, also featuring on album closer 'Death Is Not the End' are Cave's former girlfriend, singer/songwriter Anita Lane, Shane MacGowan from The Pogues and singer/songwriter PJ Harvey, who would go on to be Cave's next girlfriend.

'Some Kind of Bliss'

deConstruction: 74321 517252 **Single release:** September 1997 **Album:** *Impossible Princess*
Writers: Kylie, James Dean Bradfield, Sean Moore
Producers: James Dean Bradfield, Dave Eringa

On her sixth album *Impossible Princess*, in the last year of her twenties, Kylie finally felt ready to take chances, expose herself like never before and challenge her audience by bridging the divide between indie-rock and dance-pop. Enter the Manic Street Preachers who had tried working with Kylie in 1992, while she was still at PWL. Instead 'Little Baby Nothing' was released with porn actress Traci Lords (#29 UK). 'Some Kind of Bliss' might just be the strangest, rockiest, and most unexpected thing Kylie ever did in her career, and then it got released as her new album's first single—a Britpop rock fest blissfully celebrating heavenly feelings the week after Princess Diana died. 'Some Kind of Bliss' peaked unblissfully outside the Top 20 in both the UK and Australia. Bradfield later delivered a public apology to Kylie. 'Seeing the commercial result, I probably failed her,' he told *NME*. 'I'm eternally sorry.'

Vid Bit!

Director: David Mould

Filmed in Spain and co-starring Dexter Fletcher (later to direct Oscar-winning biopic *Rocketman*), a blue Cadillac and Kylie in barely there denim hotpants, the 'Some Kind of Bliss' video is every bit as indie as the song itself.

Remix Fix

Some kind of indie-dance? That's what John Graham's off-kilter Quivver Mix offered.

'Too Far'

deConstruction: Too Far 1 **Promo release:** May 1998 **Album:** *Impossible Princess*
Writer: Kylie
Producers: Kylie, Brothers In Rhythm

On *Impossible Princess* Kylie co-wrote all twelve tracks, garnering a sole writing credit on two. 'I wrote "Too Far" very quickly and in a very bad state,' Kylie revealed in 1997. 'I had to leave my house because there was too much in my head.' Released as a 'promotional single' to radio only, 'Too Far' is a Kylie track unlike any album opener of hers before, or since. 'Too many, too much, too hard/ Help me, this time I went too far' Kylie wails over a woozy drum and bass beat. Caught in a tussle between her UK label deConstruction and Sony BMG in the US over its release as a single (hence the US remixes), this somewhat revelatory song sank as a potential single and ended up not going far at all.

Remix Fix!

For 'Too Far', Brothers In Rhythm offered a frenetic House Mix, while Junior Vasquez and Philip Steir mixes were commissioned for US clubs. The BIR and big room Vasquez remixes appeared on the Australian-only *Impossible Remixes* album released in July 1998

'Cowboy Style'

Mushroom: MUSH01812.2 **Single release:** August 1998 (Australia only) **Album:** *Impossible Princess*
Writers: Kylie, Steve Anderson, Dave Seaman
Producers: Brothers In Rhythm

Long before Kylie turned to country-pop on 2018's *Golden*, she dabbled in its western ways here. A much more conventional Kylie track with a proper chorus, 'Cowboy Style' became the fifth and final release (in Australia only) from *Impossible Princess*. 'It's basically about my boyfriend (Stéphane Sedanoui),' Kylie explained. 'When I met him he had a very unusual look, to say the least.' 'Cowboy Style' also marked the end of her working relationship with deConstruction Records. Only Mushroom Records, her long-time Australian label, opted to release the song, minus remixes, as the fourth single from *Impossible Princess* in October 1998, but it went out of style at #39.

Vid Bit!

Director: Michael Williams

Taken from her *Intimate and Live* tour from 1998, the 'Cowboy Style' clip featured plenty of sexy, shirtless cowboys and Kylie in a cowgirl hat on a pedestal. Yee-haw!

'Did It Again'

deConstruction: 74321 535692 **Single release:** November 1997 **Album:** *Impossible Princess*
Writers: Kylie, Steve Anderson, Dave Seaman
Producers: Brothers In Rhythm

Clever girl! '"Did It Again' is, basically, I'm telling myself off,' Kylie clarified. 'Whereas some of the songs are from my heart, or my gut, or my head, this one I really feel it's just a little voice on my shoulder.' A more successful synthesis of rock and dance this was the second single from *Impossible Princess* and the album's biggest hit (#15 in Oz and one better at #14 in the UK). It was nominated for Single of the Year at the 1998 ARIA Music Awards (losing out to Natalie Imbruglia's 'Torn' cover). For her *Top of the Pops* appearance, she appeared as 'Indie Kylie' singing live with the other three 'Kylies' portrayed by a trio of messy drag queens. Backstage Kylie hung out with another of the show's performers, her ex Michael Hutchence, appearing with his band INXS to sing 'Elegantly Wasted'. It would be the last time Kylie would see Hutchence before his death on 22 November that year.

Vid Bit!

Director: Pedro Romanhi

Not one but four Kylies—SexKylie, CuteKylie, IndieKylie, and DanceKylie—catfight it out for supremacy in this clever, comical, and captivating video. When asked which one represented her most, she chose 'CuteKylie'. Awww.

Remix Fix!

After 'Some Kind of Bliss' snubbed the dance crowd, it was a different story for the second *Impossible Princess* single with Trouser Enthusiasts (still one of the best remixer names of all time!), Razor N'Guido, and Philip Steir doing it again.

'Breathe'

deConstruction: 74321 570132 **Single release:** March 1998 **Album:** *Impossible Princess*

Writers: Kylie, Dave Ball, Ingo Vauk

Producers: Dave Ball, Ingo Vauk

On the third single from *Impossible Princess*, Kylie renounced her indie cravings, skimming back into pop-dance mode. In retrospect, 'Breathe' would probably have made a more successful first single, bridging the gap between her previous album and this new adventurous Kylie. 'Breathe' was written in Japan in 1995 where Kylie was hanging out with boyfriend Stéphane Sednaoui, who later shot the 'Breathe' single cover and the *Impossible Princess* cover. '"Breathe it won't be long now" is just me saying stay calm,' Kylie mused, 'until I reason as to what is going on in my head.' 'Breathe' co-writer/producer Ball is better known as the non-singing half of Soft Cell (biggest hit: 1981's 'Tainted Love'), while Vauk is his producing partner. A charming piece of pop electronica, 'Breathe' was Kylie's last solo charting 1990s single reaching #14 in the UK and #23 in Australia. In 2018, Officialcharts.com listed 'Breathe' as 'one of Kylie's hidden gems'.

Vid Bit!

Director: Kieran Evans

Although similar to 1994's 'Put Yourself in My Place'—Kylie floating in space again in another pink outfit—this moody languid clip captures the sense of the song's lyrics where Kylie is longing to not be needy, quiet, helpless, and 'just sorting everything inside'. Evans later directed a Manic Street Preachers doco.

Remix Fix!

Todd Terry's Tee's Freeze Mix is one of the great forgotten remixes of Kylie's illustrious career. Other remixers breathing new life into the track were Sash! and Nalin & Kane.

'Say Hey'

Release: October 1997 **Album:** *Impossible Princess*
Writer: Kylie
Producers: Kylie, Brothers In Rhythm

The other song on *Impossible Princess* with a sole songwriter credit for Kylie, 'Say Hey' is a 5 a.m. rave tune as she sings of being 'in the mood to play'. From the sexy purr of her voice, it is clear this can only mean one thing. Borrowing inspiration from Iceland's Björk (called 'the weird gay's Kylie' by *The Advocate*), Kylie wrote 'Say Hey' in the bathtub trying to conjure non-verbal ways to communicate with then-boyfriend Stéphane Sednaoui, also an ex of Björk's. So beloved by fans is this track that the Kylie Minogue Forum online named itself 'SayHey'. Resurrected for 2012's Anti Tour, it became obvious the disturbingly good 'Say Hey' is one of the songs Kylie is most proud of writing and—hey—why shouldn't she be?

'Drunk'

Release: October 1997 **Album:** *Impossible Princess*
Writers: Kylie, Steve Anderson, Dave Seaman
Producers: Brothers In Rhythm

'I'm suffocated with desire/I need to save me from myself' begins this throbbing mid-90s pop-electronica odyssey detailing Kylie's emotional development and a volatile sexual relationship. It is deeply personal and 'Drunk' is probably one of the reasons why Kylie later said she would never make another record like *Impossible Princess*. '"Drunk" has nothing to do with being drunk,' Kylie pointed out, 'but the feeling of being almost angry and having so much feeling for someone and the feeling of not being satisfied until you take all.' For an artist who has always so highly prized her privacy, 'Drunk' proffers a rare glimpse behind her pop star façade and fourteen years later was revived as a highlight during 2012's Anti Tour.

'I Don't Need Anyone'

Release: October 1997 **Album:** *Impossible Princess*
Writers: Kylie, James Dean Bradfield, Nick Jones
Producers: James Dean Bradfield, Dave Eringa

The other Manic Street Preachers track on *Impossible Princess* is not a million miles away from 'Some Kind of Bliss'. In fact, 'I Don't Need Anyone' is two or more songs in one. As the first Manic Street Preachers song sent to Kylie, she rewrote the lyrics before handing them back to Bradfield who in turn merged his lyrics with Kylie's. 'This one I feel is a bit difficult to explain,' Kylie admitted. 'I like the sentiment anyway—I don't need anyone except for someone that I haven't found.' IndieKylie reclaimed her grunge past when she rocked this banger on 2012's Anti Tour, also posting a clip of her band rehearsing 'I Don't Need Anyone' to her YouTube channel.

'Jump'

Release: October 1997 **Album:** *Impossible Princess*
Writers: Kylie, Rob Dougan
Producers: Rob Dougan, Jay Burnett

'I'm saying that whatever I feel like let me be that way,' Kylie noted about 'Jump'. 'Don't be afraid of the future because it will come anyway.' Underrated expat Australian musician Dougan was a pal of Rollo from Faithless, with whom he often collaborated. Kylie and Dougan must have felt a cosmic connection, both hailing from Melbourne and 'Jump' is indeed a highlight of the album with its seductive, mesmerising electronica. The *Impossible Princess* album peaked at #10 in the UK, but received a warmer reception at #4 in Oz.

'Limbo'

Release: October 1997 **Album:** *Impossible Princess*
Writers: Kylie, Dave Ball, Ingo Vauk
Producers: Dave Ball, Ingo Vauk

Originally called 'Sweetest Summer', and reportedly Kylie's choice as first single from *Impossible Princess*, in the end 'Limbo' wound up as just an album track. 'I wrote "Limbo" in Spain, but it was actually about a time where I couldn't see the person I wanted to see because of bureaucracy,' Kylie recalled. In some ways similar to much of Ball's work with The Grid (their biggest hit 1993's *Swamp Thing* reached #3 in both the UK and Australia), 'Limbo' is literally IndieKylie battling DanceKylie for supremacy. For 2003's *Impossible Princess* reissue, Tom Parker's linernotes mention 'parts of two songs recorded with (the band) Olive in 1996 were later reworked in "Some Kind of Bliss" and "Limbo"'.

'Through the Years'

Release: October 1997 **Album:** *Impossible Princess*
Writers: Kylie, Dave Ball, Ingo Vauk
Producers: Dave Ball, Ingo Vauk

While the two Manic Street Preachers tracks seem jarringly out of place on *Impossible Princess*, in hindsight they played their part in repositioning Kylie as an artist who would take risks in her career, even if they brought lesser commercial yields and critics still did not get her. Is 'Through the Years' a veiled attempt by Kylie to analyse her relationship with Michael Hutchence (who passed away exactly one month after *Impossible Princess* was released)? 'Through the Years' provides ample evidence that when Kylie truly applies herself, and tackles something important from her life, she is a champion lyricist.

'Dreams'

Release: October 1997 **Album:** *Impossible Princess*
Writers: Kylie, Steve Anderson, Dave Seaman
Producers: Brothers In Rhythm

On the album's closing track, Kylie is in self-reflection mode as she ponders 'the dreams of an impossible princess'. Lending the album its title, *Impossible Princess* was initially released in the UK as *Kylie Minogue* due to the recent death of Princess Diana before later reverting back to its original title. Kylie actually borrowed the phrase from the 1994 book by poet and musician Billy Childish called *Poems to Break the Harts of Impossible Princesses*, given to her by the ever-thoughtful Nick Cave. On 'Dreams', originally titled 'Impossible Princess' according to Anderson in 2021, Kylie tackles melancholy electronica head first and with her usual steely conviction.

'Tears'

Release: October 1997 **Album:** *Impossible Princess*
Writers: Kylie, Dave Ball, Ingo Vauk
Producers: Dave Ball, Ingo Vauk

From the teary '50s-style pop balladry cover of late-'80s 'Tears on My Pillow' to the thudding late '90s self-penned techno-electronica of 'Tears' marked a huge progression personally and professionally for Kylie. Yet another ode to boyfriend Sednaoui (her 'urban Buddhist punk'), as the B-side to 'Did It Again' (and the original *Impossible Princess* Japanese edition bonus track), released just days after Kylie's ex Michael Hutchence had killed himself, the words of 'Tears' could not have rung, or in this case, wrung truer—'I love you to tears'.

'Stay This Way'

Release: October 2000 **Compilation:** *Hits+*
Writers: Kylie, Steve Anderson
Producer: Steve Anderson

A curiously ominous, if almost despondent, jazzy piano ballad, 'Stay This Way' finds Kylie almost predicting the death of Michael Hutchence. 'You make me feel peace/I wonder when the hearse will come' she croons quietly and sullenly. 'Stay This Way', co-written and produced by Anderson, who William Baker called 'the campest straight man in the world', first saw a proper release on 2000's *Hits+* compilation after it failed to stay on track for *Impossible Princess*.

'Love Takes Over Me'

Release: 1998/October 2000 **EPs:** *Live and Other Sides/Other Sides* **Compilation:** *Hits+*
Writers: Kylie, Steve Anderson, Dave Seaman
Producers: Brothers In Rhythm

With at least another album's worth of material left off *Impossible Princess*, the leftovers have sputtered out through the years on various compilations, including easily Kylie's worst album cover of all time, BMG's *Artist Collection*. 'I am lost in the world of you,' Kylie begins on 'Love Takes Over Me' in what appears to be the closest Kylie has ever gotten to discussing her sex life, at least in public, or on record. Perhaps because it was just a bit too intimate ('Your love takes over me/I can taste it') is why it was sidelined, despite a typically grandiose BIR production.

'Take Me with You'

Release: 1998/October 2000 **EPs:** *Live and Other Sides/Other Sides* **Compilatiion:** *Hits+*
Writers: Kylie, Steve Anderson
Producers: Brothers In Rhythm

'Take Me with You' is another *Impossible Princess* cast-off rehoused as the B-side for both the 'Some Kind of Bliss' and 'Cowboy Style' singles. It also appeared on 1998's *Live and Other Sides* EP (revamped as *Other Sides* due to Kylie's disliking of the live recordings) alongside 'Love Takes Over Me' and 'Tears' and sold as an exclusive for HMV in Australia. Like a trip-hop reprise of 'Confide in Me', here Kylie bravely confronts her own celebrity, if not her own mortality.

'This Girl'

Release: June 2000 **Compilation:** *Hits+*
Writers: Kylie, Uschi Classen
Producer: Uschi Classen

This lo-fi country-tinged mid-tempo demo boasting a bevy of sad cellos was discarded before it even got to the final production stage. 'I am not interested in fitting in/I only want to be this girl' Kylie informs us, yet the most telling lyric might be when she utters 'though I'm good at pretending/I tire easily and hurry to the ending'. 'This Girl' was finally released on the expanded *Impossible Princess* in 2003. A slight tune but also slightly revealing too.

9

Intimate and Live Album and More (1998–2000)

Intimate and Live

Original version: MUSH33183.2
Originally released: November 1998 (Australia)
Original tracklist
Disc 1

'Too Far'	6:57
'What Do I Have to Do'	4:20
'Some Kind of Bliss'	4:07
'Put Yourself in My Place'	4:51
'Breathe'	4:05
'Take Me with You'	6:29
'I Should Be So Lucky'	4:00
'Dancing Queen'	6:00
'Dangerous Game'	5:34
'Cowboy Style'	6:28

Disc 2

'Step Back in Time'	3:36
'Say Hey'	4:10
'Free'	4:01
'Drunk'	4:21
'Did It Again'	5:18
'Limbo'	4:10
'Shocked'	5:38
'Confide in Me'	6:26
'Locomotion'	3:20

'Should I Stay or Should I Go' 4:29
'Better the Devil You Know' 7:46

'German Bold Italic' (Towa Tei Featuring Kylie Minogue and Haruomi Hosono)

East West: 3984-25333-2 **Single release:** September 1998 **Album:** *Sound Museum*
Writers: Kylie, Towa Tei
Producer: Towa Tei

'You will like my sense of style!' Although recorded in Japan in 1996 prior to *Impossible Princess*, 'GBI' was included on Tei's 1997's *Sound Museum* album before getting a proper single release in 1998. This minimalist techno-pop track, where Kylie takes on the persona of a typeface, is one of the most fantastically wacky tracks of her career. Tei, previously from Deee-Lite who hit big with 1990's perennial party starter 'Groove Is in the Heart', was in the midst of making an album featuring different vocalists when Kylie sent him a fax stating, 'Music with you! Kylie. Call me.' Although 'GBI' did little on the charts (#50 in Australia and #63 in the UK), it added to her artistic vision and is a long-buried career highlight.

Vid Bit!

Director: Stéphane Sednaoui

'GBI' is a mindboggling Japanese surrealist live anime fest and who better to pull this off than Kylie's own sometime samurai. The 'GBI' video remains unreleased though it has over 100,000 views on YouTube. Clearly many people like Kylie's sense of style, even her quirkier moments.

Remix Fix!

For 'GBI', Shy FX, and Krust delivered Kylie's most eclectic, if not stylish, set of remixes. Sharp Boys even pushed the Towa Tei connection further with their nine-minute Deee-Liteful Dub.

'Sometime Samurai' (Towa Tei Featuring Kylie Minogue)

V2: TDCL-91942 **Promo release:** April 2005 (Japan/Sweden) **Album:** *Flash*
Writers: Kylie, Towa Tei
Producer: Towa Tei

Written in Japan by Kylie with Tei about then-boyfriend Stéphane Sednaoui ('cradled by your greatness') at the same time as 'GBI', in 2003 Kylie contacted Tei to say 'I can't get over that song either. I should be able to sing it better now, so I'd like to re-record it. Can you come to London?' With Tei in tow, Kylie re-recorded her vocals on the track for inclusion on Tei's sixth album, *Flash*, released in 2005. The Honshu resident has since released seven more albums.

Vid Bit!

Director: Daniel Gorrel

A gritty, sometime B&W video for 'Sometime Samurai' was issued, minus Kylie but featuring graffiti artists on mopeds. The song was later used for a geisha tour projection on KylieX2008.

Remix Fix!

Towa Tei's Japanese-only *Flasher* EP issued in December 2005 contained two spacey remixes of 'Sometime Samurai' by (Aydin Hasirci) ATFC's Bushido Groove and (Uwe Schmidt's) Don Atom.

'Dancing Queen'

Mushroom: Kylie-3 **Promo release:** November 1998 (Australia) **Live album:** *Intimate and Live*

Writers: Björn Ulvaeus, Benny Andersson, Stig Anderson

Producer: Steve Anderson

'Dancing Queen' is not just ABBA's signature song, but one of the greatest pop songs of all time. First recorded during the *Intimate and Live* concerts, and initially only released on CD in Australia, Kylie's spirited recording of 'Dancing Queen' was used to promote her live album. Referred to as 'the gayest Kylie Minogue performance ever' (no mean feat!), Kylie reclaimed her camp pop past in her inaugural pink showgirl outfit. For the 2000 Sydney Olympic closing ceremony, Kylie again sang 'Dancing Queen' for an audience of billions. As the only non-Australian song sung, ABBA's Benny and Björn sent Kylie a note to congratulate her.

'Free'

Release: November 1998 (Australia only) **Live album:** *Intimate and Live*

Writer: Kylie

Producer: Steve Anderson

Together with 'Too Far' and 'Say Hey', this offbeat, oscillating ballad/rocker completes the trifecta of tunes Kylie wrote by herself for the *Impossible Princess* project. 'Free' appeared on her Australian-only *Intimate and Live* CD/DVD, which remains the only place it has been officially released. According to Kylie's 2002 *La La La* book, 'Free' was inspired by Kylie's globetrotting with then boyfriend

Sednaoui ('this is the feeling I want for always'). On the KylieX2008 tour, elements of 'Free' were added to 'Slow' during the show's 'Xposed' fourth act.

'In Denial' (Pet Shop Boys duet with Kylie Minogue)

Parlophone: 7243 5 21857 2 6 **Release:** October 1999 **Album:** *Nightlife*
Writers: Neil Tennant, Chris Lowe
Producers: Craig Armstrong, Pet Shop Boys

Taken from Pet Shop Boys' Top 10 UK album *Nightlife*, this portentous duet was with the duo's Tennant, after Kylie had previously recorded PSB's 'Falling' for 1994's *Kylie Minogue* but changed the demo beyond recognition (see entry in Chapter 7). Thus 'In Denial' became their first true collaboration. Kylie takes on the role of an enraged young girl discovering her father's belated coming out. 'It's quite dramatic and musical, quite theatrical,' Kylie said about 'In Denial'. In 2016, *The Guardian* reassessed it as one of Kylie's ten best tracks.

'The Reflex' (Kylie Minogue & Ben Lee)

EMI: CRCD001 **Release:** November 1999 (Australia) **Compilation:** *The Songs of Duran Duran: UnDone*
Writers: Simon Le Bon, John Taylor, Roger Taylor, Andy Taylor, Nick Rhodes
Producers: Peter Min, Peter Nashel

Not quite done with covers, Kylie's 'Oz rock' duet of Duran Duran's classic with indie-rocker Ben Lee was for an Aussie compilation. Originally released by the British fab five in 1984 and remixed by Nile Rodgers, 'The Reflex' went to #1 in the UK and US, becoming the biggest hit of Duran Duran's career. Lee later covered Kylie's 'Confide in Me' in 2002 on his *The Dirty Little Secret* EP. Strangely, all mention of Lee's 1999 Kylie duet is missing from his Wikipedia page.

'The Real Thing'

Festival Mushroom: D32146 **Release:** May 2000 (Australia) **Soundtrack:** *Sample People*
Writer: Johnny Young
Producer: Josh Abrahams

Featuring in the low-budget Aussie *Sample People* movie, which Kylie appeared in, 'The Real Thing' was a suitably unreal cover of the 1969 Russell Morris Australian classic. 'It's quite faithful,' Kylie said about her cover of 'The Real Thing'. 'The original is so good you wouldn't want to veer too much from it.' The following year, Morris's original was named one of the Top 30 Australian songs of all time. Oz TV legend Ian 'Molly' Meldrum produced the original.

Remix Fix!

Quirky, left-field remixes by Sonicanimation and Pound System were sent to Australian DJs.

10

Light Years Album (2000)

Light Years

Parlophone: 7243 5 28400 2 1
Originally released: September 2000
Original tracklist

'Password' (hidden pre-gap track)	3:50
'Spinning Around'	3:27
'On a Night Like This'	3:33
'So Now Goodbye'	3:37
'Disco Down'	3:57
'Koocachoo'	4:10
'Your Disco Needs You'	4:00
'Please Stay'	3:33
'Bittersweet Goodbye'	4:08
'Butterfly'	3:43
'Under the Influence of Love'	3:24
'I'm So High'	3:33
'Kids' (with Robbie Williams)	4:20
'Light Years'	4:47
Australian tour limited edition bonus disc extra track	
'Physical'	4:42

'Spinning Around'

Parlophone: 7242 8 88795 0 7 **Single release:** June 2000 **Album:** *Light Years*
Writers: Ira Shickman, Osborne Bingham, Kara DioGuardi, Paula Abdul
Producer: Mike Spencer

Baby, baby, baby! Here's the perfect example of how the right song at the right time can turn around any spun-out career. Freshly signed to Parlophone in the UK, Kylie's debut single for her new team, 'Spinning Around', was a pure pop-disco confection about which she later declared 'it was time to be poptastic again!' Producer Spencer, a former member of '90s dance/rap act Definition of Sound, had savvily remixed 'Made It Back' for Beverley Knight (UK #19) based around Chic's 1979 disco classic 'Good Times', which spun Parlophone around. Sped up from the original R&B version, 'Spinning Around' became Kylie's first #1 in ten years in the UK and first #1 in six years in Australia. 'I'm responsible for helping Kylie Minogue come back!' co-writer Abdul bragged about 'Spinning Around', which details her 1998 divorce. 'Spinning Around' not only resurrected Kylie's career, it set up the forthcoming *Light Years* album and—most importantly of all—prepared Kylie's career to go stratospheric globally the following year. In 2020, *The Guardian* ranked 'Spinning Around' as Kylie's #1 greatest single.

Vid Bit!

Director: Dawn Shadforth

The first of many videos Shadworth made for Kylie, the sparkle, razzle and dazzle of 'Spinning Around' has all but been overshadowed by those gold lamé hotpants. Costing next to nothing from a London flea market, they helped Kylie leg it, literally, to the top of the charts.

Remix Fix!

While the original 'Spinning Around' was a seductive albeit avowedly pop affair, the Sharp and 7th District remixes were shrewdly designed for the handbag house crowd.

'Cover Me With Kisses'

Release: June 2000 (B-side of 'Spinning Around')
Writers: Kylie Minogue, Mike Rose, Nick Foster, Steve Anderson
Producer: Steve Anderson

The first of the two 'Spinning Around' B-sides, both were compositions Kylie had a hand in writing, showed the degree of confidence Parlophone had in their new signing, not just as a singer/performer, but as an evolving artist in her own right. Here Kylie steps back into a Britpop '60s-style groove with some subversive product placement. 'Cover Me In Kisses' also suggests Parlophone may have initially been keen to keep IndieKylie in the loop.

'Paper Dolls'

Release: June 2000 (B-side of 'Spinning Around')
Writers: Kylie Minogue, Steve Anderson
Producer: Steve Anderson

An acoustic valentine to the love of Kylie's life—though it is just hard to say who that was at this point—Stéphane Sednaoui, Michael Hutchence, Jason Donovan, or new *beau* James Gooding? Not exactly in keeping with the pop-disco vibe of *Light Years*, 'Paper Dolls' became something of a lost classic. In 2010, co-writer/producer Anderson uploaded a magical acoustic version of 'Paper Dolls', which was dolled up again for 2012's Anti Tour.

'On a Night Like This'

Parlophone: 7243 889310 0 7 **Single release:** September 2000 **Album:** *Light Years*
Writers: Steve Torch, Graham Stack, Mark Taylor, Brian Rawling
Producers: Graham Stack, Mark Taylor

In some ways the second single from *Light Years* had a bigger task to do than the first. 'On a Night Like This' needed to prove 'Spinning Around' was no mere fluke. This sophisticated post-disco Euro-pop bop certainly did the job. At the same time, 'On a Night Like This' provided the perfect launch pad for *Light Years*, released as Kylie's comeback album two weeks later in September. Through an extraordinary piece of PR synergy, 'On a Night Like This' was out in shops at the time Kylie performed it at the Sydney Olympics closing ceremony. Australia awarded it a #1 spot, while the UK sent it to #2 (kept from the top by Modjo's 'Lady (Hear Me Tonight)'. A regular fixture on Kylie's concerts thereafter, this by-now pop classic later found its way to 2012's *The Abbey Road Sessions* for a smoochy orchestral makeover.

Vid Bit!

Director: Douglas Avery

Inspired by fashion imagery and aiming for an atmosphere of oligarch opulence, superpower, and luxury—where better to capture that than Monte Carlo? Based around Sharon Stone's character in Martin Scorsese's *Casino* film, 'On a Night Like This' was not your average pop clip, with legendary Dutch actor Rutger Hauer appearing as her erstwhile love interest/sugar daddy.

Remix Fix!

While the single version was very much a pop radio production, the remix fest for 'OANLT' was overtly targeted at the 'pink pound'—Motiv8, Halo Varga, Rob Searle, and Bini & Martini.

'Ocean Blue'

Single release: September 2000 (B-side to 'On a Night Like This')
Writers: Kylie Minogue, Steve Anderson
Producer: Steve Anderson

A sentimental, lo-fi, acoustic guitar ballad, on 'Ocean Blue' Kylie takes 'Some time in the still/Memories lead me far away', which might be her waxing nostalgic about her beloved Australian landscape. In a 2014 article, 'Kylie The Songwriter', entertainment-focus.com dived in and declared 'the hangover from *Impossible Princess* was clearly evident in the album era's B-sides written with Steve Anderson. Songs like "Ocean Blue" and "Paper Dolls" are much simpler, acoustic songs with more spiritual and magical lyrics of love and taking time out'.

'Password'

Release: October 2000 **Album:** *Light Years*
Writers: Kylie, Johnny Douglas
Producer: Johnny Douglas

The hidden first track on *Light Years* was a little-too-obvious pastiche of Deee-Lite's 'Groove Is in the Heart' from 1990, co-written by the band's Towa Tei who Kylie worked with a few years previously. A neat trick of creating a track that does exactly what it says in its title, 'Password' was hidden in the pre-gap of track one on *Light Years* (this was not going to age well digitally, was it?). Douglas, who co-wrote a number of George Michael's big hits, including 1996's 'FastLove', contributed three other *Light Years* tracks—'So Now Goodbye', 'Disco Down', and 'Koocachoo'.

'So Now Goodbye'

Release: October 2000 **Album:** *Light Years*
Writers: Kylie, Steve Anderson
Producer: Johnny Douglas

Kicking off in true discolicious style, this is Kylie's take on Gloria Gaynor's 1979's anthem 'I Will Survive'. Another Kylie co-write with Anderson, 'So Now Goodbye' was handed over to Douglas for production duties. 'When I sat down with the people from the label to discuss what this album should be, we all agreed that I should do what I do best—a pop record,' Kylie said at the time of *Light Years*' release, calling *Impossible Princess* 'a bit of a purge' following the SAW years. In 2020, Anderson revealed 'So Now Goodbye' was written long before Kylie signed to Parlophone disclosing 'there was no "Spinning Around" then'.

'Disco Down'

Release: October 2000 **Album:** *Light Years*
Writer/Producer: Johnny Douglas

The first of two 'disco' named tracks on *Light Years*, Kylie namechecks three of the era's biggest hits—ABBA's 'Dancing Queen' (1976), Chic's 'Le Freak' (1978–79), and The Jacksons' 'Blame It on the Boogie' (1978). After being omitted from her tours during the noughties, Kylie revived this fan-favourite retro-disco nugget (which shamelessly poaches the guitar riff from ABBA's 1979 hit 'Does Your Mother Know') for 2012's Anti Tour where it became a huge crowd singalong. Kylie's joy at getting down to her own 'disco' classic was self-evident.

'Loveboat'

Release: October 2000 **Album:** *Light Years*
Writers: Kylie, Robbie Williams, Guy Chambers
Producers: Guy Chambers, Steve Power

In 2002's *La La La* book, Kylie wrote the 'key words for *Light Years* were poolside, disco, cocktails, beach and loveboat. A cruiseship where you could set your cares aside and kick your heels up with gay abandon.' If any song on *Light Years* epitomises that 'martinis and bikinis' vibe, it is 'Loveboat'. The opening number on 2001's On a Night Like This shows—her sixth concert tour by this stage—on her KylieX2008 tour Kylie segued 'Loveboat' into 'The Love Boat Theme Song' then into a full-blown cover of Barry Manilow's 'Copacabana'. Sail on, *savoir faire*!

'Koocachoo'

Release: October 2000 **Album:** *Light Years*
Writers: Kylie, Johnny Douglas
Producer: Johnny Douglas

Bringing some mod, mini-skirt, psychedelic '60s grooviness to the album for a change of pace, Kylie is ready to go-go. Goofy, a little too early musically to qualify in any way as disco, talkaboutpopmusic.com rightly christened 'Koocachoo' 'kooky'. 'Koocachoo' became a suitably Swinging Sixties outing, not to mention second opening number, during 2001's On a Night Like This concert set list. It also nabbed a literary mention in Nico Medina's 2007 award-winning novel *The Straight Road to Kylie* where it was referred to as 'musical amazingness'.

'Your Disco Needs You'

Parlophone: 7243 879025 2 7 **Single release:** January 2001 **Album:** *Light Years*
Writers: Kylie, Guy Chambers, Robbie Williams
Producers: Guy Chambers, Steve Power

The greatest Kylie single that never quite got a proper release? While Williams and Chambers's game plan with 'Your Disco Needs You' was to meld the Village People's 'YMCA' with Queen's 'Bohemian Rhapsody', it also has close roots to Village People's 'Go West', covered by Pet Shop Boys. Just squeaking into the Australian Top 20 (after fans petitioned pre-social media to have it released) and a minor hit in the Germanic territories, Parlophone made the bewildering decision not to release 'Your Disco Needs You' as a single in the UK. In 2019, Chambers confirmed 'Your Disco Needs You' was vetoed as a single for being too camp. 'As if it's ever been something to stop a song from being commercial,' he winced. 'There's always been room for camp songs—it's something we need; that part of our culture is very important.'

Vid Bit!

Directors: Todd Cole

For a needy record that got so little love from Parlophone at the time, it seems only fitting that its shoestring video budget stretched out to two versions. The first featured some natty CGI effects with one report claiming the entire budget was just $42. Kylie's German record company commissioned a re-edited video (Kylie sporting her 'Your Disco Needs You' T-shirt as seen on the single cover) and more balloons, streamers and, er, disco lips. Every disco needs that, right?

Remix Fix/Language Fix

While Almighty, Casino, and 7th District attempted to make a camp record even camper, it is Kylie's cunning linguistic skills to admire here. While the original carried a French language bridge, that switched into German, Spanish, and Japanese versions for releases in their respective countries. Her '*Deutsche*' is rather charming, not mention, rather '*sehr gut*' too.

'Please Stay'

Parlophone: 7243 889732 2 9 **Single release:** December 2000 **Album:** *Light Years*
Writers: Kylie, Richard Stannard, Julian Gallagher, John Themis
Producers: Richard 'Biff' Stannard, Julian Gallagher

One problem *Light Years* was blessed with was that literally every album track could qualify as single material. That said, its most questionable single choice was 'Please Stay'. Almost like stepping backwards in time, this slightly twee, Latin-lite pop SAW re-tread scrapped into the UK Top 10 at #10 and peaked at #15 in Australia. Performed during KylieFever2002 and the Showgirl: The Greatest Hits Tour, afterwards 'Please Stay' disappeared, undoubtedly due to the collective agreement it actually did not make such a pleasing single choice.

Vid Bit!

Directors: James Frost and Alex Smith

Silly, sexy, and with major hairography. Kylie writhes in bed in what seems to be the remainder of that gold lamé fabric from the 'Spinning Around' hotpants, while the OTT choreography is plucked directly from a drag show, but that *Light Years* pinball machine sure is pleasingly cool.

Remix Fix!

Metro, Pumpin Dolls, 7th District, and Haitras all said yes, please, to remixing 'Please Stay'.

'Bittersweet Goodbye'

Release: October 2000 **Album:** *Light Years*
Writers: Kylie, Steve Anderson
Producer: Steve Anderson

'Bittersweet Goodbye' is a potent reminder some of Kylie's greatest moments, and hits, have been ballads. It also demonstrates her fine pipes, not to mention growing strength and confidence as a lyricist ('Let the nighttime envelop us/Take us under/Bewitching spell'). 'BG' did not get any love on stage, though—was it just too personal for Kylie to sing?—until appearing on the set list for 2012's Anti Tour. In 2020, on the song's twentieth anniversary, Anderson called 'Bittersweet Goodbye' 'one of my favourite songs we've ever written.'

'Butterfly'

Blue2 Records: B2-001 **Release:** October 2000 **Album:** *Light Years*
Writers: Kylie, Steve Anderson
Producer: Mark Picchiotti

Anderson wisely decided to hand 'Butterfly' over to US producer/remixer Picchiotti to make it not just dancefloor friendly but literally fly! Parlophone were so buoyed by 'Butterfly', a month before anyone had heard 'Spinning Around', they released a one-sided white label promo 12″, minus Kylie's name, in May 2000. Such was its appeal Stateside 'Butterfly' got a club release there soaring up to #14 on the Dance Club Songs chart—Kylie's first appearance in the US charts in a decade. A limited-edition maxi CD was released there on Picchiotti's Blue2 label with remixes from Sandstorm, E-Smoove, Illicit, Trisco, Havoc, and Craig J. Staged during 2001's On a Night Like This tour, 'Butterfly' became a sexed-up club banger complete with writhing half-naked male dancers. Talk about a complete metamorphosis! In 2021, Picchiotti revealed he was originally given the choice of three demos to produce for *Light Years*—'Butterfly', 'Under the Influence of Love', and the unreleased, and still unleaked, 'Same Place Same Time'.

'Under the Influence of Love'

Release: October 2000 **Album:** *Light Years*
Writers: Paul Politi, Barry White
Producers: Richard "Biff" Stannard, Julian Gallagher

'Under the Influence of Love' was a minor Motown-esque hit for American soul singer Felice Taylor called 'I'm Under the Influence of Love' in 1967, written by the 'Godfather of lurve', Barry White. Barry's backing trio Love Unlimited slinkily covered the tune in 1973 making it a bigger hit. This is the version Kylie's is more influenced by (with a hint of John Paul Young's 'Love Is in the Air'). Stannard was a fine addition to Team Kylie—he was after all co-writer and producer of Spice Girls' debut 'Wannabe' colossus so he was influential pop company to be under.

'I'm So High'

Release: October 2000 **Album:** *Light Years*
Writers: Kylie, Guy Chambers, Megan Smith
Producers: Guy Chambers, Steve Power

'I'm So High', with its winning mix of guitar-pop and dance beats, while not a single, could certainly have been a champion contender. What other pop song in history has reminisced so poetically before about sitting poolside 'by the frangipani tree'? Co-writer Smith was an Australian singer/songwriter who fronted an unsigned girl group in the late 1990s. They recorded the original 'I'm So High' after Smith wrote it with Chambers. A no-budget B&W video of 'I'm So High' by Smith's unnamed band was uploaded in 2009 and sure enough it transpires that frangipani tree concept was all Kylie's.

'Kids' (Robbie Williams/Kylie Minogue)

Chrysalis: 7243 889577 0 0 **Single release:** October 2000 **Album:** *Light Years* (Kylie) *Sing When You're Winning* (Robbie)

Writers: Guy Chambers, Robbie Williams
Producers: Guy Chambers, Steve Power

Coupling Kylie together with former Take That bad boy Robbie Williams was a true no-brainer. EMI family labelmates and both big fans of each other, professionally and personally, it was just a matter of finding the right song for a duet. So Robbie and pal Chambers wrote one themselves, with additional uncredited input from Kylie. 'Kids' thrashes around like a big ironic indie pop statement, yet at the same time loving what it pokes fun of. An uncredited sample of Sisters Love's 1973 funk hit 'Give Me Your Love' balances out its rockier moments. 'Kids' hit #2 in the UK (kept off the top by U2's 'Beautiful Day') and went gold in Australia though it peaked at #14. Kylie and Robbie only ever performed their duet live once together that year in Manchester, though their electric *Top of the Pops* performance was swamped in sexiness. On other occasions, Kylie has had adult assistance on 'Kids' from sister Dannii, former SAW labelmate Rick Astley, and even U2's Bono at one of her 2001 'On a Night Like This' Sydney gigs.

Vid Bit!

Director: Simon Hilton

All lips, eyes, and hips, the 'Kids' clip was based around John Travolta and Olivia Newton-John's 'You're The One I Want' from 1978's *Grease* movie and the clip sizzled with sexual tension, mutual attraction, and innuendo. These two needed to get a room, or a whole album!

'Light Years'

Release: October 2000 **Album:** *Light Years*
Writers: Kylie Minogue, Richard Stannard, Julian Gallagher
Producers: Richard 'Biff' Stannard, Julian Gallagher

'Light Years' was not just the title track of Kylie's album, but a throbbing, swirling gauge of the musical direction she would plunder for at least the next two decades—electropop with an edgy, yet still vaguely familiar feel to it—using Donna Summer's 'I Feel Love' (1977) dance classic as its launchpad. During the KylieFever2002 tour, the link was even more overt with 'Light Years' mashing 'I Feel Love'. In 2008, asked if 'LY' should have been a single, Stannard replied, 'I would have swapped it (with "Please Stay"). So many people tell me "Light Years" is their favourite Kylie song. I think the record company found it a little too "pink" for their tastes.' In 2021, *Light Years* ranked as the #1 Kylie album ever as voted by fans on Facebook.

'Good Life'

Release: December 2000 (B-side to 'Please Stay')
Writers: Kylie, Steve Anderson
Producer: Steve Anderson

Not a cover of Inner City's rave classic 'Good Life', but a beachy chill-out mid-tempo track written by Kylie with Anderson who produced it. Not quite in the same league as the material that made the cut for *Light Years*, Kylie's 'living the good life' as she freestyle jams her way to the end of the song. Rarely has she sounded this relaxed, as reflected in the lyrics, which suggest finding happiness living the good life in a reality better than the dreams she had as a little girl.

'Santa Baby'

Release: December 2000 (B-side to 'Please Stay')
Writers: Joan Javits, Philip Springer, Tony Springer
Producers: Chong Lim, Steve Anderson

Years before *Kylie Christmas* Kylie's first foray into seasonal offerings came in the shape of this cover version of Eartha Kitt's 'Santa Baby' classic. Released to help 'Please Stay' compete for the coveted UK Christmas #1 slot (the single stalled at #10), Kylie's version of 'Santa Baby' has since become a perennial festive fave. She would, graciously, add 'Santa Baby' to 2015's *Kylie Christmas* album and over Christmas 2020–21 it peaked at #31 on the UK charts (granting her a Top 40 hit in five decades), certified gold for sales, and streams of over 400,000.

Vid Bit!

Director: Alasdair McLellan

For Christmas 2010, Kylie made a no-budget but too cute 'SB' video for *Love* magazine.

'Physical'

Release: March 2001 **Album:** *Light Years (Australian Tour Edition)*
Writers: Steve Kipner, Terry Shaddick
Producers: Alexis Smith, Josh Abrahams, Marius de Vries

On 'Physical', Kylie pays tribute to one of the great Australian pop divas of the past—Olivia Newton-John. 'Physical' (1981) signified a real image switch for the former *Grease* star and was definitely something Kylie could identify with. Accordingly, she transformed her 'Physical' into a more intimate, stripped-back affair. Legend has it, Kylie's 'Physical' was originally intended for the *Moulin*

Rouge! soundtrack and was a sexy highlight on 2001's On a Night Like This concerts.

'Bury Me Deep In Love' (Jimmy Little and Kylie Minogue)

Festival Mushroom: 339992 **Release:** August 2001 (Australia only) **Compilation:** *Corroboration*
Writer: David McComb
Producer: Kurt Luthy

This delightful tender duet with Aboriginal Australian legend Jimmy Little featured on the *Corroboration: A Journey Through the Musical Landscape of 21st Century Australia* compilation. 'Bury Me Deep In Love' was originally a minor, but revered, hit by seminal Australian band The Triffids in 1987 whose version played during Harold and Madge's wedding on *Neighbours* in 1989. McComb, the song's writer and lead singer of The Triffids, died aged thirty-six in 1999 from a heroin overdose, while Little died aged seventy-five in 2012 from natural causes.

'G-House Project' (Gerling Featuring Kylie Minogue)

Flying Nun Records: FNCD458R **Release:** September 2001 **Album:** *When Young Terrorists Chase the Sun*
Writers: Gerling
Producers: Gerling, Josh Abrahams

Taking a day off in London in February, 2001, Kylie added her vocals to 'G-House Project', a track for antipodean label mates Gerling. This quirky, experimental electro-rock collab was taken from Gerling's unfortunately titled *When Young Terrorists Chase the Sun* album released in September 2001. It was, prudently, retitled *Headzcleaner* for its subsequent overseas release. A radio edit promo for 'G-House Project' was pressed, but a single never eventuated.

11

Fever Album (2001)

Fever

Parlophone: 7243 535804 2 1
Originally released: October 2001
Original tracklist

'More More More'	4:40
'Love at First Sight'	3:57
'Can't Get You Out of My Head'	3:49
'Fever'	3:30
'Give It to Me'	2:48
'Fragile'	3:44
'Come into My World'	4:30
'In Your Eyes'	3:18
'Dancefloor'	3:23
'Love Affair'	3:47
'Your Love'	3:47
'Burning Up'	3:59
Australian edition bonus track	
'Tightrope'	4:27
Japanese edition bonus tracks	
'Good Like That'	3:33
'Baby'	3:49
'Burning Up'	3:59
American limited edition bonus tracks	
'Boy'	3:47
'Butterfly'	4:09

'Can't Get You Out of My Head'

Parlophone: 7243 879864 0 4 **Single release:** September 2001 **Album:** *Fever*
Writers/Producers: Cathy Dennis, Rob Davis

It is no idle boast that 'Can't Get You Out of My Head' is the song that granted Kylie the rest of her career. Can one simple song do that? When it is as good as this, then, yes, it can. And how! 'I knew a few bars in that this song was for me,' Kylie wrote in her *La La La* book in 2002. 'By the end of the track I wanted to know how quickly I could get to the studio.' Now considered Kylie's signature song, Team Kylie were so hyped about their potential winner they debuted it live six months earlier on her On a Night Like This tour. Former pop *ingénue* Dennis (see Chapter 4) wrote and produced the song with Davis for teen act S Club 7. After they, then singer Sophie Ellis-Bextor passed on it (though she later disputed this), Kylie's A&R snapped it up. 'I don't believe anyone else would have done the incredible job she did with it,' Dennis later remarked. 'CGYOOMH' justifiably topped the charts in a reported forty countries and provided Kylie with her second US Top 10 single, fourteen years after 'The Loco-Motion' became the first. It also helped Kylie's accompanying *Fever* album debut at #3 in that territory, selling over a million copies Stateside. Both *Rolling Stone* and *NME* listed 'CGYOOMH' among their Top 100 songs of the noughties and such was its cross-cultural appeal it was heard in an episode of *The Simpsons*. In 2020, *Classic Pop* magazine ranked 'CGYOOMH' as Kylie's #2 all-time single, and by 2021, it had racked up over 200 million streams. 'CGYOOMH' is also Kylie's biggest-selling single ever, at between 5 and 6 million copies and—la la la!—one of the biggest-selling singles of all time. It was more than Kylie dared to think about. For its twentieth anniversary, Kylie told BBC Radio 2 'that song and album still kinda sound fresh and modern—I'm so proud of it!'

Vid Bit!

Director: Dawn Shadforth

Just as had transpired previously in the 'Spinning Around' clip, a piece of fabric became the most important, celebrated, and freeze-framed moment from the 'CGYOOMH' video. A hooded white jumpsuit, designed by Fee Doran for Mrs Jones—which William Baker lovingly called 'pure but kind of slutty'—turned a fashion wow moment into an iconic pop culture one. With Michael Rooney's robotic hi-tech synchronised choreography and the expensive set piece of a De Tomaso Mangusta sports car as supporting characters, the 'CGYOOMH' video was a triumph of music, imagery, fashion, and zeitgeist.

Remix Fix!

Superchumbo, K&M, Plastika, Tim Deluxe, Radio Slave, Plastika, and Nick Faber were all brought on board, but it was not until Kylie performed her mashup with

New Order's pioneering '80s epic 'Blue Monday'—cleverly titled 'Can't Get Blue Monday Out Of My Head'—that it finally got its true club dues.

'Boy'

Release: September 2001 (B-side to 'Can't Get You Out of My Head')
Writers: Kylie, Richard Stannard, Julian Gallagher
Producers: Julian Gallagher, Richard 'Biff' Stannard

By default, 'Boy' and 'Rendezvous at Sunset' are two of Kylie's biggest-selling songs as 'CGYOOMH' B-sides. While Kylie could not lay claim to the songwriter royalties from her mega-hit, she instead collected a tidy sum from having co-written the single's two other tracks. 'Boy' is progressive minimalist electronica, with Kylie's deliciously gender-flipping utterances about making some 'pretty little thing' move on the dance floor. 'Boy' might just be the most underrated, intriguing track of the whole *Fever* era.

'Rendezvous at Sunset'

Release: September 2001 (B-side to 'Can't Get You Out of My Head')
Writers: Ash Howes, Ben Chapman, Julian Gallagher, Kylie, Martin Harrington, Richard Stannard
Producers: Julian Gallagher, Richard 'Biff' Stannard

'Rendezvous at Sunset' unmistakably dives back into the blissed-out Ibiza foam party (or is it after party?), of the *Light Years* vibe ('Let's rendezvous at sunset/Take it through to sunrise'). The concluding Daft Punk-esque 'rendezvous' vocoder section, however, instantly carbon-dates 'Rendezvous at Sunset' as more last century than this millennium.

'More More More'

Release: October 2001 **Album:** *Fever*
Writers: Tommy Danvers, Liz Winstanley
Producer: TommyD

More Disco! More Pop! More Kylie! *Fever* promised more, more, more, so little wonder its first track was so named and clearly influenced in style, if not in title, by 1976 dirty disco chestnut 'More More More' by The Andrea True Connection. Kylie had already announced she wanted this album to be progressive and *Fever* was the calling card that reintroduced her to American audiences. During this 'amazing and brilliant time', as Kylie later called it, *Fever* would become the sales highpoint of her career. For its twentieth anniversary in 2021, *Fever* was reissued on white vinyl.

'Love at First Sight'

Parlophone: 7243 551083 2 6 **Single release:** February 2002 **Album:** *Fever*
Writers: Kylie, Richard Stannard, Julian Gallagher, Ash Howes, Martin Harrington
Producers: Richard 'Biff' Stannard, Julian Gallagher

Fever's feel-good funky 'Love at First Sight' (as opposed to the 1988 SAW version) was cursed with having to follow 'Can't Get You Out of My Head' as the second American, and third non-US, single. To that end, there was an American remix helping 'Love at First Sight' peak there at #23. Globally the track did much better, reaching #2 in the UK (held off by Elvis Presley's 'A Little Less Conversation') and #3 in Australia. 'That was probably the first big song where I was really there since its inception,' Kylie recalled, 'and I love performing it to this day.' Euphoric, elevating, and one 'ell of a tune, 'Love at First Sight' proved there was more than just the one classic track on the *Fever* album. It is also Stannard's favourite of the tracks he has made with Kylie 'because the chorus melody is so unusual'.

Vid Bit!

Director: Johan Renck

With nods to both *Tron* and Pet Shop Boys, Renck's one-take 'Love at First Sight' video was the work of a true mad genius. In 2019, he won an Emmy for directing the *Chernobyl* mini-series.

Remix Fix!

'The music you were playing really blew my mind!' The Scumfrog, David Guetta, Kid Crème, Twin, and Joachim Garraud took it to the clubs while the Ruff & Jam versions added an urban edge. Importantly, 'Love at First Sight' was nominated for Best Dance Recording in 2003—Kylie's first Grammy nomination.

'Fever'

Release: October 2001 **Album:** *Fever*
Writers: Greg Fitzgerald, Tom Nichols
Producer: Greg Fitzgerald

The title track of her eighth studio album, Kylie called 'Fever' 'very clever lyrically'. It was one of two tracks Fitzgerald/Nichols contributed and Kylie adored them both. Inspired by their combined love of the early 1980s New

Romantic wave, the quaintly naughty medical love lyrics were tagged by some commentators as 'Carry On Kylie'. Planned as the album's fourth single—and promoted as such to radio stations in Australia—Kylie's 'Fever' was scarpered by the decision to remake 'Come into My World'. Recalling this point in her career, Kylie called it 'a stratospheric time ... I could barely believe what had just happened'. The vinyl-tastic twentieth anniversary edition of *Fever* (2021) hit Top 10 in Australia and Top 30 in the UK.

'Give It to Me'

Release: October 2001 **Album:** *Fever*
Writers: Kylie, Mark Picchiotti, Steve Anderson
Producer: Mark Picchiotti

Kylie's gameplan for *Fever* was 'to incorporate more club, dance elements to the album, but it was important to keep the songs, the pop songs'. After the terrific job Kylie, Anderson, and Picchiotti did together on *Light Years*' high-flying 'Butterfly', 'Give It to Me' is a minor disappointment. Featuring a highly annoying, early noughties bleeping computer noise throughout, at least at under three minutes 'Give It to Me' does not hang around too long. In its reappraisal of *Fever* years later *Classic Pop* magazine graciously called 'Give It to Me' an experiment that didn't quite hit the mark'. Little surprise it is one of the few *Fever* tracks Kylie has never performed live.

'Fragile'

Release: October 2001 **Album:** *Fever*
Writer/Producer: Rob Davis

With two co-writes on the *Fever* album Davis was also given the opportunity to contribute a song sans Dennis. A former pop star, he was a member of 1970s glam rocksters Mud who scored three UK #1 hits. His biggest success pre-Kylie as a songwriter was Spiller's 'Groovejet (If This Ain't Love)' featuring Sophie Ellis-Bextor. Yet after his colossal success with Kylie, he only ever wrote her a further B-side. Why? 'Kylie's a funny one,' he opined, 'because you have to please the record company before her.' Which leaves us with 'Fragile', a light, whispery confection, not quite pop and not quite dance, that has the air of being greenlit as a thank you to Davis for his other/hit contributions to *Fever*.

'Come into My World'

Parlophone: 7243 551551 0 8 **Single release:** November 2002 **Album:** *Fever*
Writers/Producers: Cathy Dennis, Rob Davis

Deconstructed, edited, and re-recorded in Melbourne as the album's fourth single—reportedly because Dennis's vocals were too prominent on the album version—'Come into My World' was a clear sign where Kylie would veer next musically. There would be no 'Can't Get You Out of My Head' retreads and Team Kylie would famously turned down 'Toxic' in 2003, co-written by Dennis. Come hither 'Come into My World' was nonetheless a Top 10 UK and Australian hit though it bombed in the US at #91 as the third *Fever* single there. Importantly, 'Come into My World' won Kylie her first Grammy, for Best Dance Recording, in 2004.

Vid Bit!

Director: Michel Gondry

Quite possibly the most ingenious Kylie video ever, Gondry's one-shot CGI trickery is a true work of art. Kylie bustles around Paris' Boulogne-Billancourt warbling 'Come into My World', but each loop finds her, and the thirty extras, multiplied. In 2018, *Billboard* ranked 'Come into My World' #71 of the 100 greatest music videos of the twenty-first century.

Remix Fix!

Remixers who came on board were Joachim Garraud, Ashtrax, and Robbie Rivera, while electroclash darlings Fischerspooner's remix was Kylie pushing the pop envelope way out.

'In Your Eyes'

Parlophone: 7243 550578 2 2 **Single release:** June 2002 **Album:** *Fever*
Writers: Kylie, Richard Stannard, Julian Gallagher, Ash Howes
Producers: Richard 'Biff' Stannard, Julian Gallagher

The somewhat delayed follow-up to 'Can't Get You Out of My Head' (due to its continued success) except in the US, 'In Your Eyes', Kylie herself noted, 'has a lot of fans. I can't believe how many people come up to me and say "I love it!" which pleases me enormously because I co-wrote it.' Synthpop defender 'In Your Eyes' was written before Kylie ventured out on 2001's On a Night Like This tour. Although overshadowed by the single on *Fever* that preceded it, 'In Your Eyes' was nonetheless a #1 hit in Australia (her first #1 as a co-writer) and #3 in the UK.

Vid Bit!

Director: Dawn Shadforth

A sequel of sorts for Shadforth's 'CGYOOMH' video, Kylie fused disco moves and robotics. While her fringe dress did not quite have the same cut through as her white-hooded 'CGYOOMH' outfit, it was probably more important for Kylie to be singing a song she co-wrote.

Remix Fix!

Besides an extended version, remixers eyeballed were Roger Sanchez, Mr Bishi, Powder Productions, Saeed & Palesh, Jean Jacques Smoothie, Knuckleheadz, and the rare RLS Re-Edit Mix, aka the Special French Remix.

'Dancefloor'

Release: October 2001 **Album:** *Fever*
Writers: Steve Anderson, Cathy Dennis
Producer: Steve Anderson

This again marks the careers of two incredibly strong, resilient female pop stars who have reinvented themselves over the years and been consistently intertwined—just in case you are wondering, we're talking about Kylie and Cathy Dennis. Way back to Kylie spinning 1989's D'Mob record 'C'Mon and Get My Love' featuring Dennis to inspire SAW for 'Better the Devil You Know', there has been a sisterly synergy between the pair. In 1992, Dennis even co-wrote a minor hit for sister Dannii, 'Love's On Every Corner'. Fast forward a decade and Dennis had just co-written the biggest hit of Kylie's career. 'Dancefloor' was Dennis teaming with Kylie's main collaborator Anderson and vibes like Brothers In Rhythm at their insistent happy house best, updated for a new millennium.

'Love Affair'

Release: October 2001 **Album:** *Fever*
Writers: Kylie, Richard Stannard, Julian Gallagher
Producers: Richard 'Biff' Stannard, Julian Gallagher

'What we set out to do with *Fever* was to make it a culmination of everything I've learned and everything I've done,' Kylie declared. Some critics considered 'Love Affair' a strong contender for a fifth single from the *Fever* album. It certainly sounds like a hit, but perhaps not a big enough hit, especially when you consider the big four that had just come before it. At that moment, Kylie reflected, 'the future looks good … the planets are in alignment, but I like being me right now.'

'Your Love'

Release: October 2001 **Album:** *Fever*
Writers: Kylie, Pascal Gabriel, Paul Statham
Producers: Pascal Gabriel, Paul Statham

Light Years offered ten Kylie co-writes, but on *Fever* that number halved. With Kylie ever in demand for touring, merchandise, appearances, and—get this—having a life, time was tight for the simple task of songwriting. Having co-written two of the singles on *Fever* she could definitely point to having a decent batting average. The deliriously sweet 'Your Love' was, as per the BBC review of *Fever*, 'a rare serene moment in what is primarily a bit of an arse-shimmying, glitzy-disco affair.'

'Burning Up'

Release: October 2001 **Album:** *Fever*
Writers/Producers: Greg Fitzgerald, Tom Nichols

One of those sneaky records that begins as a ballad before it fires up into a space-age mirror ball glitter bomb, 'Burning Up' was the next logical sonic cosmos after *Light Years*. The second of the Fitzgerald/Nichols offerings on *Fever*, Fitzgerald had previously worked with Madonna on the poetic pop demo 'Revenge' which she later passed on to Sophie Ellis-Bextor. After his Kylie writing gig, Nichols moved on to work with two other Aussie pop divas, Tina Arena and Holly Valance. Meanwhile down at the electro disco in 2013, Canadian musician Andrew Huang covered 'Burning Up' using a direct sample from Kylie's version.

'Tightrope'

Release: October 2001 **Album:** *Fever*
Writers: Kylie, Pascal Gabriel, Paul Statham
Producers: Pascal Gabriel, Paul Statham

'Tightrope' was the second of the Gabriel/Statham collabs with Kylie for *Fever*, but after this, it would be almost another decade before Gabriel would work with Kylie again. Some critics suggested B-side 'Tightrope' was as good as its A-side 'In Your Eyes' and considering Kylie included it on 2012's Anti Tour then there is a good chance she might agree. With a killer chorus, some raw personal lyrics courtesy of Kylie's diary ('There's so much I want to share/For so long I've been too scared') 'Tightrope' is a true highlight from the *Fever* era.

'Baby'

Release: October 2001 **Album:** *Fever*
Writers/Producers: Liz Winstanley, Bottolf Lødemel, Lars Aass

As someone touted as a Kylie rave-pop rival in 1990, it must have seemed ironic a decade later that British singer/songwriter Winstanley was now penning tracks for Kylie's biggest-selling album of all time. Winstanley's second co-writing credit for the *Fever* album (after 'More More More') was hidden away as a Japanese Edition bonus, in addition to appearing on the 'Love at First Sight' single. Post Britney's 1998 '...Baby One More Time' hit, Kylie's 'Baby' likely already seemed past its use by date.

'Good Like That'

Release: February 2002 (B-side to 'In Your Eyes')
Writers/Producers: Joe Belmaati, Mich Hansen, Kara DioGuardi

It must have seemed like a major comedown for DioGuardi to be demoted from first single release on *Light Years* with 'Spinning Around' to B-side of 'In Your Eyes' single and Japanese edition bonus track of *Fever*. 'Good Like That' lifts inspiration from Stardust's 1998 'Music Sounds Better With You' hit, but there must have been the feeling at Parlophone that 'Good Like That', produced with Belmaati and Hansen aka Cutfather & Joe, already sounded a little too last millennium.

'Harmony'

Festival Mushroom: 020672 **Release:** February 2002 (Australian B-side to *In Your Eyes*)
Writers: Kylie, Steve Anderson
Producer: Steve Anderson

Included as one of two B-sides with the Australian 'In Your Eyes' single, 'Harmony', written on a warm summer day according to Anderson, finds Kylie gushing about a suitor. Just who was it making Kylie's heart sing? Presumably 'Shoreditch Travolta' model James Gooding whom she dated from 2000–2003. After a very public split at the 2003 Brit Awards the 'love rat' sold his story to the tabloids admitting to having cheated on Kylie. Never performed live but one of Anderson's personal faves, 'Harmony' now probably no longer exists for Kylie, just like Gooding.

'Never Spoken'

Release: February 2002 (Australian B-side to *In Your Eyes*)
Writers: Kylie, Steve Anderson
Producer: Steve Anderson

It is the tossed away B-sides on *Fever* where we really get to see what is going on in Kylie's heart and soul, never mind getting her out of our heads! The intense lyrics for 'Never Spoken' read like a conflicted woman contemplating some serious relationship issues, making it one of Kylie's most overlooked B-sides. In many ways 'Never Spoken' is the perfect flip, musically, lyrically, and emotionally, to its 'In Your Eyes' A-side.

'Whenever You Feel Like It'

Lava: 7567-83543-2 **Release:** June 2002 **Soundtrack:** *Scooby-Doo: Music From and Inspired by The Motion Picture*
Writers: Kylie, Billy Steinberg, Rick Nowels
Producer: Rick Nowels

It must have been a thrill for Kylie to write with songwriting legends Steinberg and Nowels. Steinberg has co-penned some iconic songs (Madonna's 'Like a Virgin', Bangles' 'Eternal Flame', and Cyndi Lauper's 'True Colours' to name but three), while Nowels is no slouch having co-written hits for Celine Dion, Madonna, and Dido. 'Whenever You Feel Like It' is, alas, a very much an of-its-era disco-pop track that never truly achieves the right feels. It was included on the 2002 *Scooby-Doo* soundtrack, which peaked at #24 in the US.

12

Body Language Album (2003)

Body Language

Parlophone: 7243 595758 2 7
Originally released: November 2003
Original tracklist

'Slow'	3:15
'Still Standing'	3:40
'Secret (Take You Home)'	3:16
'Promises'	3:17
'Sweet Music'	4:11
'Red Blooded Woman'	4:21
'Chocolate'	5:00
'Obsession'	3:31
'I Feel for You'	4:19
'Someday'	4:18
'Loving Days'	4:26
'After Dark'	4:10
Australian limited edition bonus track	
'Slow Motion'	4:18
Japanese edition bonus tracks	
'You Make Me Feel'	4:19
'Slow Motion'	4:18
North American edition bonus tracks	
'Cruise Control'	3:55
'You Make Me Feel'	4:19

'Slow'

Parlophone: 7243 553383 2 7 **Single release:** November 2003 **Album:** *Body Language*
Writers: Kylie Minogue, Dan Carey, Emilíana Torrini
Producers: Sunnyroads (aka Dan Carey, Emilíana Torrini)

'Slow' was very much a risqué risk—brimming with sexual tension, more electro than pop, and a soundscape that made radio at the time curl its toes. 'We just tried to picture a scene where someone came round and said, "I've got the new Kylie single and it's really cool,"' co-writer Carey later remarked. 'It's a weird sounding record.' It also came replete with a steamy video that completely upstaged the song. If anything, however, 'Slow' proved Kylie was not just about a formula, or reheating past successes. How different would Kylie's career have been though, especially in the US, if she had said yes to Cathy Dennis' 'Toxic' instead of releasing the self-penned 'Slow'? That we can only guesstimate in hindsight. Regardless, 'Slow' hit #1 in the UK and Australia, was nominated for a Grammy for Best Dance Recording (losing, yup, to Britney Spears' recording of 'Toxic') and a decade later Kylie selected it as her own favourite song from her career, ranking as her greatest success as a songwriter (her sole UK #1 co-write to date). In the US it became Kylie's last single to chart in the Top 100, stalling at #91, though it reached #1 on the Dance Club Songs chart. Sonically innovative and lyrically daring, 'Slow' is still, without question, the sexiest song Kylie has ever recorded. Read her body language!

Vid Bit!

Director: Baillie Walsh

Those skimpy speedos and bikinis! That pastel towel choreography! That flimsy Balenciaga frock! This was a true prick tease of a Kylie video in all senses of the word. Filmed at an Olympic swimming pool in Barcelona, in 2018 Kylie selected 'Slow' as one of her two favourite videos (the other being 'Come into My World'). In 2007, Walsh directed the movie *Flashbacks of a Fool.*

Remix Fix!

Radio Slave and Medicine 8 did the business, but The Chemical Brothers' remix speedily became a fan favourite. For 2020's Infinite Disco gig, Donna Summer's 'Love to Love You Baby' sexed 'Slow' up.

'Soul on Fire'

Release: November 2003 (B-side to 'Slow')
Writers: Kylie, Emilíana Torrini, Dan Carey
Producers: Sunnyroads

The first 'Slow' B-side was written by the same dream team who composed the A-side. Torrini is an Icelandic singer/songwriter who as a member of dance collective GusGus had a number of minor dance hits (the standout being 2002's 'David') and subsequently released three solo albums. Surprisingly, after the success of their work with Kylie on 'Slow' Sunnyroads (aka Torrini and Carey) never worked with her again. 'Soul on Fire' sure does give the impression of being a great half-finished idea, with a lyric suggesting major relationship issues at the Minogue homestead ('Can't we go back to bed'), and at 101 bpm is neither dance nor ballad.

'Sweet Music'

Release: November 2003 (B-side to 'Slow')
Writers: Kylie, Ash Thomas, Karen Poole
Producer: Ash "Baby Ash" Thomas

The second of the two 'Slow' B-sides was a slightly more upbeat (112 bpm) track that could have fallen off any number of Prince albums between the '80s and '90s. 'Sweet Music' really is too good to have been tossed away as just a B-side and finds Kylie delicately tiptoeing the musical tightrope between funky pop and urban R&B. Lyrically 'Sweet Music' features a rather glib self-referential lyric ('Let's make this demo right'), plus a knowing reference to Michael Hutchence ('new sensation' refers to the 1988 INXS hit of the same name).

'Still Standing'

Release: November 2003 **Album:** *Body Language*
Writers: Ash Thomas, Alexis Strum
Producer: Ash 'Baby Ash' Thomas

In many ways, *Body Language* was the album Kylie always wanted to make—fusing her love of Prince-style funk and Janet Jackson pop/R&B from the mid-80s with excursions into electro-disco and post-new wave dance. 'Still Standing' was the opener for Kylie's special invite-only one-off Money Can't Buy gig in London to launch *Body Language*. *The Guardian* called 'Still Standing' 'a magnificent blend of Prince's "Kiss" and Peter Gabriel's "Sledgehammer"'. The UK's Official Charts website in 2018 named it one of Kylie's 'hidden gems and deep cuts you need in your life'. That 'Still Standing' was track #2 on *Body Language* proves Parlophone considered it one of the album's most immediate tracks. Ex-pop star Strum is now a stand-up comedian—still.

'Secret (Take You Home)'

EMI: KYLIESAMPLER 551 666 **Promotional single release:** January 2004 (Taiwan only) **Album:** *Body Language*
Writers: Reza Safinia, Lisa Greene, Niomi McLean-Daley, Hugh Clarke, Paul George, Gerard Charles, Brian P. George, Curtis T. Bedeau, Lucien J. George
Producers: Rez, Johnny Douglas

At the 2003 Brit Awards, British rapper Ms. Dynamite (McLean-Daley) won awards as British Female Solo Artist and British Urban Act. For an album leaning heavily on '80s pop and R&B, it was a canny move to add her street cred to *Body Language*. The lengthy list of songwriters credited for 'Secret (Take You Home)' is due to the interpolation of Lisa Lisa and Cult Jam with Full Force's 'I Wonder If I Take You Home' 1985 freestyle hit. On 'S(TYH)' Kylie also irresistibly raps, while the song took on a secret life of its own in Taiwan becoming a #1 hit in 2004.

'Promises'

Release: November 2003 **Album:** *Body Language*
Writers: Kurtis el Khaleel, David Billing
Producers: Kurtis Mantronik, Johnny Douglas

Mantronik was the electronic-funk pioneer behind Mantronix who during their 1984–91 lifespan shapeshifted from hip-hop to house. While Kylie had no writing involvement in the chic R&B pop of 'Promises', it is a clear kiss-off to an unpromising ex ('The promises we used to keep have gone/And with them all the words that kept us both from seeing what was wrong'). Released as a promotional single in Ireland, 'Promises' was a true album highlight.

'Red Blooded Woman'

Parlophone: 7243 548223 2 2 **Single release:** March 2004 **Album:** *Body Language*
Writers: Johnny Douglas, Karen Poole
Producer: Johnny Douglas

'Red Blooded Woman', as single #2, was an abrupt change in genre, style, and mood from 'Slow'. *Billboard* called it 'a cousin of Justin Timberlake's "Cry Me a River"'. Interesting chart fact: the same week 'Red Blooded Woman' debuted at #5 in the UK, Britney Spears debuted at #1 with 'Toxic'. Although 'Red Blooded Woman' peaked at #4 in Australia, it failed to chart in the US. It did feature in one of the great TV moments of Kylie's career during the Australian satire series *Kath & Kim*. Strangely, it was not Kylie who sang it but her 'mum' Kim (Gina Riley) as a karaoke classic—'Here's a blast from the past!'—to which Epponnee-Rae

(Kylie) yells, 'Don't give up your day job, mum!' Noice, different, unusual, to coin a very *Kath & Kim* phrase.

Vid Bit!

Director: Jake Nava

Kylie's in a real jam here, a traffic jam, as it turns out. What is a girl to do? Jump out and strut her footloose stuff, a decade before folks did similar in the Oscar-winning *La La Land* movie.

Remix Fix!

At this point in Kylie's career, Parlophone were not only making interesting single choices for Kylie from *Body Language*, but less obvious remix choices for 'Red Blooded Woman' too—Narcotic Thrust, Whitey, and Play Paul (not released commercially but leaked in 2011).

'Chocolate'

Parlophone: 7243 549822 2 4 **Single release:** June 2004 **Album:** *Body Language*
Writers: Johnny Douglas, Karen Poole
Producer: Johnny Douglas

Uncut unkindly called 'Chocolate' 'trip hop for tweenies'. Tweaked slightly in its single/radio edit release, pumping up the vocal and with a minute bumped from its running time, the wispy whispery 'Chocolate' dipped in at #6 in the UK, but peaked at a disappointing #14 in Australia. A rapid-fire raunchy rap by Ludacris ('The bedroom we lose calories in it/Start families in it') was recorded but nixed (rumoured by Kylie herself) though it leaked in 2006. Saucy stuff indeed.

Vid Bit!

Director: Dawn Shadforth

At least a decade before Hollywood rediscovered musicals, Kylie was taste-testing it with 'Chocolate'. That coy smile, and nod to French chic, just had to be because of beau Olivier Martinez.

Remix Fix!

'Chocolate' sourced just two remixers—Tom Middleton (future electro) and EMÓ (slinky).

'Obsession'

Release: November 2003 **Album:** *Body Language*
Writers: Kurtis el Khaleel, David Billing, Mim Grey
Producers: Kurtis Mantronik, Johnny Douglas

Rather than running from, or recreating her past, Kylie was now at a point where she could almost self-reverentially acknowledge it for inspiration—such was the cheeky borrowing here of the opening riff from 'Better the Devil You Know'. Asked in 2004 if the lyrical content of 'Obsession' referred to the end of a troubled relationship, Kylie told *The Independent*, 'if it wasn't that I loved the song so much, it would not be on my album 'cos I just thought, "Eugh, I know I'm gonna be asked about this."' Kylie only performed 'Obsession' at the Money Can't Buy one-off.

'I Feel for You'

Release: November 2003 **Album:** *Body Language*
Writers: Jason Piccioni, Liz Winstanley, Stefano Anselmetti
Producer: Electric J

The most experimental track on *Body Language* (with some bonus rain effects for extra feels) includes an unacknowledged sample from underground UK garage/electronic record 'It's My House' by New Horizons issued in 1997. *Metro Weekly* wrote about the album, 'if you're expecting *Body Language*, Minogue's ninth studio album, to be a sequel to her massive 2002 hit *Fever,* you'll be sorely disappointed.' *Slant Magazine* opined instead that '*Body Language* is less immediate and more experimental, a midway point between the alternative/electronica of 1997's *Impossible Princess* and Minogue's more mainstream post-millennium work'.

'Someday'

Release: November 2003 **Album:** *Body Language*
Writers: Kylie, Emilíana Torrini, Ash Thomas
Producer: Ash 'Baby Ash' Thomas

Mantronik was not the only living legend to feature on *Body Language.* Green Gartside, better known as the mainstay of '80s art-pop funksters Scritti Politti, lent vocals to 'Someday', although he and Kylie were never actually in the studio together. Critically-revered Scritti Politti and their white boy funky soul style is very much part of the ''80s babies' musical tapestry of 'Someday'. *The Guardian* decreed 'Someday' 'as close to a chill-out track as Kylie has ever made, and indeed co-written'. In 2007, 'Someday' was sampled by Panda Bear for his twelve-minute-plus musical odyssey 'Good Girl/Carrots', alongside other snatches from Kraftwerk and Lee 'Scratch' Perry.

'Loving Days'

Release: November 2003 **Album:** *Body Language*
Writers: Kylie, Richard Stannard, Julian Gallagher, Dave Morgan
Producers: Richard 'Biff' Stannard, Julian Gallagher

It was a rollercoaster year for Kylie personally in 2003. After her public bust-up with model James Gooding post-Brit Awards in London on 20 February, she moved on to dashing French actor Olivier Martinez who she met three days later at the 2003 Grammy awards in New York. That means Kylie was single for a mere three days! 'Loving Days' was her final co-write on *Body Language*, and while she preferred not to air her dirty laundry on her records, she was more than happy to let us in on her private joy. 'We were just in a romantic mood and went for it,' Stannard recalled of 'Loving Days'. The same team also wrote the unreleased 'Attention Seeker'.

'After Dark'

Release: November 2003 **Album:** *Body Language*
Writers/Producers: Cathy Dennis, Chris Braide

The big question here has to be—why did Team Kylie opt for Dennis' lesser 'After Dark' and hand over 'Toxic' to Britney Spears, originally pegged for *Body Language*? Could it be Kylie herself had just come out of a rather toxic personal relationship and the lyrics cut a little too close to home? 'I wasn't at all angry when it worked for her,' Kylie insisted later. 'It's like the fish that got away. You just have to accept it.' The final track on *Body Language*, 'After Dark' is the perfect comedown for an album that takes a journey to music terrain hitherto unknown to her fans, if not Kylie herself. The sole live outing of 'After Dark', as a girl group affair, was at 2003's Money Can't Buy one-off gig. In 2019, Kylie gave her own blunt appraisal of *Body Language*: 'I'm not sure as a body of work it stands up, but "Slow" was a no-brainer for the first single'.

'Slow Motion'

Release: November 2003 **Album:** *Body Language*
Writers: Kylie, Andrew Frampton, Mark Stent, Wayne Wilkins
Producer: The Auracle

This sexy electro-R&B groover was a *Body Language* bonus track on the Australian and Japanese editions of the album. Presumably it was initially spelt 'slo' to avoid confusion with *Body Language*'s lead single 'Slow'. This is Kylie in sensual mode ('everything's wide open now that you're here!'), getting freaky about skin-on-skin action, though realising 'it's love I've fallen into'. Chalk up another sexy song clearly inspired by Martinez. The pair remained lovebirds until 2007. In 2010, he began dating future wife Halle Berry. The pair had a son, Maceo, in 2013.

'You Make Me Feel'

Release: November 2003 **Album:** *Body Language*
Writers: Kylie, TommyD, Felix Howard, Marius de Vries
Producer: TommyD

'You Make Me Feel' is another Kylie co-write banished from the standard *Body Language* album. Double, or even triple-tracked, vocals give the impression of a Kylie girl group *a la* Destiny's Child. Kylie may be 'your girl Friday/seven days a week', but 'You Make Me Feel' feels more plodding than progressive. Co-writer Howard was a former child model/actor who appeared in Madonna's 'Open Your Heart' video, became a major songwriter for the likes of Sugababes and Amy Winehouse, then rose to A&R executive at EMI where he signed Calvin Harris and Lana Del Rey. After departing EMI in 2012, he signed a likely lad called Lewis Capaldi. de Vries, Madonna and Massive Attack's bestie, won a Grammy in 2017 for *La La Land*.

'Almost a Lover'

Release: March 2004 (B-side to 'Red Blooded Woman' single)
Writers: Kylie, Karen Poole, Ash Thomas
Producer: Ash 'Baby Ash' Thomas

Speaking of 'almost', seven Kylie co-writes for *Body Language* ended up as either single B-sides, or bonus tracks. 'Almost a Lover' is a slinky electropop ditty again owing a major *merci* to Madonna's work with French producer Mirwais (on 2000's 'Music' and 2003's 'American Life' albums). Decidedly heavy on the Moog bassline, but light on a truly catchy chorus, 'Almost a Lover' is saddled with one of Kylie's most cumbersome, if not combustible, lyrics—'We've got the flame/I want the fire'. Thomas later worked with Jessie J and Emile Sandé (as Ash Millard).

'Cruise Control'

Release: March 2004 (B-side to 'Red Blooded Woman' single)
Writers: Kylie, Johnny Douglas, Karen Poole
Producer: Johnny Douglas

It is here that we can evaluate what *Body Language* might have been if Team Kylie had spun more doggedly into R&B. With a touch of bhangra beats and a slightly juvenile tween feel, the most interesting thing about 'Cruise Control' is the uncredited, practically obscured, dancehall rap assumed to be by Sean Paul ('I move like a spiderman' is one of the few decipherable lines), or a close proximity to him if it is not. Years later, Entertainment.focus.com listed 'Cruise Control' as one of the best Kylie B-sides, while a version minus the rap also surfaced on the net.

'City Games'

Release: June 2004 (B-side to 'Chocolate' single)
Writers: Kylie Minogue, Julian Gallagher, Karen Poole, Richard Stannard
Producers: Richard 'Biff' Stannard, Julian Gallagher

The final track to be released during the *Body Language* era, a sluggish electro-funk number that enthusiastically echoes Britney Spears' early hits, was already more (in)famous as the title of Kylie's next album reported in early 2003, long before *Body Language* was confirmed (see Appendix I). If the *City Games* album was a hoax, it was an elaborate one and may have slightly derailed fans' expectations once the official *Body Language* track list was announced.

13

Ultimate Kylie Compilation (2004)

Ultimate Kylie

Parlophone: 7243 875365 2 4
Originally released: November 2004
Original tracklist
Disc One

'Better the Devil You Know'	3:53
'The Loco-Motion' (7″ Mix)	3:14
'I Should Be So Lucky'	3:24
'Step Back in Time'	3:04
'Shocked' (DNA 7″ Mix)	3:09
'What Do I Have to Do' (7″ Mix)	3:33
'Wouldn't Change a Thing'	3:14
'Hand on Your Heart'	3:51
'Especially for You'	3:56
'Got to Be Certain'	3:19
'Je ne sais pas pourquoi'	4:01
'Give Me Just a Little More Time'	3:06
'Never Too Late'	3:21
'Tears on My Pillow'	2:29
'Celebration'	3:57

Disc Two

'I Believe in You'	3:21
'Can't Get You Out of My Head'	3:49
'Love at First Sight'	3:57
'Slow'	3:13

'On a Night Like This'	3:33
'Spinning Around'	3:27
'Kids'	4:20
'Confide in Me'	4:26
'In Your Eyes'	3:18
'Please Stay'	4:04
'Red Blooded Woman'	4:20
'Giving You Up'	3:30
'Chocolate'	4:01
'Come into My World'	4:06
'Put Yourself in My Place'	4:11
'Did It Again'	4:14
'Breathe'	3:40
'Where the Wild Roses Grow'	3:57
Digital Edition	
'Dancing Queen' (from *Live and Intimate*)	3:45

'I Believe in You'

Parlophone: 7243 876333 2 2 **Single release:** December 2004 **Compilation:** *Ultimate Kylie*
Writers: Kylie, Scott Hoffman, Jason Sellards
Producers: Babydaddy, Jake Shears

The first of two new tracks from 2004's *Ultimate Kylie* compilation, the unbelievably infectious 'I Believe in You' was a co-write with Babydaddy (Hoffman) and Shears (Sellards) from America's swinging Scissor Sisters. 'I Believe in You' returned Kylie to the top ten in Australia (#6), #2 in the UK (kept off the top by Band Aid 20's 'Do They Know It's Christmas'), #3 on the US Dance Club Songs chart, and was nominated for a 2006 Grammy for Best Dance Recording (losing to Chemical Brothers 'Galvanize'). 'I Believe in You' did, however, contain an ominous lyric, in light of Kylie's cancer diagnosis the following year: 'The joker's always smiling in every hand that's dealt/And I don't believe that when you die your presence isn't found'. In 2020, 'I Believe in You' was finally certified silver for sales of 200,000 in the UK.

Vid Bit!

Director: Vernie Yeung

When director Yeung was sent the track, he recalls: 'they wanted something disco. I thought of using a mirrorball'. He proceeded to create a spherical cage with Kylie captivatingly in the centre. The glamorous and ethereal videoshoot was choreographed by Rafael Bonachela.

Remix Fix!

Kylie snared Myles MacInnes aka Mylo for his percolating, almost threatening, mix, while Skylark's Balearic trance beat was perfect for an Ibiza pool party! In 2007, a ballad version debuted on *The Kylie Show* TV special, thereafter used during the KylieX2008 tour and later leaking online, then lovingly and touchingly re-recorded for 2012's *The Abbey Road Sessions*.

'BPM'

Release: December 2004 (B-side to 'I Believe in You')
Writers: Kylie Minogue, Richard Stannard, Julian Gallagher
Producers: Richard 'Biff' Stannard, Julian Gallagher

Kylie's irresistible, if not irrepressible 'BPM' (123 beats per minute) was reportedly first tackled during the *Body Language* sessions. Not wanting to take anything away from the glossy shimmering pop of A-side 'I Believe in You', 'BPM' truly deserved better than a B-side. Kylie herself must have thought so too, digging it out for 2012's Anti Tour—the only song from this era to make the cut. '"BPM" is a classic case of knowing I had a great song but never really getting the production right,' Stannard admitted years later.

'Giving You Up'

Parlophone: 7243 8 69638 2 6 **Single release:** March 2005 **Compilation:** *Ultimate Kylie*
Writers: Kylie, Miranda Cooper, Brian Higgins, Tim Powell, Lisa Cowling, Paul Woods, Nick Coler
Producers: Brian Higgins, Xenomania

The one-stop-shop appeal of *Ultimate Kylie* was it gathered together the biggest hits from all three of her labels on one double album with 'Giving You Up' the second new track to entice diehard fans. While the Xenomania-crafted 'Giving You Up' was a decent enough stomping electropop tune, in hindsight its more adventurous and memorable B-side, 'Made of Glass', would likely have made a better single. Nonetheless 'Giving You Up' went Top 10 in both Australia and the UK (#8 and #6 respectively). Its one live outing was at 2005's Showgirl gigs.

Vid Bit!

Director: Alex and Martin

Look out, viewers, it is the *Attack of the Giant Kylie* video nasty! French directors Alex Courtes and Martin Fourgerol's dated CGI-heavy clip does at least convey a surreptitious sense of humour.

Remix Fix!

Riton's bleepy tech takes now seem locked in a time vacuum, while German techno outfit Alter Ego offered a distinctly Teutonic alternative.

'Made of Glass'

Release: March 2005 (B-side to 'Giving You Up')
Writers: Kylie, Miranda Cooper, Brian Higgins, Lisa Cowling, Tim Powell, Matt Gray
Producers: Brian Higgins, Xenomania

Leaking on the internet before its official release, 'Made of Glass' is arguably the greatest Kylie Minogue B-side of all time. Reportedly also recorded by former S Club 7 member Rachel Stevens, 'Made of Glass' is IndieKylie does DanceKylie with a dash of PopKylie thrown in for good measure and lyrically offers a veiled insight into Kylie's relationship with Olivier Martinez ('a million beats in a Parisian heart'). Released in March 2005, 'Made of Glass' would also mark the last piece of new Kylie music until '2 Hearts' in November 2007. The title 'Made of Glass' could not, it transpired, have been more prophetic, though mercifully Kylie proved to be only momentarily shattered not irreparable. Phew!

'Over the Rainbow'

Parlophone: 00946 350495 2 7 **Promo single release:** December 2005 **Live Album:** *Showgirl Homecoming Live*
Writers: Harold Arlen, Yip Harburg
Producer: Steve Anderson

Written for classic 1939 film *The Wizard of Oz* and a signature song for Judy Garland, its then-teen star who played Dorothy, 'Over the Rainbow' was released by Kylie's label for Christmas as a digital single. Coupled with 'Santa Baby', it marked the first release after her cancer diagnosis halted the Showgirl: The Greatest Hits Tour, after the European leg had finished and before the Australian leg. Fittingly some proceeds from 'Over the Rainbow' went towards breast cancer research. The song has also been a UK hit for Cliff Richard, Eva Cassidy, and Ariana Grande.

'The Magic Roundabout'

Milan: M2-36164 **Release:** February 2006 **Soundtrack:** *Doogal (Music from the Motion Picture)*
Writers: Andrea Remanda, Jon O'Mahony, Michael Harwood, Nick Keynes
Producers: Steve Anderson, Goldust

Although the *Doogal* movie, from where 'The Magic Roundabout' came, opened in Europe in February 2005, it was released in significantly revised form a year later in the US along with the soundtrack. A family film version of the classic *The Magic Roundabout* TV show, *Doogal* featured Kylie and Robbie Williams' voices. Produced by the now infamous Harvey Weinstein, Kylie and Ian McKellen were the only voices retained from the UK version for American audiences. Kylie was also given the task of warbling the movie's newly written theme song and, ever the pro, Kylie sings this not-so-magical childish fluff with gusto. Not exactly a magical blockbuster either, *Doogal* barely made back its $US20 million budget. A planned sequel was eventually cancelled.

14

The *X* Files Leaks (The Unofficial *Xtra* Tracks)

As its title suggests, this book's primary focus is on the officially released songs from Kylie Minogue's extensive, and impressive, catalogue. Anything extra of interest, or note, or just too good to ignore, should hopefully be found in Appendix I. The *X* era, however, merits a special *X*-tra chapter.

Although Kylie's tenth album X was not officially released until November 2007, in February that year ten demos/songs from her comeback project, including 'In My Arms' pencilled as the lead single, appeared on file sharing networks. By May 2007, internet chatrooms were full of chatter that a three-disc CDR set containing forty-nine Kylie demos was in the hands of a Kylie collector. Some of the tracks even had titles the same as old demos and releases. At least seven of the songs were tracks pitched to Kylie and sung by session singers, but the other demos appeared to be true blue Kylie demos and outtakes. The bulk of them leaked fully a decade later.

During an interview that year on his first promotional visit to Australia, Calvin Harris let slip the source of the leak. 'A guy from her record company had his laptop stolen and they got put on the internet,' Harris fumed. At the end of 2007, Kylie confirmed to me in an interview that much of what did not make it on to *X* was her more personal tracks.

In February 2017, the additional songs from the *X* era finally leaked online. Almost like a purge, in light of Kylie having signed a new record deal with BMG, was this Parlophone/EMI doing some early spring cleaning of their digital cupboards?

Here is an alphabetised overview of the project's leaked tracks, misfits, and curiosities that did not appear on *X* (or get any kind of proper release be it as a B-side, bonus track, or iTunes extra, unless otherwise noted).

'Acid Min': If her sister can be known as 'Disco Dannii' then why not Kyles as 'Acid Min'? A distant comedown afterglow cousin of 'Slow' but less acid house and more sensual spoken word.

'Boombox': See separate entry in Chapter 16.

'Classical Transit': Kylie makes some 'orchestral moves' here on this throbbing three-minute electro-bass heavy demo giving a knowing nod to Giorgio Moroder that is so busy it gets stuck in a dead end.

'Come Down': Based on Kevin Lyttle's Indian-influenced 'That Vibe' (whose 'Turn Me On' was a 2003 hit), with 'That Vibe' released on his 2008 album *Fyah*. Is he the rapper on Kylie's retake?

'Down Down': A pounding Cutfather and Jonas Jeberg *X* reject lifting its backing track a touch too obviously from Justin Timberlake's ground-breaking/Grammy winning 2006 'SexyBack' hit.

'Fall for You': A frantic techno-pop track co-written with the Biffco team. 'We wrote it over this track I wrote with Greg Kurstin,' Richard Stannard recalled. 'A lot of people love this track.'

'Flower': See separate entry in Chapter 17.

'Give Up to Love': Another noughties-trapped electro track thought to be by Hannah Robinson (on vox too?), Martin Harrington and Ash Howes which might have been a better fit for *Body Language*.

'Guess': 'Guess who's back/Don't disrespect!' Kylie has a message for the masses as she raps her way through this under-100-second disco-funk track insisting 'I was only gone for a while'.

'I Am Ready (Survivor)': Reportedly by Boy George with shady lyrics ('I felt compassion with knives in my back') and swirling ready-made disco strings. Kylie previously covered Culture Club's 'Victims'.

'I Can't Help That': Landing somewhere between '70s disco and '80s funk, Kylie sashays in on this cute clubby, dubby affair with lyrics that manage to mention disco, movies and even 'a pot of coffee'.

'In the Mood for Love': Sexy electronica courtesy of Mylo. He got so upset at Kylie/Parlophone for not including this on *X* he briefly uploaded it to his MySpace page claiming he had a 'beef' with her. Ouch.

'Like Love (Hold On)': At long last, Kylie lyrically realises she is close to godliness ('I'm a deity'), but the music cannot decide if it is '90s Prince or '00s Madonna before—hold that thought—abruptly ending.

'Lose Control': Energetic indie electronica so good Kish Mauve grabbed it back from Kylie when she dumped it from *X*, releasing their version as an identikit single under their name in 2008.

'Love Attack (So Safe)': Lovingly produced by Calvin Harris (reportedly written by Hannah Robinson/Joe Dworniak) this sonically ahead-of-its-time big room anthem features a huge 'hands in the air' chorus.

'My Love is Real': Assumed to be a Karen Poole/Kylie/Soul Mechanics collab this pumping, squelchy, electro-disco ditty is another *X* offcut that is a true spurned corker. Team Kylie were spoilt for choice.

'Never Be Lonely': Reportedly by Jens Bergmark and Henrik Johan Korpi from the Murlyn stable with singer Therese Grankvist (on vox?). Borrows Monsoon's 1982 'Ever So Lonely' #12 hit chorus.

'One to One': Synth-heavy, mid-tempo Rob Davis effort with Biffco production that does not quite sound like Kylie singing. Stannard later admitted, 'I don't think I even played it to Kylie!'

'Ooh': Not to confused with another demo of the same name from the *Ultimate Kylie* era this has a somewhat hypnotic *X* groove but, ooh, it is a hot groundhog mess minus a proper chorus.

'Osmondosis': Jokey title aside (mixing Mormon boy band The Osmonds with 'osmosis'), this Studio 54 throwback neatly samples their 1979 'I, I, I' track produced by Bee Gees' Maurice Gibb.

'Right Here Right Now (Thing Called Love)': Not to be confused with her other two songs of the same name (1991's SW production and 2015's Giorgio Moroder collab) this formulaic funk-pop is definitely the lesser of the three.

'Ruffle My Feathers (Everlasting Love)': Moroder-influenced disco-pop camouflaging a not-so-veiled attack on someone's ego trip. Performed on KylieX2008 with a Bitrocka remix, Stannard called it 'very personal to Kylie'.

'Sexual Gold (Hush Hush)': Steve Anderson/Richard Stannard/Kylie minimalist electropop collab inspired by Goldfrapp. Anderson said this version is the 'weaker' of the many versions discarded after it leaked.

'Simple Boy': 'Slow'-like Biffco demo with Kylie putting on a brave face ('Turn around and walk away/Can't take it no more'). 'One of the best sessions of my life,' Stannard declared.

'Something to Believe In': Uplifting anthem with Kylie trawling her diary fits perfectly between 'No More Rain' and 'Stars'. 'My attempt at a PWL song,' Stannard said, 'but the record company didn't get it!'

'Spell of Desire': A simmering piece of Euro-pop electronica by Mylo meant for *X* that somehow missed the cut. Initially leaked by Mylo in 2007 on his MySpace page (where he called it 'Spell for Desire').

'Taprobane (Extraordinary Day)': Poignant, lush synth Biffco ballad with deeply personal lyrics about the private Sri Lankan island Kylie went to heal post-cancer treatment. Stannard called the song 'cathartic' for Kylie.

'That's Why They Write Love Songs': See entry in Appendix II for 2012's Anti Tour.

'To the 9's': Shimmering, strutting, if slightly disjointed, electropop with vox that might be Karen Poole and/or Kylie in unison. Best line: 'Let the music take you up to the 9s so I can have you'.

'What's It Gonna Take': The second Calvin Harris demo (two more—'In My Arms' and 'Heart Beat Rock'—made *X*) this bouncy tune is a foretaste of what Harris would soon perfect with other female vocalists.

'When the Song Comes On': Kylie's sass, attitude and simpering vocals ('I get it, ooh, when the song comes on') wrestle with a somewhat overthought/overwrought demo. Even a 'na-na-na' refrain comes on too.

'White Diamond': See entry in Chapter 15.

'You Make Me Feel': Not the *Body Language* track of the same name but a jangly guitar stomper co-written by Kylie with Kish Mauve who later released their own version on 2009's *Black Heart* album.

'You're Hot': The final of the snubbed *X* offcuts and while initially promising some heat sonically with its jittery urban-electro bleepiness 'You're Hot' goes cold due to a tepid, unmemorable chorus.

... and the *Xtra* Extras!

Over the years, the titles below have been mentioned in regards to the *X* leaks, but remain not just unconfirmed but no longer available on the net, if they ever existed, or indeed did leak at some point. The word 'Pitch' in brackets next to a demo indicates the song was sung by someone other than Kylie as it was proposed to her A&R team for consideration for the *X* album project. Any writers/producers mentioned are rumoured.

'Boys Boys Boys': Cathy Dennis co-write with Mark Ronson.

'Can't Get Enough' (Pitch).

'Drop the Pressure': Pitch by Mylo, though seems unlikely as he had a hit himself in 2005 with a remix called 'Doctor Pressure'—mixing in Miami Sound Machine for a UK Top 30 hit.

'Into The Light' (Pitch).

'Tell You Why'.

'Tell It Like It Is': Stuart Crichton with Biffco.

'Tell Me That It's Over' (Pitch): Richard Stannard, Stuart Crichton, Rob Davis, Kylie.

'The Reason'.

'We Are' (Pitch).

Buyer Beware!

'Excuse My French' (Pitch): *Pardon moi*! It is clear why Kylie was not keen to use this track as she had just split with Olivier Martinez. It is reportedly sung by Mia Crispin (Mia J) autotuned to sound like Kylie.

'I Think I Love You': Stomping pop bop tribute to R&B legend Marvin Gaye. Yes, really! Reported from *X* and again likely voiced by session singer Mia J—although it sure does sound Kylie-esque.

'When The Cat's Away' (Pitch): Another rejected tune—which sure sounds like a purr-fect hit—voiced by Mia J who supposedly co-wrote it (and 'Excuse My French') with Daniel Sherman/Kurtis Mantronik.

15

The X Album (2007)

X

Parlophone: 50999 513952 2 3
Originally released: November 2007

Original tracklist	
'2 Hearts'	2:51
'Like a Drug'	3:18
'In My Arms'	3:32
'Speakerphone'	3:54
'Sensitized'	3:57
'Heart Beat Rock'	3:24
'The One'	4:05
'No More Rain'	4:02
'All I See'	3:05
'Stars'	3:41
'Wow'	3:10
'Nu-di-ty'	3:04
'Cosmic'	3:09
CD-Rom bonus track	
'Rippin' Up the Disco'	3:29
Australian and New Zealand iTunes Store bonus tracks	
'Magnetic Electric'	3:16
'White Diamond'	3:03
European iTunes Store bonus track	
'Heart Beat Rock' (Benny Blanco remix Featuring MC Spank Rock)	3:13
Japanese Edition bonus tracks	

'King or Queen'	2:39
'I Don't Know What It Is'	3:18
US edition bonus tracks	
'All I See' (featuring Mims)	3:51
'Carried Away' (Amazon digital bonus track)	3:14
Mexican special edition bonus track	
'Do It Again'	3:22

'I Talk Too Much' (Just Jack Featuring Kylie)

TVT Records: TV-2980-2 **Release:** September 2007 **Album:** Overtones
Writers: Jack Allsopp, Ali Love
Producer: Jack Allsopp

British musician/rapper Allsopp, aka Just Jack, scored a #2 hit in January 2007 with his single 'Starz In their Eyes'. His sophomore album, *Overtones*, was released two weeks later. When the album was reworked for a US release, 'I Talk Too Much', featuring Kylie on backing vocals, was added to raise his profile in the States. A great match of electropop and artful noise—the question has to be asked why this funky music maverick wasn't on board for *X*? In 2009, Just Jack mused about his talkative duet with Kylie calling it 'very cool and very strange'.

'Love Is the Drug'

Universal Music TV: 5302508 **Release:** October 2007 **Compilation:** *Radio 1 Established 1967*
Writers: Andy Mackay, Bryan Ferry
Producers: Steve Anderson, Calvin Harris

Kylie's crisp cover of Roxy Music's 1975 classic had production chores shared by Anderson and Harris (who also mixed it). 'Love Is the Drug' arrived in stores via BBC's *Radio 1 Established 1967* compilation to commemorate the British pop music station's fortieth anniversary. Kylie's version sticks closely to the addictive original (also released as a single in 1980 by the iconic Grace Jones), one of the Rock and Roll Hall of Fame's '500 Songs That Shaped Rock and Roll'.

'2 Hearts'

Parlophone: 50999 513903 0 3 **Single release:** November 2007 **Album:** *X*
Writers: Mima Stilwell, Jim Eliot
Producers: Kish Mauve

The first single from Kylie's tenth album—hence the Roman numeral *X*—was also her first official release and first new material after her cancer diagnosis, treatment, and recovery. The big statement '2 Hearts' made was there was no big statement to make. Instead, it was just another great stomping example of what Kylie does best—world-beating pop forever and ever. The writers of '2 Hearts', Stilwell and Eliot, were British electropop duo/husband-and-wife Kish Mauve who released the original retro-electro glam rock version, then titled 'Two Hearts', in 2005 on their self-titled EP. 'I loved "2 Hearts" when I first heard it and it was a joy to record,' Kylie cooed in 2007. Her final Australian #1 to date and tenth in total, '2 Hearts' peaked at #4 in the UK, though a month prior the single and its remixes leaked, which surely impacted sales.

Vid Bit!

Director: Dawn Shadforth

Despite having recruited a group of drag queens from London club BoomBox and secured outfits by Gareth Pugh and Christopher Kane, '2 Hearts' was a more sedate performance piece for the first half with Kylie singing atop a grand piano. In the second half, she swaps it for a sexy black latex catsuit, strutting her way about a stage living out her best glam rock fantasies.

Remix Fix!

Kish Mauve provided their own remix, while others on board were Alan Braxe, Studio Version, Paul Harris, and Mark Brown. Freemasons' unofficial Dirty Hands remix mashed in Beyoncé.

'I Don't Know What It Is'

Release: November 2007 (B-side to '2 Hearts')
Writers: Kylie, Richard Stannard, Paul Harris, Julian Peake, Rob Davis
Producers: Richard 'Biff' Stannard, Paul Harris, Julian Peake

This hidden glam-house fusion gem from the Biffco team continues a long tradition in Kylie songs of jaunty music disguising some heavy emotions, if not heartbreak. 'Why do you always put me down/It's better when you're not around' and then later 'I'm choking inside/I love you to death in the afterlife' are not your typical 'la-la-la' pop sentiments. Is this Kylie distilling her relationship with Olivier Martinez who she once called 'the love of my life'? Only she knows!

'King or Queen'

Release: November 2007 (B-side to '2 Hearts')
Writers: Kylie, Karen Poole, Greg Kurstin
Producer: Greg Kurstin

Is Kylie pushing the pansexuality button on this Prince-lite pop-funk written with Kurstin and Poole? 'This one is much more of a celebration than anything I've done before,' Kylie said of *X*, 'with some room for reflection as well, which was good.' Released in November 2007 '2 Hearts' was the Kylie single on sale when she appeared on TV's *Doctor Who* in the 'Voyage of the Damned' episode, in a role written specifically for her, which became a huge UK ratings success.

'Like a Drug'

Release: November 2007 **Album:** *X*
Writers: Mich Hedin Hansen, Jonas Jeberg, Engelina Andrina, Adam Powers
Producers: Cutfather, Jonas Jeberg

Kylie's second 'drug'-titled song in the one year, 'Like a Drug' was initially sent to Britney Spears' A&R team who decided it sounded too much like a Kylie Minogue song—so guess where it ended up? 'It's one of those songs where I knew it would be cut up, so the recording can seem a bit fractured, or something, because I'm not singing it as you do a live vocal,' Kylie recapped. As for the subject matter of the song's title, Kylie was eager to clarify that for her dancing was the drug. 'I love that feeling to be out and to be just swept away by a song,' she opined at the time. 'You grab your friend and you go, "C'mon we've got to get on the dancefloor!"'

'In My Arms'

Parlophone: 50999 212984 2 4 **Single release:** February 2008 **Album:** *X*
Writers: Kylie, Calvin Harris, Richard Stannard, Paul Harris, Julian Peake
Producers: Calvin Harris, Richard 'Biff' Stannard

Calvin Harris released his debut album, *I Created Disco*, in 2007, aged twenty-three, and he was quickly snapped up to work on Kylie's comeback album including this, the third single. 'I thought they were joking,' he recounted. 'Two weeks later I was in the studio working with her. I had loads of backing tracks I couldn't fit my voice around because I'm not a natural singer, so it worked really well for Kylie.' For her part, Kylie stated that recording 'In My Arms' 'with Biff is a lot of fun and he brings out that camp side of me. I don't think Calvin Harris quite knew what had hit him (laughs).' Harris described 'In My Arms' to *NME* as 'like 500 men with their tops off dancing'. 'In My Arms' was the second global and third UK/Australian single from *X*. It peaked at #10 in the UK, but a disappointing #35 in Australia (her lowest chart hit in a decade). The Asian/Chinese album version of 'In My Arms' featured Taiwanese popstar Jolin Tsai, while Mexican singer Aleks Syntek featured on a Spanglish version of *X* in that territory.

Vid Bit!

Director: Melina Matsoukas

Filmed in LA by Matsoukas, who also directed the 'Wow' video, 'In My Arms' was a perfect visual match for this retroelectro hit. Gareth Pugh was responsible for the stunning outfits.

Remix Fix!

On the dance floor front Sébastien Léger, Chris Lake, Steve Pitron & Max Sanna, Spitzer, and Death Metal Disco Scene took 'In My Arms' into theirs. Oddly Harris did not remix his own track.

'Speakerphone'

Release: November 2007 **Album:** *X*
Writers: Christian Karlsson, Pontus Winnberg, Henrik Jonback, Klas Åhlund
Producers: Bloodshy & Avant

The same year this team delivered 'Speakerphone' and 'Nu-di-ty' for Kylie's *X* album, they penned 'Piece of Me' for Britney Spears. Considering 'Piece of Me' is based on what was going on in Britney's life at the time, does this mean 'Speakerphone' ('rock hard like a sinner block') and 'Nu-di-ty' ('I like it') were what was happening in Kylie's life post-cancer? Kylie herself loved 'Speakerphone': 'it's so catchy'. In August 2009, a competition was held for fans to create a video for 'Speakerphone'. The winner was an animation/art piece by Hungarian Rudolf Pap shown prior to Kylie's 2009 concert in LA. That same year, the outstanding Steve Anderson Studio Static Version of 'Speakerphone' was an iTunes bonus track on her *Live in New York* album.

'Sensitized'

Release: November 2007 **Album:** *X*
Writers: Guy Chambers, Cathy Dennis, Serge Gainsbourg
Producers: Guy Chambers, Cathy Dennis

While Chambers made a welcome return on *X*, this marked Dennis's last appearance in the Minoguesphere. 'Sensitized' contained an interpolation of 'Bonnie and Clyde' by legendary French pop artist Serge Gainsbourg and French movie icon Brigitte Bardot, plus a sample from 'Requiem pour un con' by Gainsbourg who died in 1991. 'I am so over the moon that we got permission to use it,' Kylie squealed. 'It's hot.' Kylie also recorded a *très chic* Franglais version of 'Sensitized' with Christophe Willem (see entry in Chapter 16).

'Heart Beat Rock'

Release: November 2007 **Album:** *X*
Writers: Kylie, Karen Poole, Calvin Harris, John Lipsey
Producer: Calvin Harris

Harris's second offering on *X* is a true throwback to early '80s funk-pop/dub rock. In 2019, Kylie told *Billboard* that Harris 'was possibly a bit nervous I think he confessed as much afterward ... it's no surprise he's gone on to crush everything.' Kylie also recalled 'Heart Beat Rock' was penned 'when I wrote "I Believe in You"—the same day I met Jake Shears and Babydaddy.' The hip-swaying Benny Blanco Remix of 'Heart Beat Rock' featuring MC Spank Rock ('Can you make it hot for me, Kylie?') was a European iTunes Store bonus track.

'The One'

Parlophone: 50999 514973 2 3 **Single release:** July 2008 **Album:** *X*
Writers: Kylie, Richard Stannard, James Wiltshire, Russell Small, John Andersson, Johan Emmoth, Emma Holmgren
Producers: Richard 'Biff' Stannard, Freemasons

Literally 'the one' that got away! Originally titled 'I'm the One' and released in 2006 by Laid Featuring Emma, Kylie's fifth and final single from *X* was a blast of pure unadulterated pop-house bliss with the Freemasons duo on board as co-producers. 'I just worked with Biff on the track and we were just delighted to get the word Michelangelo in there,' Kylie tittered. 'It's the little things that float our boat. "The One" is more traditional Kylie.' A digital download fifth single release, with the physical release cancelled, 'The One' peaked at #36 in the UK, but missed the Australian chart altogether. In 2018, 'The One' was ranked as Kylie's sixth best song of all time by Melbourne's *Herald-Sun*. That same year, when asked which non-single album track she would have wanted as a single, Kylie replied, 'I would have loved "The One" to have a full scale release.'

Vid Bit!

Director: Ben Ib

Ib was responsible for the concert visuals on KylieX2008 tour and Aphrodite: Les Folies Tour. 'Kylie sent me a really detailed brief with loads of amazing images, from Man Ray to Rodchenko, through Donna Summer and The Jackson 5,' Ib explained. 'I came up with a treatment inspired by some of her references, heavily based on the era of the 1940s.' It was all shot in a Manchester studio on a day off from her tour with dancers Jason Beitel and Nikki Trow.

Remix Fix!

Since Freemasons delivered such a powerhouse club mix, it was only fitting the video for 'The One' used their single edit too. Popjustice judged the full-length Freemasons mix 'exquisite'. It was and still is.

'No More Rain'

Release: November 2007 **Album:** *X*
Writers: Kylie Minogue, Karen Poole, Christian Karlsson, Pontus Winnberg, Jonas Quant
Producers: Greg Kurstin, Karen Poole

The lost opportunity on *X* was to turn it into a triumph of Kylie's will, spirit, and 'second hand chances'. Was the deliberate move to mostly avoid mentioning cancer a serious miscalculation in retrospect? Should the dramatic, poignant and glitter-dripping 'No More Rain' have been *X*'s lead single? 'My goal throughout the illness and afterwards was to get back on stage,' Kylie explained, 'and I guess I wrote "No More Rain" as almost like a mantra, positive thinking.' Debuting 'No More Rain' on the KylieX2008 tour, Kylie called it 'my favourite moment every show, because there was no choreography, there was no nothing. I'd just stand there with the microphone and just enjoy the shower of emotion I felt. It was about coming out of the other side.' Reign on, Kylie!

'All I See'

Capitol Records: 50999 2 13764 2 9 **Single release:** March 2008 **Album:** *X*
Writers: Jonas Jeberg, Mich Hedin Hansen, Edwin Serrano, Raymond Calhoun
Producers: Jeberg, Cutfather

This was the first single release from *X* in the US with lots of big appointment TV appearances (including *Dancing with the Stars* and *Ellen*). 'All I See' contains an interpolation of 'Outstanding' by The Gap Band, a minor US pop hit but a #1 R&B hit in 1982. Co-writer Serrano, aka stage name Lil' Eddie, recorded his version of 'All I See' on his album *City of My Heart,* released in Japan in 2009. Adding a rap to the US version was rapper Shawn Mims (an acronym for 'Music Is My Saviour'). Kylie, a lifelong R&B devotee, adored 'All I See', a punchy album cut but featherweight single contender. Released on CD single in the US and digitally in Oz, it failed to chart in both territories.

Vid Bit!

Director: William Baker

Filmed in minimalist monochromatic in just a couple of hours with fetish-ish outfits and dancer Marco Da Silva, all-seeing Kylie sure seemed to be enjoying playing dress up for Baker.

Remix Fix!

Kylie's American dance champion/stalwart Mark Picchiotti unveiled a slew of house and funk mixes, which helped it reach #3 on the US Hot Dance Club Play chart. The 'All I See' Remix Featuring Mims ('I see you watch me watch Kylie') was a US edition bonus track.

'Stars'

Release: November 2007 **Album:** *X*
Writers: Kylie, Richard Stannard, Paul Harris, Julian Peake
Producers: Richard 'Biff' Stannard, Paul Harris, Julian Peake

'"Stars" is a really different track for me,' Kylie said prior to *X*'s release, and along with 'No More Rain' and 'Cosmic', it completes the album's trifecta of reflective, self-penned songs. Ultimately, it sums up Kylie's life's philosophy and recovery mantra in its contemplative lyrics: 'You never know what you find/ Because stars don't shine in singular places'. In 2008, Stannard recalled with 'Stars' he and Kylie 'wanted to rock out a bit to keep us going late at night'. Added to 2012's Anti Tour set list, the guitar-led, meaning of life searching 'Stars' proved truly blissful.

'Wow'

Parlophone: 50999 520940 0 2 **Single release:** February 2008 **Album:** *X*
Writers: Kylie, Karen Poole, Greg Kurstin
Producers: Greg Kurstin, Karen Poole

Twisted disco inferno 'Wow' was *X*'s second single. In the UK 'Wow' hit #5 (where it went silver with sales of 200,000) and in Australia reached #11, though it limped in to US Hot Dance Airplay chart at #19. '"Wow" was recorded in Ibiza the afternoon after we arrived,' Kylie reminisced. 'We wrote "Wow" because this place was wow.' In 2018, 'Wow' was duly described by the *Herald-Sun* as if 'someone's shaking up a bottle of soda for three minutes until everything gets more and more hectic and you're out of breath when it finally explodes. A joyful noise.'

Vid Bit!

Director: Melina Matsoukas

Filmed simultaneously with 'In My Arms', 'Wow' was crammed with pizzazz and razzmatazz, and Kylie zipped up in snug catsuits and blonde wigs. Matsoukas's template for 'Wow' was put to good use when she next directed the debut clip, 'Just Dance', for a fledgling artist called Lady Gaga. Matsoukas later became the first woman to win a Grammy for directing a music video—Rihanna's 'We Found Love'—ironically written/produced by Kylie 'discovery' Calvin Harris.

Remix Fix!

Brazilian rock act C.S.S. (aka Cansei de Ser Sexy) smoothed out the original's electro edges and beefed up the percussion for their Latin American remix. Other mixers on duty were David Guetta & Joachim Garraud, MSTRKRFT, and DJ Rokk & Pixel 82, while the Death Metal Disco Scene version was the one Kylie made a wow moment during her Aphrodite: Les Folies Live tour.

'Nu-di-ty'

Release: November 2007 **Album:** *X*
Writers: Karen Poole, Christian Karlsson, Pontus Winnberg
Producers: Bloodshy & Avant

'I think "Nu-di-ty" is great,' Kylie affirmed in 2007 of this cocksure tossback to 'SexKylie' with risqué lyrics about popping zippers, daring to bare and 'one button at a time'. 'The first time I heard it,' Kylie admitted, 'I didn't get it. I liked it, but I didn't get it. It took me maybe three listens to figure it out and once you have figured it out it's really fun latching on to the odd beats in it.' An impromptu acoustic version of 'Nu-di-ty' recorded backstage in 2011 at the Aphrodite: Les Folies Tour with Kylie hanging with her band on the sofa might just be its defining version.

'Cosmic'

Release: November 2007 **Album:** *X*
Writers: Kylie Minogue, Eg White
Producers: Eg White, Matt Prisne

Kylie conceived ethereal *X* closer 'Cosmic' in Melbourne towards the end of her cancer treatment. 'I didn't write anything throughout most of my therapy (cancer therapy),' she reflected. 'I wanted to write a song called "Cosmic" … it felt quite floaty as well. It's such a joy when lyrics, or an idea, have found their place and what's more people like them.' Possessing one of Kylie's most deeply personal lyrics ('It's like I was asleep yet now I'm here') she rues not saying no, her self-worth and being destructive. Sung on *The Kylie Show* special 'Cosmic' certainly lived up to its title.

'Rippin' Up the Disco'

Release: November 2007 **Album:** *X*
Writers: Mich Hedin Hansen, Jonas Jeberg, Jasmine Baird
Producers: Cutfather, Jeberg

Included on the USB edition/CD-Rom bonus track/access to online *X* bonus track (it was a late noughties thing!), 'Rippin' Up the Disco' was an ahead of its time slice of pre-Gaga strobe-light-lovin' nu-electro disco. 'I don't know how many songs I've done for this album,' Kylie pondered in 2007. 'There's a lot of songs I recorded for my album which didn't make it, but meant a lot to me at the time in any case.' 'Rippin' Up the Disco' with its love for electro ladies, retromatic fashion and foxy funkadelic might well have been a display of sisterly love for 'Disco Dannii'. Kylie does sing 'I'm ambitious now' after all. There would be more disco Kylie to come too. Obvs.

'Magnetic Electric'

Release: November 2007 **Album:** *X*
Writers: Kylie, Karen Poole, Greg Kurstin
Producer: Greg Kurstin

This fan fave scorcher, originally planned as the title track for her tenth album, was co-written by Poole. 'Writing with Kylie has always been really easy and quick,' she declared, 'she's brilliant.' Poole comes from sturdy pop music stock—her father was Brian Poole, lead singer of 1960s British pop band The Tremeloes. It was thanks to another Minogue that she got her big break. 'Dannii's "Put the Needle On It" was the first thing I really did that got me noticed,' Poole explained. The too hot, sizzling 'Magnetic Electric' accordingly opened 2012's Anti Tour.

'White Diamond'

Release: November 2007 **Album:** *X*
Writers: Kylie, Scott Hoffman, Jason Sellards
Producers: Babydaddy, Jake Shears

Introduced during William Baker's documentary *White Diamond: A Personal Portrait of Kylie Minogue*, 'White Diamond' had its premiere on 2006's Showgirl: The Homecoming Tour as a perky dance number. A sweeping downtempo version ('Like a pure white diamond I'll shine on and on'), however, was what was eventually released. In 2018, *Billboard* listed 'White Diamond' as one of the twenty best songs about diamonds—alongside Rihanna's 'Diamonds', Marilyn Monroe's 'Diamonds are a Girl's Best Friend', and Prince's 'Diamonds and Pearls'.

'Carried Away'

Release: November 2007 **Album:** *X*
Writers: Kylie, Karen Poole, Greg Kurstin
Producer: Greg Kurstin

Why the slightly underbaked 'Carried Away' was included as an *X* extra and so many other great songs recorded for the album weren't ('My Love is Real', 'Sexual Gold', and 'Something 2 Believe In' to mention but three) seems a roadmap of what not to do when an album leaks and you lose the plot (see Chapter 14). On the upside, 'Carried Away' is one of the few instances on *X* where you can genuinely hear Kylie's strong vocal skills and prowess unprocessed.

'Cherry Bomb'

Release: November 2007 **Album:** *X*
Writers: Kylie, Christian Karlson, Pontus Winnberg, Jonas Quant, Karen Poole
Producers: Bloodshy & Avant

Kylie's delicious 'Cherry Bomb' in many ways predates/predicts Lady Gaga's dominant era of dance-pop ushered in by her 'Just Dance' debut a month before Kylie's fortieth birthday in May 2008. Included on 2012's Anti Tour, that same year MuuMuse.com described the juicy 'Cherry Bomb' as 'the *X*-era Bloodshy & Avant smash ... rudely tacked on as a B-side to "Wow" back in 2008 (despite being more than amazing enough to have made the album tracklisting, or even a single)'. B&A were on a major diva roll having just worked with Madonna, Britney, and Kelis.

'Do It Again'

Release: November 2007 **Album:** *X*
Writers: Kylie, Karen Poole, Greg Kurstin
Producer: Greg Kurstin

From 'Did It Again' to 'Do It Again', Kylie certainly covered diverse musical terrain in a decade. A fine slither of ear candy, on this Euro-pop stormer, our gal contemplates not being able to stop falling in love—a consistent theme not just in her songwriting, but her personal life too. Like a mashup of 'Wow' and 'Carried Away', that 'Do It Again' is a little too similar to and lesser than both is presumably why it was tossed away on *X*'s Mexican special edition.

16

Boombox Compilation and More (2008–2010)

Boombox: The Remix Album 2000–2008

Parlophone: 50999 268198 2 2
Originally released: December 2008
Original tracklist

'Can't Get Blue Monday Out of My Head'	4:05
'Spinning Around' (7th District Club Mental Mix)	4:09
'Wow' (Death Metal Disco Scene Mix)	4:01
'Love at First Sight' (Kid Crème Vocal Dub)	3:41
'Slow' (Chemical Brothers Remix)	4:45
'Come into My World' (Fischerspooner Mix)	4:18
'Red Blooded Woman' (Whitey Mix)	3:36
'I Believe in You' (Mylo Vocal Mix)	3:24
'In Your Eyes' (Knuckleheadz Mix)	3:48
'2 Hearts' (Mark Brown's Pacha Ibiza Upper Terrace Mix)	4:20
'On a Night Like This' (Bini & Martini Club Mix)	4:04
'Giving You Up' (Riton Re-Rub Vox)	4:13
'In My Arms' (Sébastien Léger Vocal Remix)	3:49
'The One' (Bitrocka Remix)	4:43
'Your Disco Needs You' (Casino Radio & Club Mix)	3:40
'Boombox' (LA Riots Remix)	3:58
Japanese edition bonus tracks	
'All I See' (featuring Mims)	3:49
'Wow' (CSS Remix)	3:13
'Can't Get You Out of My Head' (Greg Kurstin Mix)	4:06

Digital Edition bonus tracks

'Can't Get You Out of My Head' (Greg Kurstin Mix) 4:06

'Butterfly' (Mark Picchiotti Sandstorm Dub) 9:03

'The Winner Takes It All' (Dannii Minogue and Kylie Minogue with the BBC Concert Orchestra)

EMI TV: 50999 2 42016 2 9 **Release:** October 2008 **Soundtrack:** *Beautiful People*
Writers: Björn Ulvaeus, Benny Andersson
Producers: Ian Masterson, Steve Anderson, Terry Ronald

To accompany the BBC's *Beautiful People* comedy series set in 1997, siblings Kylie and Dannii recorded a fabber-than-ABBA version of the super Swedes' greatest heartbreak hit. Featuring the BBC Concert Orchestra, their swishy hi-NRG sister act rendition of 'The Winner Takes It All' was somewhat overshadowed by Oscar winner Meryl Streep's version in 2008's hugely successful *Mamma Mia!* movie. 'The Winner Takes It All' was later included on Dannii's 2013 *This Is It: The Very Best of* compilation. Maybe one day we will hopefully get a complete 'KyliexABBA' album!

'Lhuna' (Coldplay and Kylie Minogue)

(RED)Wire: 2008 **Release:** December 2008
Writers: Guy Berryman, Jonny Buckland, Will Champion, Chris Martin
Producers: Markus Dravs, Brian Eno, Jon Hopkins, Rik Simpson

Recorded during sessions for Coldplay's fourth album, 2008's *Viva la Vida or Death and All His Friends*, the hauntingly gloomy 'Lhuna' was released as a digital download charity single on World AIDS Day, 1 December. Martin's original intention was to have Kylie and David Bowie on 'Lhuna', but after Bowie heard it he refused, telling Martin via a text message that the song was 'not one of your best'. Martin and Kylie teamed up again on stage at Glastonbury in 2019 for a teary rendition of 'Can't Get You Out of My Head', the song Coldplay performed at Glastonbury in 2005 in Kylie's honour when she cancelled due to her cancer diagnosis.

'Boombox' (LA Riots Remix)

Release: December 2008 **Compilation:** *Boombox: The Remix Album 2000–2008*
Writers: Andrew Frampton, Danielle Brisebois, Jimmy Harry, Mark Stent, Wayne Wilkins
Producers: Andrew Frampton, Mark 'Spike' Stent, Wayne Wilkins

Kylie's debut Oz single, 1987's 'Locomotion' (featuring photography by Andrew Lehmann), was produced by SAW underling Duffy. Upon hearing this version, Pete Waterman bluntly proclaimed it 'rubbish'. SAW's 1988 update retained the Aussie-ified lyrics, which replaced 'railroad' with 'railway', but reinstated Little Eva's original full 'The Loco-Motion' title.

The singular *Kylie* 1988 debut album featured photography by Lawrence Lawry and sleeve design by PWL co-owner David Howells (no credit for that hat, unfortunately). On the inside sleeve, Kylie wrote: 'To my wonderful family, my dearest pups, my manager Terry and my great friends—my sincere thanks to you all for your continued care and support'. Awww.

Kylie's 1988 mega duet with Jason Donovan, 'Especially for You', featured photography from Grant Matthews, who had previously shot numerous album covers for INXS. The B-side 'All I Wanna Do Is Make You Mine' was shortened to 'All I Wanna Do' on the actual UK single—the same title as sister Dannii's 1996 single, which became her biggest hit and biggest seller.

On the inside sleeve of Kylie's sophomore album, 1989's *Enjoy Yourself* (cover by Simon Fowler), she gave a special shout out to the PWL team (deeming them the 'house of fun'), her manager Terry Blamey ('for working overtime and laughing at my jokes'), and dedicated the album 'to all my fans—I couldn't have done this without your support! Enjoy. Kylie."

1990's *Rhythm of Love* album (cover by Markus Morianz) featured four of SAW's finest works ('Better the Devil You Know', 'Step Back in Time', 'What Do I Have to Do', and 'Shocked') plus Kylie's first forays into songwriting. Reviewing it for *Smash Hits* that year, I called this turning point record 'a cracking pop outing', awarding it 8 out of 10. Gadzooks!

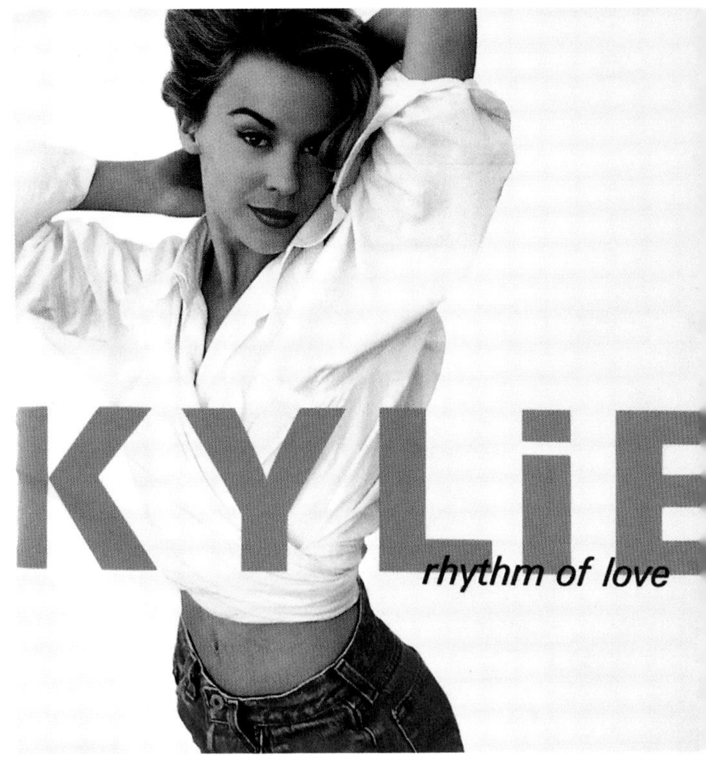

1991's *Let's Get to It* album was twenty-something Kylie in moody B&W mode on the cover by Juergen Teller (though the Hysteric Glamour dress is actually lime green with pinks, yellows and darker greens). The album's shady swing-beat lead single, 'Word Is Out', was penned by a newly slimmed down Stock & Waterman about Kylie's break-up with Michael Hutchence.

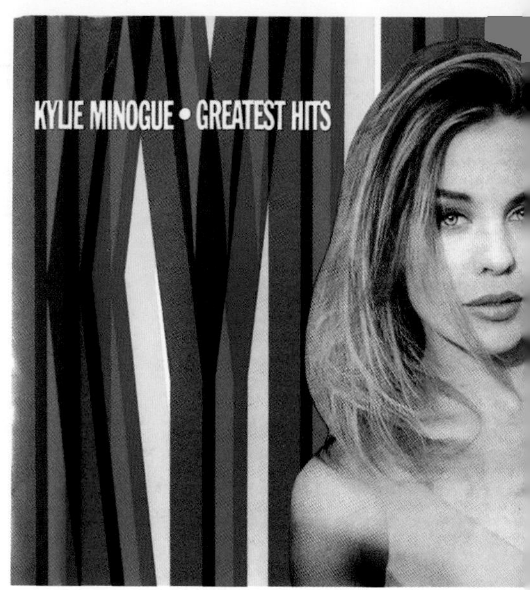

Kylie dedicated 1992's *Greatest Hits* 'to the many wonderful people I have had the pleasure to work with and all of you who have believed in me and stayed loyal'. The original Australian *Greatest Hits* is arguably the most garish Kylie cover of all time boasting dayglo lettering and a badly-cropped pic, wisely reverting to the classy PWL cover some time after.

Snapped by Rankin and designed by Mark Farrow (renowned for his minimalist Pet Shop Boys covers), Kylie dedicated her 1994 eponymous album 'to all who played a part—many thanks for your inspiration, guidance and belief'. Pet Shop Boys contributed the hypnotic 'Falling' to Kylie's deConstruction debut and five years later duetted with her on the melodramatic 'In Denial'.

Stills of an eerie, lifeless Kylie and a murderous Nick Cave from the 'Where the Wild Roses Grow' video by David Tonge graced the cover of their 1995 single together with The Bad Seeds. The inside sleeve also featured another photo of a beaming Kylie and bemused Cave snapped backstage together at the T in the Park concert in August 1995, taken by John Gunion.

Photographed by then-boyfriend Stéphane Sednaoui, 1997's candid *Impossible Princess* album was again designed by Mark Farrow. Kylie thanked Sednaoui on the sleeve gushing, 'Stéphane, merci et je t'adore'. He provided the standard and 3D covers for an album attributing all lyrics to Kylie, bar 'I Don't Need Anyone' where she shared credit with the Manics' James Dean Bradfield.

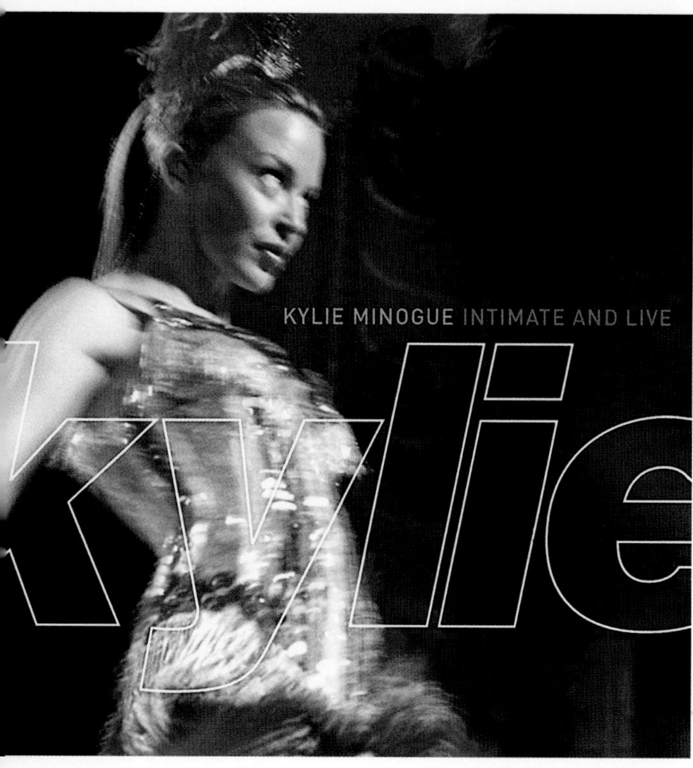

An Oz-only release after her contract with deConstruction met an impossible pass, Kylie's first live album was duly titled *Intimate and Live* after her tour of the same name. Recorded at her 1998 Sydney shows, it was, Kylie declared, 'an experience I will always treasure.' The album cover was by Campbell Knott with, notably, creative design/styling by BFF William Baker.

Kylie's Parlophone debut, 2000's poptastic *Light Years*, was photographed by Vincent Peters on the glitzy Spanish island of Ibiza, overseen by William Baker with design by Mark Farrow. Launched with a #1 single courtesy of the shimmering 'Spinning Around' and some simpering gold hotpants, Kylie affirmed *Light Years* was 'light and fun … like being on summer holiday'.

Kylie's family-friendly 2000 duet with Robbie Williams, 'Kids', came in two CD single versions, both shot by Hamish Brown and designed by Tom Hingston Studio. Robbie's line 'Press be asking do I care for sodomy/I don't know yeah probably' did not harm its gay appeal, though one B-side was his hard rock solo coming of age song, 'John's Gay', detailing him losing his virginity.

Coming off the hottest single of her career, 'Can't Get You Out of My Head', 2001's *Fever* album was photographed by Vincent Peters, styled by William Baker and designed by Adjective Noun. After nine co-writes by Kylie on *Light Years*, that number dipped to five on *Fever*. Kylie pledged on the sleeve 'to my fans, I hope you like this and thank you for your wonderful support.'

Fashion mavericks Mert Alaş and Marcus Piggott read Kylie's *Body Language* for her 2003 album cover, with visual direction and Bardot-esque styling by William Baker, plus sleeve direction and design by Tony Hung. *NME* opined at the time that *Body Language* was 'really the only appropriate title for an album by a woman about whose bottom so much has been written'.

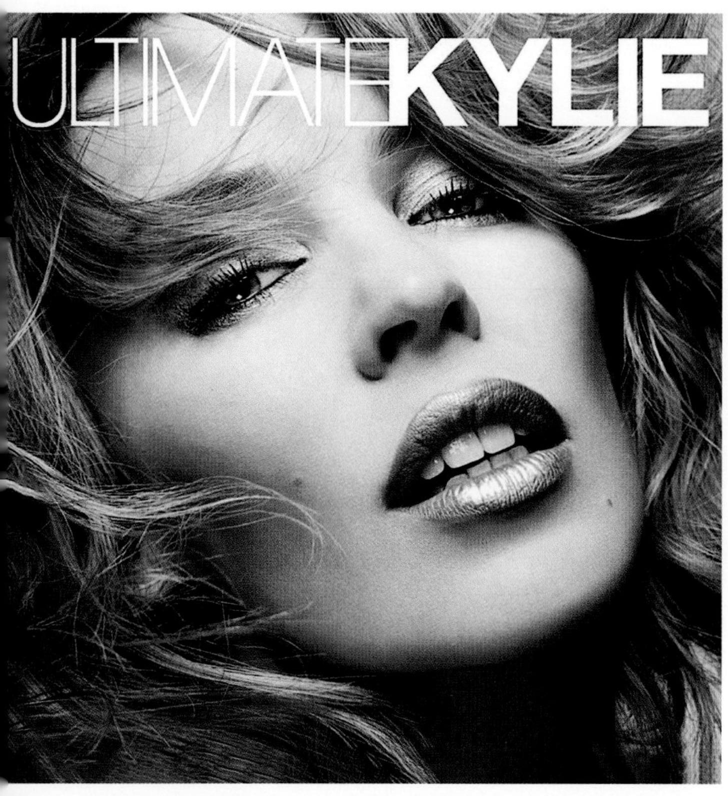

Kylie's second proper hits compilation (not including 2001's intentionally disruptive *Hits+*) was 2004's *Ultimate Kylie* splicing together hits from across all three of her labels up to that time, plus two new singles she had co-written. Its cover was shot by Simon Emmett, with visual direction/ styling by William Baker and astute liner notes from Neil Rees and Nigel Goodall.

For 2007's *X* album, William Baker was finally upgraded to photographer, with digital imaging/ production by Provision Studio. The sleeve direction/design (including the sleeve's challenging typeface) was by Adjective Noun. Post-cancer/ recovery Kylie reflected: 'my love and thanks to everyone who played a part in the making of this album, both near and far'.

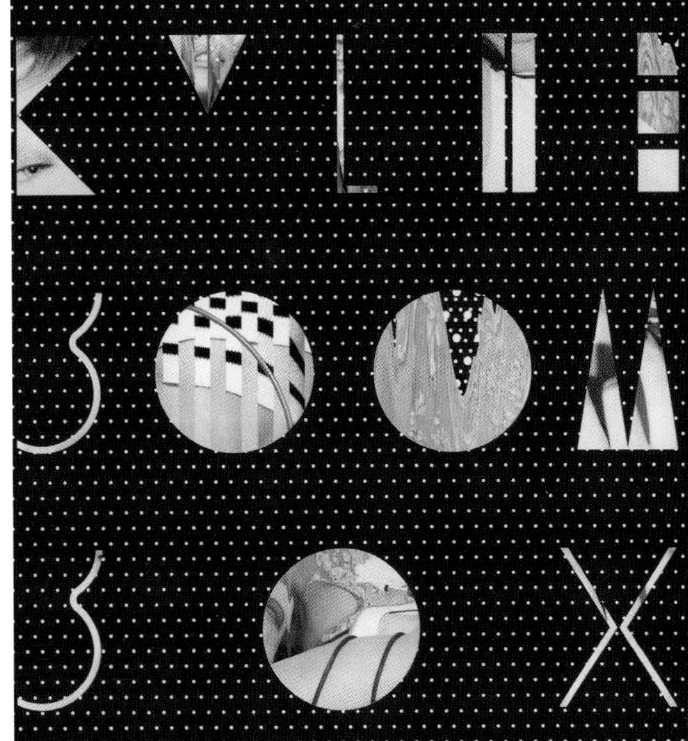

To date, Kylie has released twelve remix albums, but just three were issued in the UK—1998's *Mixes* (nine *Impossible Princess* remixes) 2008's *Boombox*, and 2021's *Disco: Extended Mixes*. For *Boombox*, Adjective Noun were responsible for its fly design, with collective photography from William Baker, Rankin, Vincent Peters, Nick Knight, Liz Collins, and Mert & Marcus.

2010's *Aphrodite* album cover descended via photography by William Baker, photographic post-production from Digital Light, and art direction/design by Adjective Noun. Executive produced by Stuart Price, Kylie thanked him 'for tying the whole thing up in the most magical fashion'. Unlike predecessor *X*, which contained seven co-writes, *Aphrodite* shrank down to a mere two.

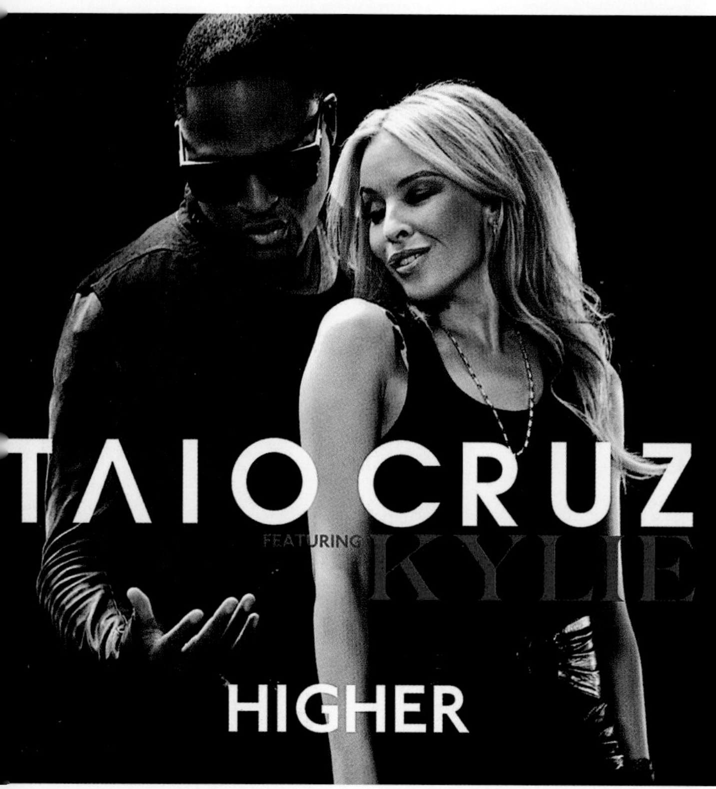

2010's duet between Taio Cruz and Kylie, 'Higher', remains her last UK Top 10 hit to date. Thanks to a version between Cruz and Travie McCoy, 'Higher' also became a million seller in the US. A third take on 'Higher', featuring Cruz with both Kylie and McCoy called—they wish!—the 'three-way version', was included on certain versions of the CD/digital bundles.

The stylised B&W cover photography (and sumptuous inside sleeve colour photography) for 2012's *The Abbey Road Sessions* was shot by William Baker. Six months earlier, Baker had photographed *The Best of Kylie Minogue* compilation cover, which many fans assumed to be a model wearing a jacket adorned with a wealth of badges bearing the face of the real Kylie.

Kiss Me Once (2014) was Kylie's one and only album with RocNation management, one and only album executive produced by Sia and final studio album with Parlophone. Photographed by William Baker with design by Adjective Noun, on the sleeve Kylie gave thanks 'to my fans who always inspired me.' Kylie later diplomatically called the album 'a bit of a tricky time'.

Kylie Christmas was such a stellar concept, idea, and success in 2015, the album was re-released a year later as an expanded version with an extra name: *Snow Queen Edition*. On *Kylie Christmas* she gave thanks 'for everything' to then-boyfriend Justin Sasse who featured in the video for 'Every Day's Like Christmas', which a reunited Stock Aitken Waterman lovingly remixed.

Although they had previously sung together and recorded a version of ABBA's 'The Winner Takes It All', Kylie and sister 'Disco Dannii' finally made good in 2015 on their promise to release an all-new duet. '100 Degrees', a track initially only on the *Kylie Christmas* deluxe edition, campily and cannily reappeared later in 2016 as '100 Degrees (Still Disco to Me)'.

For 2018's *Golden*, her BMG label debut, Kylie co-wrote all the country-tinged material—the first time she had done so on an album since *Impossible Princess*, two decades earlier. Simon Emmett returned after over a decade's absence as the album's photographer with art director/ designer Leif Podhajsky replacing Kylie's banished 'gay husband' William Baker.

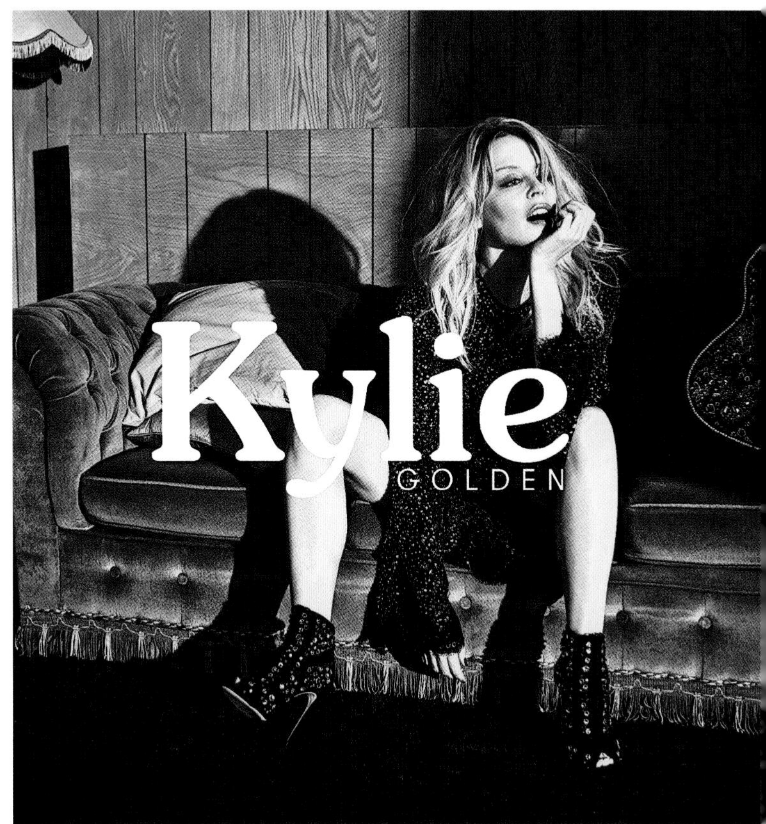

After just one BMG studio album, Kylie issued her fourth greatest hits set. Timed to hit shops the same week as her legendary Glastonbury set (its most watched TV moment in history), *Step Back in Time: The Definitive Collection* hit #1 in the UK and Oz. An expanded edition was released for Christmas and BMG, going on to win an award for Catalogue Marketing Campaign.

Clearly Kylie was so chuffed with Simon Emmett's honey-hued work on *Golden* that he returned again to happy-snap her as the ultimate '70s dancefloor icon for 2020's *Disco* album. Kylie had already referred to the London based photographer, who had also snapped her for fashion mags, as 'the one and only' on Instagram, so there was plenty of discolicious love between them.

For 2021's *Disco: Guest List Edition*, Kylie's cover muses were clearly Donna Summer and Diana Ross, alongside Euro-discotheque spirit animals Amanda Lear, Germany's Silver Convention, ABBA's Agnetha and Frida, Sweden's Madeleen Kane, Italy's late Raffaella Carrà, and French/Egyptian diva Dalida, who died in 1987, the same year Kylie released her debut single.

In 1994, I interviewed Kylie for *Smash Hits* (Australia) during my three-year run as editor. Throughout our intimate and lively chat at the Ritz-Carlton Hotel in Sydney's Double Bay, Kylie addressed all manner of drug and Michael Hutchence-related topics for the first time. Three years later, spookily, it would be the very same hotel where Hutchence would be found dead.

In 2011, I got to rub shoulders with Kylie at a Sydney Mardi Gras event thanks to her then-Australian publicist, also called Kylie! We had last chatted for an interview in 2007 for *DNA* magazine (her response to my last question 'Are you happy?' was the telling 'No … I still have a lot of searching to do!'). Thankfully, she seemed much more content four years later. Phew!

Above: The hotpants that (re)started a career! In 2012, to celebrate Kylie's twenty-five-year career, six figurines were produced by her Darenote company. In addition to the naughty-but-nice 'Spinning Around' one pictured were also 'So Lucky', 'Showgirl', 'Aphrodite', 'Homecoming', and 'La La La' (the iconic 'Can't Get You Out of My Head' white dress). Collect the set, lovers!

Left: 'I was probably meant to be a one-hit wonder,' Kylie told an interviewer in 2020 with a laugh. 'I was written off so many times.' To that end, her *Disco* album, which kept Little Mix from the #1 spot in the UK charts, afforded her a new chart record—the only woman to have a #1 album in five consecutive decades. To say something else, that's pure Minogue magic! (*Photo: Kylie - Infinite Disco. Credit: David Lopez-Edwards*)

Just in time for Christmas, Parlophone plundered Kylie's back catalogue for fifteen of her most sought-after remixes, plus one 'new' track, the title track left over from *X*, remixed by LA Riots. Peaking at #28 in the UK and #72 in Australia, the album reached the Top 10 of the US Electronic Album Chart. At just under four minutes, LA Riots' retake of 'Boombox' was 'the sound of the underground', unlike the original *X* demo (or possibly even further back to the *Body Language* album) that leaked in 2015, which married rock and electro less successfully.

'Sensitized' (Christophe Willem duet with Kylie Minogue)

Sony Music: 88697473242 **Release:** May 2009 **Album:** *Caféine*
Writers: Guy Chambers, Cathy Dennis, Serge Gainsbourg
Producers: Guy Chambers, Cathy Dennis

This 'Sensitized' was a Franglais version of the *X* track with French singer Christophe Willem, winner of *Nouvelle Star*, the French version of *Pop Idol*, in 2006. Produced by Chambers and Dennis, who produced Kylie's original, it appeared on Willem's second album *Caféine*, which hit #1 in France and #2 in Belgium. Chambers also wrote/produced the all-English 'Heartbox', the album's third single, which would have been perfect for Kylie. Drats. (See also Appendix I.)

'Chiggy Wiggy' (Kylie Minogue with Sonu Nigam and Suzanne D'Mello)

SCI: SFCD 1-1444 **Release:** October 2009 **Soundtrack:** *Blue*
Writers: AR Rahman, Abbas Tyrewala
Producer: AR Rahman

Goodbye Hollywood, hello Bollywood as Kylie trysts with Indian 'playback' artist Sonu Nigam on a tune clashing bhangra with R&B, written by music legend/Oscar winner AR Rahman, taken from the 2009 film *Blue*. In the movie sequence where she dances with Akshay Kumar, Kylie seems as if she has mistakenly gate-crashed an Indian wedding in a Mumbai nightclub (dressed in a teeny weeny thingy). 'Chiggy Wiggy' is surely the most deeply dippy thing Kylie's ever wriggled her way through. 'Working with AR Rahman was a real thrill,' she recalled to *Times of India* in 2021. 'It was a rather different style for me and it kind of lived in its own world, but what is surprising is how many people remember it and mention it to me.'

'Monkey Man' (The Wiggles Featuring Kylie Minogue)

ABC Music: R-301512-2 **Release:** February 2009 **Album:** *Go Bananas!*
Writer: Toots Hibbert
Producer: Anthony Field

Auntie Kylie finally gets to hang with Aussie act The Wiggles for some toddler pop as the 'Pink Wiggle'. There is even a dance—and video! Recorded to raise funds for UNICEF (and possibly impress her three nephews Ethan, Charles, and James), 'Monkey Man' was a cover of the 1969 Toots & The Maytals ska hit. Released in February 2009 on *Go Bananas!*, the thirtieth album by The Wiggles, 'Monkey Man' later appeared on The Wiggles's 2017 *Duets* compilation. According to Wigglepedia, Kylie to date remains the only Pink Wiggle—and shortest Wiggle, too.

'Everybody Hurts' (Helping Haiti)

Syco Music: 88697661102 **Release:** February 2010
Writers: REM
Producers: Steve Robson, John Shanks

A cover of REM's '90s classic, 'Everybody Hurts' was conceived by British music impresario/reality TV judge Simon Cowell to help raise money after an earthquake hit Haiti. The UK's fastest-selling charity record of the twenty-first century (selling over 600,000 copies) 'Everybody Hurts' topped the charts for two weeks, as well as being a sizeable hit in many other territories. Besides Kylie, this big blustery ballad featured Leona Lewis, Rod Stewart, Mariah Carey, Cheryl, Mika, James Blunt, Take That, Susan Boyle, JLS, Miley Cyrus, Michael Bublé, Jon Bon Jovi, Alexandra Burke, James Morrison, Westlife, and (yes, him again!) Robbie Williams.

Vid Bit!

Director: Joseph Kahn

This moving black and white clip featured the Helping Haiti crew interspersed with footage from the Haitian disaster. Kylie and many of the other celeb singers end up covered in dust to signify the rumble the earthquake had caused. Despite this, Kylie must have enjoyed working with Kahn because she nabbed him to direct the video for her new single.

17

Aphrodite Album (2010)

Aphrodite

Parlophone: 50999 268198 2 2
Originally released: June 2010
Original tracklist

'All the Lovers'	3:20
'Get Outta My Way'	3:38
'Put Your Hands Up (If You Feel Love)'	3:37
'Closer'	3:09
'Everything Is Beautiful'	3:25
'Aphrodite'	3:45
'Illusion'	3:21
'Better Than Today'	3:25
'Too Much'	3:16
'Cupid Boy'	4:26
'Looking for an Angel'	3:49
'Can't Beat the Feeling'	4:09
Japanese edition bonus track	
'Heartstrings'	3:16
iTunes Store Experience Edition bonus track	
'Mighty Rivers'	4:01
Amazon MP3 and BigPond bonus track	
'Go Hard or Go Home'	3:42

'All the Lovers'

Parlophone: 50999 646767 2 2 **Single release:** June 2010 **Album:** *Aphrodite*
Writers: Jim Eliot, Mima Stilwell
Producers: Jim Eliot, Stuart Price

The lead single from her Price-produced eleventh album *Aphrodite*, the joyous 'All the Lovers' instantly became another signature Kylie song, if not one beloved by her LGBTQ+ fan base as a positive, uplifting, and empowering gay anthem. 'I'd worked with (Eliot and Stilwell) before, because they wrote "2 Hearts",' Kylie said, 'and this was just delicious when we heard it. They had written it for me with 'Human' from The Killers in mind which Stuart had produced ... as I was recording it, I knew "All the Lovers" had to be the first single; it sums up the euphoria of the album perfectly.' Classic Kylie, 'All the Lovers' peaked at #3 in the UK (her final solo UK Top 10 to date), #1 on the US Dance Club Songs chart, but sputtered out at #13 in Australia. 'All the Lovers' has been a constant fixture during her subsequent tours, cited as a queer anthem (Kylie called it a 'homage' to her gay audience), plus Kylie now refers to her fans as her 'lovers'. Aww.

Vid Bit!

Director: Joseph Kahn

Watch as Kylie singlehandedly builds a human tower of underclad lust in the city of Angels, based on the nude human installation photoshoots of American photographer Spencer Tunick. Banned in some Asian countries for being what gay magazine *The Advocate* deemed 'orgiastic', in 2017 Kahn revealed those censors requested Kylie remove the same sex content, but she refused. Bigger issue: whatever happened to the video's huge floating white elephant?

Remix Fix!

WAWA & MMB, Michael Woods, Dada Life, XXXChange and Fear of Tigers got all loved up, while Peter Rauhofer's Reconstruction Mix earned its own Kylie-revisits-*Barbarella* remix video.

'Go Hard or Go Home'

Single release: June 2010 (B-side to 'All the Lovers')
Writers: Damon Reinagle, Daniel Davidsen, Lucas Secon, Mich Hansen, Thomas Sardorf
Producers: Cutfather, Daniel Davidsen, Thomas Sardorf, Damon Sharpe, Lucas Secon

It took five writers—none Kylie—to come up with the breathless but autopilot Euro-pop of 'Go Hard or Go Home', housed on the B-side of 'All the Lovers'. Dane Secon is better known by his stage name of Lucas, or to paraphrase his

Grammy-nominated 1994 hit, 'Lucas With the Lid Off'. 'Go Hard or Go Home' was the first of two songs Secon wrote for the *Aphrodite* project.

'Los Amores'

Single release: June 2010 (B-side to 'All the Lovers')
Writers: Jim Eliot, Mima Stilwell
Producers: Jim Eliot, Mima Stilwell, Stuart Price

This is the bit where having a Spanish model boyfriend comes in handy, as surely Catalonian Andrés Velencoso must have assisted Kylie with her '*en español*'. 'Los Amores' was—*correcto!*—the Spanish version of A-side 'All the Lovers'. Kylie launched *Aphrodite* on the Spanish island of Ibiza that year with a bash at the legendary Pacha club, on the same day sister Dannii gave birth to son, Ethan. Hello Auntie Kylie, or should that be Tía Kylie.

'Any Which Way' (Scissor Sisters)

Polydor: 273810 **Release:** June 2010 **Album:** *Night Work*
Writers: Jason Sellards, Scott Hoffman, Ana Lynch, Stuart Price
Producers: Stuart Price, Scissor Sisters

Released two days prior to Kylie's *Aphrodite* album on Scissor Sisters's third album *Night Work*, Kylie went uncredited for her work on 'Any Which Way'. The unashamedly camp disco pop 'Any Which Way' was the second single from *Night Work* in September 2010 reaching #81 on the UK singles chart. Although there were remixes for the single from 7th Heaven and Carte Blanche, whispery Kylie did not feature in the video. She did pop up on stage to join the Sisters for a rendition of 'Any Which Way' during their 2010 Glastonbury set.

'Get Outta My Way'

Parlophone: 50999 9 08748 2 6 **Single release:** September 2010 **Album:** *Aphrodite*
Writers: Lucas Secon, Damon Sharpe, Peter Wallevik, Daniel Davidsen, Mich Hansen
Producers: Cutfather, Peter Wallevik, Daniel Davidsen, Damon Sharpe, Lucas Secon, Stuart Price

The album's ebullient second single, 'Get Outta My Way', peaked at #12 in the UK (Kylie's first single to not reach the Top 10 since 'Breathe' in 1998) and a grim #69 at home in Australia, though again it was a US Dance Club Songs #1.

Despite the lowly chart returns in a sadly ageist pop music market, fan fever for 'Get Outta My Way' has refused to dissipate, which is why the song was included on the set list for Kylie's White Party appearance in Palm Springs and at New York Pride both in 2018. Five years after 'Get Outta My Way' was released, it found new life, sampled for Swedish DJ/artist Alesso featuring Roy English's way 'Cool' UK Top 10 hit.

Vid Bit!

Director: AlexandLiane

With an aerial overhead shot picking up where her 2003 'Slow' video left off, 'Get Outta My Way' was another glittering example of Kylie's mastery of the music video art form. Directors Alex Lage and Liane Sommers are visual artists. A year later, a semi-official video for the Bimbo Jones Radio Mix appeared, filmed at a photoshoot for *Vs* magazine, directed by Chris Bisagni.

Remix Fix!

Realising they had a dance monster on their hands with 'Get Outta My Way', Parlophone went out of their way to enlist a dozen remixers—Bimbo Jones, 7th Heaven, Paul Harris, Kris Menace, Matt Zo, Sidney Samson, Daddy's Groove, BeatauCue, Penguin Prison, Yasutaka Nakata, SDP (aka Stuart Price), and Steve Anderson.

'Put Your Hands Up (If You Feel Love)'

EMI: 5099908438058 **Single release:** May 2011 **Album:** *Aphrodite*
Writers: Fin Dow-Smith, Miriam Nervo, Olivia Nervo
Producers: Starsmith, Stuart Price, Miriam Nervo, Olivia Nervo

Aphrodite's somewhat shunned fourth single was originally intended for former Girls Aloud singer/tabloid bait Cheryl. After the disappointing reaction to 'Better Than Today', Kylie announced there would be no more singles from *Aphrodite*, but her American label, Astralwerks, had other ideas. They prepped 'Put Your Hands Up (If You Feel Love)', which meant Parlophone reluctantly came on board, scrapping together some measly pennies for a lyric video. The goods news first—Kylie's handy euphoric track was another #1 on the US Dance Club Songs chart and by reaching #50 in Australia a significant improvement on *Aphrodite*'s two previous singles. Then there was the UK: #93. This is one single that truly deserved more love.

Vid Bit!

A lyric video for the old school Pete Hammond remix was posted on Kylie's YouTube channel.

Remix Fix!

Two words—Pete Hammond! It was as if it was 1989 all over again. Hammond's PWL-esque remix became the focal point of the single, which included mixes from NERVO, Bimbo Jones, Basto, Muscles, and Retromatik. In 2015, former PWL staffer Hammond released his autobiography, *Get Down Here and Mix Yourself a Hit: Mixmaster: My Story.*

'Closer'

Release: June 2010 **Album:** *Aphrodite*
Writers: Stuart Price, Beatrice Hatherley
Producer: Stuart Price

Not to be confused with Kylie's 1992 rave tune of the same name, this 'Closer' was, as Kylie pointed out, 'a little gem of Price's'. When Price and Kylie were compiling the track list for *Aphrodite*, they agreed, said Kylie, 'we have plenty of bangers and that's when we decided we needed songs like "Closer" to bring it down a little.' Performed live on 2011's Aphrodite: Les Folies Tour, Kylie flew in and above the crowd on a hunky black angel, highlighting the operatic, cinematic, and magical aspects of 'Closer'. Hatherley's mum is English actress Patricia Franklin.

'Everything Is Beautiful'

Release: June 2010 **Album:** *Aphrodite*
Writers: Tim Rice-Oxley, Fraser T. Smith
Producer: Fraser T. Smith

It was something of a coup for Kylie to have a hypnotic song written for her by post-Britpop band Keane (Rice-Oxley) and super-producer Smith (who the following year co-wrote and produced Adele's 'Set Fire to the Rain'). 'To have those kinds of songwriters come in on this project just gives it another dimension, particularly lyrically,' Kylie cooed. The closest thing to a ballad on the *Aphrodite* album, Rice-Oxley rhapsodised, 'everyone's a fan of Kylie. You can't not be.' He also described writing a song for Kylie as 'a privilege, really'. Keane reunited in 2019.

'Aphrodite'

Release: June 2010 **Album:** *Aphrodite*
Writers: Nerina Pallot, Andy Chatterley
Producers: Nerina Pallot, Andy Chatterley, Stuart Price

Should the celestial title track from *Aphrodite* have been the album's third single instead of 'Better Than Today'? Naming her album after the goddess of love and including tracks titled 'Looking for an Angel' and 'Cupid Boy', Kylie realised herself 'these names suggest a bit of a divine intervention'. Some years later, PopJustice asked Kylie to reassess *Aphrodite*. 'It would have been great to have songs I'd written about that dark period in my life,' she acknowledged, 'not, "Hey I saw you across the dancefloor!"' Pallot, meanwhile, has tallied up six solo albums.

'Illusion'

Release: June 2010 **Album:** *Aphrodite*
Writers: Kylie Minogue, Stuart Price
Producer: Stuart Price

The first of the two Kylie co-writes on *Aphrodite*, 'Illusion' was also the only track she wrote with Price. Detailing an unravelling relationship, you could certainly take your pick of targets for whom Kylie was referring to. When it came to selecting tracks for *Aphrodite*, having learned the lessons from the previous *X*, Price said 'we didn't just do 50 or 60 songs and see which ones worked. It was a very focused exciting way of making a record.' On the Aphrodite: Les Folies Tour, a revamped 'Illusion' was reimagined as a gloriously opulent Middle Eastern harem-meets-Cecil B DeMille extravaganza, no illusion required.

'Better Than Today'

Parlophone: 50999 9 46629 2 4 **Single release:** December 2010 **Album:** *Aphrodite*
Writers: Nerina Pallot, Andy Chatterley
Producers: Nerina Pallot, Andy Chatterley, Stuart Price

Written by pop singer/songwriter Pallot with husband Chatterley, 'Better Than Today' had been released on her *Buckminster Fuller* EP a year earlier as an acoustic-based folk-pop ditty. A perfectly fine album track, 'Better Than Today' proved a controversial choice as third single from *Aphrodite*. Idolator summed up the situation in 2019 declaring 'the Gays [™] are still fuming that "Better Than Today" was released as the third single from *Aphrodite* ahead of literal classics like "Closer" and "Cupid Boy"'. In that respect, 'Better Than Today' failed miserably—#32 in the UK and #55 in Australia, though it reached #1 on the US Dance Club Songs chart.

Vid Bit!

Director: Kylie (with assistance from William Baker and TeamKylie)

More a performance clip of 'Better Than Today' live from her For You, for Me (KylieUSA200) tour the previous year. More fun was Kylie's goofball 'BTT' dance tutorial she later posted.

Remix Fix!

The 'BTT' remixes (from Bills & Hurr, Bimbo Jones, Starlab, Club Junkies, Bellatrax, Monarchy, and The Japanese Popstars) were, like the song itself, more workmanlike than wonderful.

'Too Much'

Release: June 2010 **Album:** *Aphrodite*
Writers: Kylie, Calvin Harris, Jake Shears
Producer: Calvin Harris

After first teaming up for 2004's 'I Believe in You' and 2007's 'White Diamond', Shears was back on board for *Aphrodite* with Harris, who by this stage had gone from being a pop wannabe to a major music somebody. The fact 'Too Much' was the only song from the album not on the set list for Aphrodite: Les Folies Tour suggests Team Kylie justly accepted 'Too Much' was below par. 'Too Much' did finally find some belated love when Kylie included it on 2012's Anti Tour where it literally raised the rafters in a moment of way too much fun.

'Cupid Boy'

Release: June 2010 **Album:** *Aphrodite*
Writers: Sebastian Ingrosso, Magnus Lidehäll, Nick Clow, Luciana Caporaso
Producers: Stuart Price, Sebastian Ingrosso, Magnus Lidehäll

Kylie only had a hand in two *Aphrodite* tracks, ranking as her smallest creative input for any of her five Parlophone studio albums. Recovered from cancer and in remission, she was happily dating hunky model Andrés Velencoso and if any song on *Aphrodite* stands as a valentine to him it must be 'Cupid Boy'. In case anyone missed that point, during Kylie's performance of it during her Aphrodite: Les Folies Tour the following year, photos of Velencoso and his glistening torso took centre stage. Bleepy Stereogamous 'CB' remixes featured on the 'Put Your Hands Up' single.

'Looking for an Angel'

Release: June 2010 **Album:** *Aphrodite*
Writers: Kylie, Stuart Price
Producer: Stuart Price

The first track Kylie and Price worked on together, the second of her co-writes on *Aphrodite*, and the penultimate track on the album, synth-poppy 'Looking for an Angel' is an almost conscious nod to her made in heaven days at PWL. 'Stuart asked me, "Have you ever had a song called angel?",' Kylie recounted. 'I literally had to think back because one would imagine I had done so, but no, we hadn't.' In 2015, Kylie told British TV host Jonathan Ross that former boyfriend Michael Hutchence was her guardian angel, on tour at least.

'Can't Beat the Feeling'

Release: June 2010 **Album:** *Aphrodite*
Writers: Hannah Robinson, Pascal Gabriel, Børge Fjordheim, Matt Prime, Richard X
Producers: Stuart Price, Pascal Gabriel, Børge Fjordheim

The final of *Aphrodite*'s dozen tracks and planned as a single at some stage, with remixes reportedly commissioned, 'Can't Beat the Feeling' was mashed with 'Love at First Sight' on 2011's Aphrodite: Les Folies Tour. An official studio projection version leaked soon after. In 2020, Retropopmagazine.com selected 'CBTF' as one of their 'Five Kylie Albums Tracks That Should Have Been Singles' alongside 'Secrets', 'Sexy Love', 'Rollin'', and 'Disco Down'.

'Heartstrings'

Release: June 2010 **Album:** *Aphrodite*
Writers: Brian Higgins, Gerard O'Connell, Jason Resch, Jaxon Bellina, Kieran Jones, Matt Gray, Miranda Cooper
Producers: Xenomania

With Stuart Price firmly in control as executive producer of the *Aphrodite* project that meant the two tracks Kylie recorded earlier with the Xenomania crew were quietly shuffled off as bonus tracks. 'Heartstrings' is cute electro disco-pop conceived by seven people—none of them Kylie—with a regulation Xenomania production. Price and Team Kylie clearly thought it was a bit of old rope. Cooper later co-write the musical version of David Walliams's *Billionaire Boy*.

'Mighty Rivers'

Release: June 2010 **Album:** *Aphrodite*
Writers: Brian Higgins, Gerard O'Connell, Jason Resch, Jaxon Bellina, Miranda Cooper, Carla Marie Williams, Tim Deal
Producers: Xenomania

With a few switches in the Xenomania composer department—none again Kylie—'Mighty Rivers' is a trancey and lyrically intriguing *Aphrodite* bonus track.

One of the early 'organic pop' tracks from the original direction for Kylie's eleventh album, 'MR' had its moment in the sun when Kylie performed it during 2012's Anti Tour concerts. Asked by a fan in 2020 on Twitter to release 'MR' as a single, Kylie wittily replied with a cartoon of a screaming baby. In 2021, 'MR' was rightfully reassessed by a fan on YouTube as 'the mother of The Weeknd's "Blinding Lights"'.

'Devotion' (Hurts Featuring Kylie Minogue)

RCA Label Group: 88697666682 **Release:** August 2010 **Album:** *Happiness*
Writers: Theo Hutchcraft, Adam Anderson
Producers: Hurts, Jonas Quant

Released at the end of August, 2010, the stately 'Devotion' came from the English synth-pop duo's 2010 debut album *Happiness*. 'Since we have enjoyed an illicit life-long love affair with Kylie Minogue, we mustered up every ounce of courage we had and asked her if she would like to sing the song with us,' Hurts member Theo Hutchcraft explained. The deluxe edition of Hurts's *Happiness* album included a live cover of Kylie's 'Confide in Me' and the original demo, minus Kylie, of 'Devotion'. Hitting #4 in the UK, *Happiness* was an even bigger album success in Germany where it reached #2.

'Wonderful Life'

Sony Music: 88697793392 **Release:** October 2010 **Compilation:** *BBC Radio 1's Live Lounge—Volume 5*
Writers: Theo Hutchcraft, Adam Anderson, Joseph Cross
Producers: BBC

Continuing a wonderful thing, two months later, Kylie's gorgeous, acoustic-plus-strings cover of Hurts's elegiac ballad 'Wonderful Life', originally recorded for *BBC Radio1 Live Lounge* program, was released on the *Volume 5* compilation. The session, recorded at the end of September 2010, boasted a live string accompaniment and was filmed and posted by the BBC. When Kylie harmonises with those violins 'Wonderful Life' is a true wonder.

'Higher' (Taio Cruz Featuring Kylie Minogue and/or Travie McCoy)

4th & Broadway: 00602527593531 **Single release:** November 2010 **Album:** *Rokstarr*
Writers: Taio Cruz, Sandy Wilhelm
Producers: Taio Cruz, Sandy Vee

The fifth single from Cruz's sophomore album *Rokstarr*, 'Higher' was originally intended for Kylie's *Aphrodite*. When that did not happen, Cruz recorded 'Higher' himself, before the revised Cruz/Kylie duet version was released in all territories, outside of the US, a year later. The American label decided to replace Kylie with a guest rap from Travie McCoy of Gym Class Heroes where it reached #24 in the charts. 'Higher' reached #8 in the UK, #25 in Australia, but hit #1 on the US Dance Club Songs chart. Due to its myriad of mixes, 'Higher' was certified platinum for a million sales in the US and remains Kylie's biggest hit to date in Germany.

Vid Bit!

Director: Alex Herron

Cruz was a busy guy; he filmed two versions of the 'Higher' video on the same day-the European version with Kylie and the McCoy one for American audiences.

Remix Fix!

The 'Higher' remix package was a true 'camp Kylie' affair with 7th Heaven, Club Junkies, and Wideboys. DJ Wonder added grime and dubstep, while Ultimate High did Cruz/McCoy only. Jody Den Broder's mix got the true ultimate high, however, by featuring all three.

'Let It Snow'

EMI: Digital download **Release:** November 2010 **EP:** *A Kylie Christmas*
Writers: Sammy Cahn, Jule Styne
Producer: Steve Anderson

This jazz-pop festive classic came with the previously issued 'Santa Baby' on *A Kylie Christmas* EP. Five years later, both tracks would be revamped for 2015's *Kylie Christmas* and 2016's *Kylie Christmas: Snow Queen Edition* reissue, her final Parlophone releases. Another EP, *A Christmas Gift*, was released in December 2010 as a free download for a day containing 'Aphrodite', 'Can't Beat the Feeling', and 'Santa Baby'. To celebrate the release of 'Let It Snow', a minimalist 'video' featuring a photo of Kylie in a snow globe surrounded by falling snow was posted to her YouTube channel. Frank Sinatra, Dean Martin, and Michael Buble have all had hit versions of 'LIS'.

'We Are One' (Kylie Minogue x Verbal)

YouTube: Uploaded track for donation **Release:** April 2011
Writer/Producer: John Fontein

Japanese hip-hopper Verbal was one of Kylie's support acts for the Japanese leg of her Aphrodite: Les Follies Tour. The pair teamed up on charity single 'We Are One'—Verbal rapping in Japanese and Kylie singing in English, as well as the international 'na-na-na'—for the Tōhoku earthquake that had struck Japan a month earlier. A bland, fairly generic copy of Black Eyes Peas's hits of the era ('gotta share the pain') is likely why 'WAO' was not afforded a proper release and simply uploaded to YouTube with donations requested for UNICEF Japan.

'Silence'

Release: May 2011 (B-side to 'Put Your Hands Up')
Writers: Henry Samuel, Chris Bruce, Stuart Price
Producer: Stuart Price

Before we farewell Kylie-as-goddess in her *Aphrodite* era there is 'Silence', an enjoyable, if stylistically derivative, nu-disco pop affair, given short-shift as a fourth single B-side and never with the sniff of being performed live. Henry Samuel is actually the real name of singer Seal, whose 2007 fifth album *System* was produced by Price. Some digital platforms erroneously credit Price and/or Kylie with 'Silence'. During her 2011 Australian tour, Kylie told *Perth Now* she felt 'let down with my releases from *Aphrodite*.' Luckily, help was just down the road.

18

The Abbey Road Sessions Album and More (2012–2013)

The Abbey Road Sessions

Parlophone: 509990 15022 2 0
Originally released: October 2012
Original tracklist

'All the Lovers'	3:22
'On a Night Like This'	3:00
'Better the Devil You Know'	3:58
'Hand on Your Heart'	3:36
'I Believe in You'	2:48
'Come into My World'	3:32
'Finer Feelings'	3:35
'Confide in Me'	4:08
'Slow'	4:08
'The Loco-Motion'	2:34
'Can't Get You Out of My Head'	3:33
'Where the Wild Roses Grow'	4:05
'Flower'	3:31
'I Should Be So Lucky'	3:14
'Love at First Sight'	3:35
'Never Too Late'	3:01
Australian JB Hi-Fi edition bonus track	
'Wow'	3:04
Japanese and Australian David Jones edition bonus track	
'In My Arms'	3:41

'Timebomb'

Parlophone: 5099931951128 **Single release:** May 2012
Writers: Karen Poole, Matt Schwartz, Paul Harris
Producers: Matt Schwartz, Paul Harris

Released as a standalone single after Kylie completed her Anti Tour concerts, 'Timebomb' was a 128-bpm grimy electro, apocalyptic-accepting dance tune that returned her to the upper echelons of the chart in Australia (#12) and provided another #1 on the US Dance Club Songs chart, though it detonated in the UK at #31. Intended for yet another compilation, *The Best of Kylie Minogue*, it was scrapped when Parlophone selected tracks based on a fan survey. The previous year, Parlophone issued a boxset, *The Albums 2000–2010*, a kind of clearing house notice signifying Kylie's near end-of-contract. In October 2012, her Australian label released *K25 Time Capsule*, containing forty-nine Kylie singles including 'Timebomb'. Arguably the most interesting thing about 'Timebomb' is it is not the song with the same name written by Michael Jackson. In 2001, British press reports stated the King of Pop had written two songs—'I'll Try Anything Once' and 'Time Bomb'—for Kylie. Neither of these Jacko tracks ever materialised.

Vid Bit!

Director: Christian Larson

The bum was back! Twelve years after it steamed up screens in the 'Spinning Around' clip, Kylie decked out her highly-prized behind in a pair of denim cut-offs proudly paraded around the streets of London's Soho for the 'Timebomb' video. Whoop!

Remix Fix!

Besides an extended version, mixes came from DADA, Steve Redant & Phil Romano, Style of Eye and Italia3. Poignantly, Peter Rauhofer's lamentably overlooked retro-electro remix would be one of his last before dying of a brain tumour in 2013.

'Who Were We?' (Kylie Minogue and Berlin Music Ensemble)

Pierre Grise Productions: Digital download **Release:** July 2012
Writers: Leos Carax, Neil Hannon
Producer: Andrew Skeet

The melodramatic, cinematic, and symphonic 'Who Were We?' was taken from French surrealist film *Holy Motors* featuring Kylie in a charming supporting role. *The New York Times* in their review of *Holy Motors* crowed that 'French filmmaker Leos Carax opens the door to a world full of laughter, horror and rapture', while *The Telegraph* called it 'jaw-droppingly bonkers'. 'Who Were We?' was written by the movie's director/writer Carax with The Divine Comedy's Hannon. Carax's follow-up, *Annette*, won Best Director at 2021's Cannes Film Festival.

'Flower'

Parlophone: 50999 4 16468 2 3 **Single release:** September 2012 **Album:** *The Abbey Road Sessions*
Writers: Kylie, Steve Anderson
Producer: Steve Anderson

Unkindly chopped from 2007's *X* album, this delicate, heartfelt ballad with Kylie's vulnerable musings on death, the afterlife, and her longing for a child was first performed live on the KylieX2008 tour. 'It's a love letter to the child I may or may not ever have,' Kylie said at the time. Properly recorded four years later as a free download for pre-orders of 2012's *Abbey Road Sessions*, after the album's release, this fragile but potent 'Flower' squeaked into the UK Top 100.

Vid Bit!

Director: Kylie!!!

Such a personal Kylie song demanded a director who knew her intimately—so Kylie herself directed this moving, yet still hopeful, black and white clip, shot in beautiful coastal Cornwall.

The Abbey Road Sessions (Album)

Release: October 2012
Writers: (See previous individual song listings)
Producers: Steve Anderson, Colin Elliot

Kylie might not have convinced Parlophone to let her record an album of Blossom Dearie's jazz standards, but *The Abbey Road Sessions* album by turns bewitched, bothered, and bewildered her audience. It presented newly recorded jazz-pop versions of fifteen Kylie classics spread across her twenty-five-year back catalogue as if she had been reborn as Blossom Minogue. 'Flower' was the only new song and solely produced by Anderson. Backed by the Royal Philharmonic Orchestra, Kylie also lured Nick Cave back to re-record 'Where the Wild Roses Grow'. The new big band retake of 'On a Night Like This' was the album's second single after the wistful 'Flower'. While reviews for *The Abbey Road Sessions* skewered from hit (*Q* magazine called it 'quality stuff' and *The Guardian* awarded it four stars) to miss (*NME* gave it 3/10 and *The Daily Express* called it 'a little daft'), *The Abbey Road Sessions* debuted at #2 in the UK, hit #7 in Australia, and peaked in the US at #120. Dearie, who died in 2009, would have approved.

'Whistle' (Kylie Minogue with Múm)

Parlophone: Kyliepro1 **Promo single release:** February 2013
Writers: Gunnar Örn Tynes, Örvar Þóreyjarson Smárason
Producers: Múm, Árni Rúnar Hlöðversson

Recorded with Icelandic band Múm, this was an ethereal experimental folk track from the Björk school of indie Scandi pop, composed for the 2012 romantic horror movie *Jack and Diane*, which Kylie also had a role in. Released as a promotional digital single, the opening line of 'Whistle' is Kylie singing 'I bleed like a pig'. Little wonder this was severely testing Kylie's relationship with Parlophone! *Jack and Diane*, starring Riley Keough, bombed at the box office with thewrap.com complaining, 'unless you're dying to watch Elvis' granddaughter make out with Kylie Minogue there's not much to recommend'. *Smilewound* (2013) was Múm's last LP.

'Limpido' (Laura Pausini and Kylie Minogue)

Atlantic: 5053105982219 **Single release:** September 2013 **Compilation:** *20—The Greatest Hits*
Writers: Laura Pausini, Virginia Simonelli
Producers: Laura Pausini, Paolo Carta

Kylie continued her plan for world domination on 'Limpido', one language group at a time. Here she stopped off in Italy with Italian artist Pausini, although Kylie's vocals are in English. A *molto* Italo-rock track, Pausini also recorded 'Limpido' (meaning 'clear/clean') solo in English (called 'Radiant') and Spanish ('Limpio'). The Pausini/Minogue version went to #1 in Italy and was a minor hit in some other territories. In 2021, Pausini was Oscar nominated for 'lo si'.

Vid Bit!

Director: Gaetano Morbioli

Filmed in Rome this unfathomably boasts an African dancer in rope braids and Kylie and Pausini writhing about in pools of glitter at the end. A three-minute making of the video can also be found online.

19

Kiss Me Once Album and Garibay and More (2014-2015)

Kiss Me Once

Parlophone: 2564632807
Originally released: March 2014
Standard Edition

'Into the Blue'	4:08
'Million Miles'	3:28
'I Was Gonna Cancel'	3:32
'Sexy Love'	3:31
'Sexercize'	2:47
'Feels So Good'	3:37
'If Only'	3:21
'Les Sex'	3:47
'Kiss Me Once'	3:17
'Beautiful'	3:24
'Fine'	3:36
Special Edition Bonus Tracks	
'Mr President'	4:11
'Sleeping With the Enemy'	3:54

'Skirt'

Parlophone: Digital download **Promo single release:** June 2013
Writers: Kylie, Chris Elliot, Chris Lake, Terius Nash
Producers: Nom de Strip

Kylie's 'buzz single' release via new management Roc Nation came about because she 'had an epiphany in 2012 that I just felt like a change.' Premiering on her forty-fifth birthday, 'Skirt' became a digital release hitting #1 on the US Dance Club Songs chart, her tenth #1 on that chart to that point. At year's end, *Billboard* ranked 'Skirt' as one of 2013's Top 50 game-changing EDM (electronic dance music) tracks. That deal with Roc Nation, however, lasted barely two years.

Vid Bit!

Director: Will Davidson/William Baker

Australian fashion photographer Davidson called his stop-motion montage of 1,000 still images of Kylie in a hotel room for 'Skirt' a 'lyric video'. Afterwards he shot Kylie for the cover of *Vogue* ('How Kylie got her sparkle back!') then filmed her 'Sexercise' video.

Remix Fix!

With 'Skirt' skirting around a hard dance sound, the mixes were not your typical pop fare—Nom de Strip (gritty minimal dubstep), GTA (a crop circle-shaped rave), Switch (robotic house), and Hot Mouth (freaky EDM).

'Into the Blue'

Parlophone: 0825646319695 **Single release:** January 2014 **Album:** *Kiss Me Once*
Writers: Kelly Sheehan, Mike Del Rio, Jacob Kasher Hindlin
Producers: Mike Del Rio, Kelly 'Madame Buttons' Sheehan

As the first true blue dive into *Kiss Me Once*, Kylie's twelfth studio album, 'Into the Blue' was classic PopKylie but in a visibly different musical landscape. 'A song like "Into the Blue" is a Kylie song. It's what everyone tells me and it's what I feel myself,' Kylie chuffed. 'There's some melancholy in the lyrics, but ultimately it's hopeful, even euphoric at some points. It's sparkling!' Australian singer/songwriting powerhouse Sia Furler acted as co-executive producer on *Kiss Me Once*, but 'Into the Blue' peaked at #12 in the UK, a harsh #46 in Australia (her first lead single not to go Top 40), but—phew!—#1 on the US Dance Club Songs chart. In 2018, Melbourne's *Herald-Sun* called 'Into the Blue', 'easily the best thing on the dog's breakfast *Kiss Me Once* album where they tried a bit of everything'.

Vid Bit!

Director: Dawn Shadforth

'For "ITB" there was no brief at all,' Shadforth admitted. 'On the day we were very loose and intuitive.' French actor/director Clément Sibony was cast as Kylie's handsome arm candy.

Remix Fix!

After the edgy 'Skirt', things returned to safer turntables for 'ITB'—Roger Sanchez, Tracy Young, Patrick Hagenaar, Country Club Martini Crew, Vanilla Ace, and Morlando. The superior retake from J-pop legend Yasutaka Nakata (his second for Kylie) was so good some labelled it kismet!

'Sparks'

Release: January 2014 (B-side to 'Into the Blue')
Writers/Producers: Karen Poole, Matt Schwartz

From the same team behind 2012's 'Timebomb' single, 'Sparks' was the world music-flavoured B-side to 'Into the Blue', her first proper single for Roc Nation, the entertainment company from Jay-Z (i.e. Mr Beyoncé!). With lyrics by Poole that might be a veiled attempt to motivate Kylie to move on from a bad relationship ('Sometimes the love that you wasted/Becomes the love that you've lost'), 'Sparks' is one of the most fascinating Kylie B-sides and a something of a vocal revelation. There is no way a 'Singing Budgie' could have pulled this off. Truly sparkly.

'Million Miles'

Parlophone: Digital download **Promo single release:** March 2014 **Album:** *Kiss Me Once*
Writers: Chelcee Grimes, Daniel Davidsen. Peter Wallevik, Mich Hansen
Producers: Peter Wallevik, Daniel Davidsen, Cutfather

Asked about her new album's executive producer, Kylie could not stop gushing about Sia. 'Her talent is crazy, out of this world and undeniable,' Kylie declared. 'I had a lot of songs, so she was able to help me get some clarity with those and be my buddy.' British co-writer Grimes's first songwriting success actually came with 'Million Miles', inspired by being away from home. 'I just sang, "I feel like I'm a million, million, million, feel like I'm a million miles away" and that was the hook,' she recalled. A promotional only track and never performed live, the feisty 'Million Miles' baffled many fans that it was never in contention as a single.

'I Was Gonna Cancel'

Parlophone: 825646289493 **Single release:** May 2014 **Album:** *Kiss Me Once*
Writer: Pharrell Williams
Producers: Pharrell Williams, Kelly Sheehan

The story behind 'I Was Gonna Cancel', the second and ominously final single from *Kiss Me Once*, might actually be more interesting than the song itself. 'I was just having a pretty lousy day,' Kylie recalled, 'but Pharrell was super cool and talked me through that and then wrote "IWGC" which is a very positive song about not letting those things get you down and just get on with your day.' Williams was at the time still on his hot streak with 'Get Lucky' for Daft Punk and his own 'Happy' single. 'When I recorded the song I was still in a relationship and it doesn't take a lot of time when life can change dramatically,' Kylie noted of her split with Andrés Velencoso, 'so by the time that song was connecting with the public it really felt like it was destined to be a song about me.' All of which means that if anything on the album hints at the personal turmoil in Kylie's life it could be 'IWGC'. As a single 'IWGC', spent one week in the UK charts at #59, reached #5 on the US Dance Club Songs chart, but—gulp!—failed to chart in Australia.

Vid Bit!

Director: Dimitri Basil

Shot in Melbourne, this heavily panned, slightly washed-out clip with slo-mo-then-go interpretative dance section was clearly heavily influenced by Sia's clips. Kylie described it as 'an abstract look at pedestrian life'. Basil's movie debut, *High Weirdness*, was due in 2022.

Remix Fix!

While the original 'IWGC' left some fans underwhelmed, the remixes (The Presets, KDA, Maze & Masters, Steph Seroussi, Rene Amesz, and Guy Scheiman) were its saving grace. One more than the rest. In 2014, RuPaul tweeted '"I Was Gonna Cancel" by Kylie Minogue is playing on a loop in me head. @MotoBlanco RMX is heaven' to which Kylie replied 'Thank u RU!' A year later, the original 'IWGC' was immortalised during a 'lip sync for your life' battle on *RuPaul's Drag Race*. The happy house Moto Blanco remix of 'IWGC' truly cancelled out the original's lacklustre vibe.

'Sexy Love'

Parlophone: Digital download **Promo single release:** March 2014 **Album:** *Kiss Me Once*

Writers: Wayne Hector, Autumn Rowe, Peter Wallevik, Daniel Davidsen, Mich Hansen

Producers: Daniel Davidsen, Peter Wallevik, Cutfather

Like Stuart Price on *Aphrodite*, Kylie brought Sia in to executive produce *Kiss Me Once* to afford it a sense of cohesion. 'There was a point where Sia and I were looking at the songs we had so far,' Kylie recalled. 'We thought there were nice ones, but we didn't feel like we had a sexy one. Then I ended up within a short space of time with three songs that had "sex" in the title.' Planned as the album's third single, the cutesy 'Sexy Love' was released to Australian radio as a promotional single, but withered when cut from the Kiss Me Once Tour. A loveable video posted online by Kylie in 2015, directed by Ellen Von Unwerth, was culled from photoshoot footage.

'Sexercize'

Warner Bros. Records: Sampler **Promo single release:** March 2014 **Album:** *Kiss Me Once*
Writers: Sia Furler, Marcus Lomax, Jordan Johnson, Stefan Johnson, Clarence Coffee Jr, Nella Tahrini
Producers: The Monsters & The Strangerz, Kelly Sheehan

The first time Sia showed her muse the title of this song, Kylie duly blushed thinking it sounded wrong. 'But that's the genius of Sia,' Kylie enthused later. 'She can make it cool and make it hot and I can probably put the little wink into it, so you know it's going to be more fruity than sleazy.' Retitled 'Exercise' on the censored version of *Kiss Me Once*, this 'tongue and cheek song', as Kylie liked to call it, was also one of the album's four promotional singles, along with 'Million Miles', 'Les Sex', and 'Beautiful'. The bouncy 'Sexercise' failed to chart, apart from reaching #30 on the US Hot Dance/Electronic Songs.

Vid Bit!

Directors: Roman Coppola and Will Davidson

Two 'Sexercise' clips were filmed: one by Coppola based on the 1965 gay soft-porn short film *Kustom Kar Kommandos*; and the other more widely eyeballed 'bouncing ball' version filmed in a pool in Oxfordshire, England. High heels on an exercise ball? No wonder Kylie has great glutes!

'Feels So Good'

Release: March 2014 **Album:** *Kiss Me Once*
Writer: Tom Aspaul
Producers: MNEK, Wayne Wilkins

With dreamy vocals, atmospheric sunset 'n' cocktails production and wistful lyrics, 'Feels So Good' seemed a natural as a single from *Kiss Me Once*. That it did not and was never granted a live outing suggests its loved-up content was too upsetting for someone going through another painful breakup. Originally a moody dance demo, 'Indiana', by 'unapologetically queer' British musician Tom

Aspaul, 'Feels So Good' was produced by Uzoechi Emenike (aka MNEK). *Instinct* later dubbed Aspaul 'a songwriter in his own right with an impressive number of credits under his belt, including the creator of homosexuality, Kylie Minogue'.

'If Only'

Release: March 2014 **Album:** *Kiss Me Once*
Writers: Ariel Rechtshaid, Justin Raisen, Dan Nigro
Producer: Ariel Rechtshaid

PopJustice described 'If Only' as 'reflective and dramatic, like Cyndi Lauper's "Time After Time" put through a 2014 enormoballad blender'. Was the audience dividing, hard-to-peg 'If Only' one of the reasons *Kiss Me Once* sold just 200,000 copies worldwide? Speaking to Australian press, Kylie admitted, 'maybe it wasn't successful because it wasn't good enough, or it didn't deserve more. Who knows? Even in retrospect, it's hard to say why something works, or it doesn't.' *Kiss Me Once* would not just be the only album she released via Roc Nation, but her last album of new material released by Parlophone. If only things had been different.

'Les Sex'

Warner Music Argentina: KM-LS-1 **Promo single release:** March 2014 **Album:** *Kiss Me Once*
Writers: Amanda Warner, Peter Wade Keusch, Joshua 'J.D.' Walker, William Rappaport, Henri Lanz, Sia Furler
Producers: Joshua 'J.D.' Walker, GoodWill & MGI

The final of the 'sex' triple play on *Kiss Me Once*, the unashamedly camp 'Les Sex' was coyly retitled 'We Could Call It' on the censored album. Opinion again was divided on 'Les Sex'. Was it tongue in cheek, or just more cheeky tongue? *Time Out* magazine singled it out in their review of *Kiss Me Once* saying 'best of all is the ludicrous "Les Sex", on which Minogue, 46 next birthday, carries off lines like "Les love, les sex, les hand on les leg". Seriously, what a pop star.'

'Kiss Me Once'

Release: March 2014 **Album:** *Kiss Me Once*
Writer: Sia Furler
Producer: Jesse Shatkin

Kylie's favourite song on *Kiss Me Once* was its anthemic title track written for her by Sia. 'It's not the most obvious one on first listen,' Kylie informed *The*

Huffington Post, 'compared with other songs on the album that are more shiny.' Many critics and fans thought 'KMO' should have been a single, if not the album's first single. A centrepiece of the Kiss Me Once Tour and a dazzling laser light display at the same time, this quintessentially Kylie song—'Me and you, baby we made it through'—is truly like a love letter to her fans. Intothepopvoid.com called 'KMO' 'one of Kylie's greatest moments—a shoo-in for her all-time top ten'. PopMatters agreed saying this dreamy, arm-waving anthem 'really nails the essence of the Kylie sound'.

'Beautiful' (with Enrique Iglesias)

Universal Music Group (Australia/NZ): Digital download **Warner Music Group (US)/Warner Music Japan: CD Promo single release:** March 2014 **Album:** *Kiss Me Once*
Writers: Enrique Iglesias, Mark Taylor, Alex Smith, Samuel Preston
Producers: Mark Taylor, Alex Smith

The fourth and final promotional single from *Kiss Me Once* was released to radio in Japan and the US as a one-track promotional single, while Iglesias's Australian label Universal released it as a digital download on the same day as Kylie's album. A video for slowly building powerballad 'Beautiful' was planned but nixed after the single peaked at #47 in Australia and failed to chart in New Zealand. Cameron Adams wrote on news.com.au, 'the team behind Enrique's "Hero" and Cher's "Believe" try and merge the two songs ... but the inconvenient truth is there's no real hooks on this song'. Kylie performed an acoustic rendition, with just piano and minus Iglesias, during her live *Spotify Sessions*, which redeems, if not reclaims, this honestly beautiful song.

'Fine'

Release: March 2014 **Album:** *Kiss Me Once*
Writers: Kylie, Karen Poole, Chris Crowhurst
Producer: Chris Loco

If Kylie was in the throes of another break-up with another 'love rat', you would hardly have guessed it from her twelfth studio album, *Kiss Me Once*. The only hint of trouble on the standard album is this reassuring post-breakup detachment theory album closer she co-wrote ('When you feel everything's impossible/Just know you'll be fine'). So why so little writing input? It is likely Kylie's time was stretched, simultaneously being a coach on *The Voice UK* and *The Voice Australia*. Doing press for 2019's *Step Back in Time* compilation, it was pointed out no tracks from *Kiss Me Once* were included. 'At some point the stars are aligned and everything is on your side,' she told *Paper* diplomatically, 'and they had their own pattern on that album, let's say.'

'Mr President'

Release: March 2014 **Album:** *Kiss Me Once*
Writers: Kylie, Kelly Sheehan, Jacob Kasher Hindin
Producers: Thomas Olsen, Kelly Sheehan

Here is Kylie's other album co-write, one of the two bonus tracks for *Kiss Me Once*. Co-writer/producer Sheehan also goes by her recording engineer name of 'Madame Buttons'. Thomas Olsen is better known as Australian DJ/producer/ remixer Tommy Trash, and on the basis of this track—which sounds like it slid in on a grotty basement dance floor between *Body Language* and *X* with Kylie channelling screen legend Marilyn Monroe (from her famous birthday song for US President John F. Kennedy)—it is a shame he was not the Aussie artist who was EP on *Kiss Me Quick*. Three months after the release of *Kiss Me Once*, a non-Kylie/Marilyn, instrumental, dirty electro version of 'Mr President' leaked. Look for it as the 'karaoke' version.

'Sleeping With the Enemy'

Release: March 2014 **Album:** *Kiss Me Once*
Writers: Claude Kelly, Greg Kurstin
Producers: Greg Kurstin, Joe Kearns

Borrowing heavily sonically from Massive Attack's 1991 classic 'Unfinished Sympathy' before sweeping in with a Pet Shop Boys-style chorus, it is hard to understand why Kylie and Sia decided to give 'Sleeping With the Enemy' (and 'Mr President') the big kiss-off from *Kiss Me Once*. Perhaps their fangirling superseded their better judgement. 'Having a female and Australian girl, one of the coolest girls I know who has rewritten the rules of pop for herself, I'm in awe,' Kylie rhapsodised about Sia. The two would, however, never work together again.

'Golden Boy'

Parlophone: 825646320875 7" **Single release:** April 2014 **Album:** *Kiss Me Once*
Writers: Ariel Rechtshaid, Justin Raisen, Dan Nigro
Producer: Ariel Rechtshaid

Here is the team from 'If Only' back for a song initially palmed off as the HMV Digital bonus track on *Kiss Me Once*. One month later, 'Golden Boy' was released as a limited edition (1,000 copies) 7″ vinyl single, with some minimalist 'etchings' by Kylie and graphic designer Tony Hung on its B-side, for World Record Store Day in 2014. 'Golden Boy' is Kylie back in slightly left-of-centre pop terrain with a brain-bursting chorus. The shiny irony of that 'Golden Boy' title is that it provided a segue of sorts to Kylie's next proper studio album, 2018's *Golden*.

'Crystallize'

Parlophone: Digital download **Single release:** June 2014
Writers: Kylie, Jason Sellards, Devonté Hynes
Producer: Scott Hoffman (Babydaddy)

A charity single for the 'One Note Against Cancer' campaign, Kylie bestie Jake Shears was in on the action again, as was co-writer Hynes, better known as Blood Orange (born in 1985, two years before Kylie had her first hit). Prior to the release of the single, fans were allowed to bid on one note in the song on an auctioning website, and once all notes were sold, Kylie released the song. While 'Crystallize', which marked a decade since Kylie's first Scissor Sisters collab, had a brief visit to the UK chart at #60, it failed to make any impact in her native Australia. In 2016, *The Guardian* selected it as one of Kylie's ten best tracks dubbing it 'a beautiful pop confection'.

Vid Bit!

Director: Alice Moitié

Directed by French fashion photographer Moitié, 'Crystallize' does not feature Kylie but in her place a young woman tripping on being a bedroom pop star. The second half is dedicated to the thousands of donors who bid on every note of 'Crystallize'. Now that is truly giving back!

Sleepwalker EP (Kylie and Garibay)

Parlophone: Digital download **Release:** September 2014

'Glow': **Writers:** Kylie, Fernando Garibay, Amanda Warner
'Wait': **Writers:** Peter Wade Keusch, Amanda Warner, Fernando Garibay
'Break This Heartbreak': **Writers:** Kylie, Fernando Garibay, Amanda Warner
'Chasing Ghosts': **Writers:** Kylie, Sterling Fox, Fernando Garibay, Amanda Warner;
Producer (all tracks): Fernando Garibay.

What is a gal to do when she is dateless, label-less, and management less? Get busy creatively! With a running time of just over fifteen minutes the *Sleepwalker*

EP is certainly short if not sweet. Garibay told *Billboard* he met the 'extraordinary' Kylie when she was looking for producers for *Kiss Me Once* and he was on a hot streak having produced Lady Gaga's *Born This Way* #1 in 2011. 'It was a beautiful thing, because we did it in our own time,' Kylie explained. 'It was just about expression and kind of mashing things up.' MTV deemed this Kylie's 'experimental EP' while *Billboard* called the songs 'ethereal, left-of-centre cuts'. Being free to download from Kylie's SoundCloud page meant the *Sleepwalker* songs were ineligible to chart.

Vid Bit!

Director: William Baker

Three of the EP's four tracks ('Glow', 'Wait', and 'Chasing Ghosts') appeared in the short film *Sleepwalker*, directed by Baker, shown before Kylie's Kiss Me Once Tour.

'Crave You (Reprise)' (Flight Facilities Featuring Kylie Minogue)

Future Classic: FCL119CD **Release:** October 2014 **Album:** *Down To Earth*
Writers: Giselle Rosselli, Hugo Gruzman, James Lyell
Producers: Hugo Gruzman, James Lyell

Originally released in 2010 featuring the vocals of co-writer Rosselli (known as Giselle), 'Crave You' became a cult underground EDM hit in Australia. Four years later, it featured on Flight Facilities's *Down to Earth* debut album which peaked at #3 down under. Prior to the album's release, the band uploaded a video of Kylie performing this brief *a capella* reprise in an apartment directed by 'Uncle Friendly', which *Spin* magazine justifiably termed 'bizarre'.

'Bette Davis Eyes'

Warner Music TV: WMTV237 **Year:** November 2014 **Compilation:** *Sounds of the 80s*
Writers: Donna Weiss, Jackie DeShannon
Producer: Stuart Price

One of thirty-seven cover versions recorded for the BBC's *Sounds of the 80s* compilation, Kylie delivers a glossy dance version of Kim Carnes's early '80s 'Harlow gold' classic, eye-catchingly produced by a briefly returning Price. Upon its release, Idolator declared 'the camp cover wouldn't sound of place on the diva's *Light Years* LP, which is a really big compliment'. A sweetly ferocious/precocious acoustic version leaked in 2016.

'Right Here Right Now' (Giorgio Moroder Featuring Kylie Minogue)

RCA: 0886445051308 **Single release:** January 2015 **Album:** *Déjà Vu*
Writers: Giorgio Moroder, Patrick Jordan-Patrikios, Karen Poole, David Etherington
Producers: Giorgio Moroder, Roman Lüth, Patrick Jordan-Patrikios

Released in January 2015 as the lead single from Moroder's *Déjà Vu* comeback album, 'Right Here Right Now' was performed on the Australian leg of Kylie's Kiss Me Once Tour with Moroder calling her 'an Australian treasure'. Kylie's second release with the 'Right Here Right Now' title hit #1 in Argentina, but wound up at #125 in the UK. While 'Right Here Right Now' was not rightfully the big hit it deserved to be, music legend Moroder had only good things to say about Kylie. 'She's a professional and such a great lady,' he told *Rolling Stone.*

Vid Bit!

Director: Daniel Börjesson

Like the song itself, the 'Right Here Right Now' video was a flawless, inventive piece of music video art with Kylie in full pop princess mode and moody Moroder stalking the shadows.

Remix Fix!

Eight official remixers (DJ Sneak, Felix Da Housecat, Ant LaRock, Kenny Summit, 7th Heaven, Whiiite, Zoo Brasil, and Ralphi Rosario) helped 'Right Here Right Now' hit #1 on the US Dance Club Songs chart—Kylie's fifteenth and Moroder's first, aged seventy-four. Five years later for World Record Day in 2020, a 12″ vinyl edition with remixes by Kenny Summit was issued.

'Absolutely Anything and Anything At All'

Fireweheel/Menlo Park Music: Digital download **Promo single release:** August 2015
Writers: John Greswell, Christopher Taylor
Producers: Dreamtrak, Menlo Park

This absolutely forgettable oddity was taken from the British sci-fi comedy *Absolutely Anything*, directed by former Monty Python member Terry Jones, and starring Simon Pegg, Kate Beckinsale, Eddie Izzard, and Joanna Lumley. The movie was released three days after another of its stars, Robin Williams, tragically took his own life. Not only was it Williams's last movie (in a voice-only role), but Jones's. *Absolutely Anything* earned a paltry $7 million globally and the not so triple-A 'Absolutely Anything and Anything At All' failed to chart.

Vid Bit!

Directors: Bill Jones, Ben Timlett

Like the movie itself, the 'Absolutely Anything and Anything At All' video is corny, the effects look cheap, and it has a bad smell of bygone children's television to it.

Kylie + Garibay EP (*Black and White*)

Parlophone: Digital download **Release:** September 2015

'Black and White' (featuring Shaggy): **Writers:** Kylie, Fernando Garibay, Whitney Phillips

'If I Can't Have You' (Featuring Sam Sparro): **Writers:** Fernando Garibay, Sam Sparro, Brian Lee

'Your Body' (Featuring Giorgio Moroder): **Writers:** Kylie, Fernando Garibay, Jamie Hartman, Whitney Phillips, Max McElligott; **Producer (all tracks):** Fernando Garibay

Released little more than a year after their first EP, the second (and to date final) *Kylie + Garibay* EP was just three tracks, all with special guests and a running time of under thirteen minutes. 'There's a sense of purity. It's liberating for us to be able to do an EP like this, where there is no agenda,' Garibay told *Billboard* saying he and Kylie wanted to 'write songs for the sake of writing songs, and not for anything else.' Shaggy was brought in to spice-up 'Black and White', the focus track, Australian expat Sparro was her duet partner on 'If I Can't Have You' and then there was next Minogue/Moroder collab, 'Your Body'. Described as a 'low-key experimental project', the second *Kylie + Garibay* EP, also known as *Black and White*, made a minimal impact on music services.

Vid Bit!

Director: Katerina Jebb

One of Kylie's long-time gal pals, photographer Jebb, captured her frolicking, having fun, and being silly by a pool for the 'Black and White' video. In 'damaged footage' style, very in vogue at the time, it is as if Kylie (minus Shaggy) was finally letting her guard down. Kylie also posted Jebb's body-conscious B&W clip for 'Your Body'.

'The Other Boys' (NERVO featuring Kylie Minogue, Jake Shears & Nile Rodgers)

Dr2 Records: 12C2LD017 **Single release:** October 2015 **Album:** *Collateral*
Writers: Miriam Nervo, Olivia Nervo, Nile Rodgers, Fred Falke
Producers: NERVO, Nile Rodgers, Fred Falke

Kylie had previously worked with the Australian Nervo twins in 2010 on *Aphrodite*'s 'Put Your Hands Up (If You Feel Love)'. There was obviously still plenty of love there after her pal Jake hauled her in to be included as 'the other girl' on this record and hang around long enough for a video shoot. Such was their combined pulling power even Chic's legendary Nile Rodgers joined the party. While the EDM-flavoured 'The Other Boys' topped the Dance Club Songs chart in the US and went Top 5 in Argentina, this pansexual dance explosion undeservingly failed to find a wider audience due to being just a few years ahead of the queer-pop-goes-mainstream boom.

Vid Bit!

Director: Hannu Aukia

Shears called the filming in London's Brick Lane, 'Aussie overload in the best way'.

Remix Fix!

The Ultra label commissioned a swag of remixes, some of which arguably rank among the best Kylie has ever been associated with (Mr Gonzo, Michael Mandal & Forbes, BOJAN, Florian Picasso, Teenage Mutants, Viglietti, and Rhythm Masters).

20

Kylie Christmas & *Snow Queen Edition* Albums (2015–2016)

Kylie Christmas

Parlophone: 0825646004898
Originally released: November 2015
Standard Edition

'It's the Most Wonderful Time of the Year'	2:44
'Santa Claus Is Coming To Town'	2:15
'Winter Wonderland'	1:53
'Christmas Wrapping'	5:05
'Only You'	3:05
'I'm Gonna Be Warm This Winter'	2:29
'Every Day's Like Christmas'	4:13
'Let It Snow'	1:56
'White December'	3:07
'2000 Miles'	3:34
'Santa Baby'	3:22
'Christmas Isn't Christmas 'Til You Get Here'	3:03
'Have Yourself A Merry Little Christmas'	3:22
Deluxe Edition bonus tracks	
'Oh Santa'	2:38
'100 Degrees'	4:31
'Cried Out Christmas'	3:44

Kylie Christmas: Snow Queen Edition

Parlophone: 0190295890728
Originally released: November 2016
Additional tracks added to *Kylie Christmas* tracklist

'Stay Another Day'	3:40
'At Christmas'	3:46
'Wonderful Christmastime'	3:42
'I Wish It Could Be Christmas'	4:14
'Christmas Lights'	4:06
'Everybody's Free (To Feel Good)'	2:10
French exclusive	
'Night Fever'	3:15

'It's the Most Wonderful Time of the Year'

Release: November 2015 **Album:** *Kylie Christmas*
Writers: Edward Pola, George Wyle
Producer: Steve Anderson

First there was 'Santa Baby' in 2000, then 'Let It Snow' in 2010, which snowballed into *Kylie Christmas*, and a year later *Kylie Christmas: Snow Queen Edition*. That is a lot of snow for a girl from Melbourne who grew up without the cold, wet, white stuff. 'It's the Most Wonderful Time of the Year', Kylie's own personal favourite Christmas song, was the lead track for 2015's festive offering *Kylie Christmas* (better renamed 'Kyristmas'?), which despite being a collection of old and new material is considered her thirteenth proper album. Released in November 2015, Kylie was back on Parlophone in the UK for a special one-off deal (even they had to see this would be a big seller) and Warner Music for the rest of the world including Australia.

'Santa Claus Is Coming To Town' (Featuring Frank Sinatra)

Release: November 2015 **Album:** *Kylie Christmas*
Writers: John Frederick Coots, Haven Gillespie
Producers: Charles Pignone, Steve Anderson

Originally a hit in 1934 for Eddie Cantor and most recently in 2011 by Michael Bublé, how did Kylie get to duet with legendary crooner Sinatra, who actually passed away in 1998? His label Capitol (part of the EMI family with Parlophone) had previously compiled two duet albums in 1993/1994 digitally without Sinatra alive with superstar names (including Barbra Streisand, Liza Minnelli, and Tony Bennett), which became million sellers. Sinatra first recorded 'Santa Claus Is

Coming To Town' in 1948 and the version used for Kylie's album came from a recording he made for a 1957 TV special, *Happy Holidays With Bing and Frank* (featuring Bing Crosby beloved for his *White Christmas* standard).

'Winter Wonderland'

Release: November 2015 **Album:** *Kylie Christmas*
Writers Felix Bernard, Richard B. Smith
Producer: Steve Anderson

The shortest track on the album at just 1:53, 'Winter Wonderland' was also written in 1934 in the midst of the Great Depression. Lyricist Smith penned the words while being treated from tuberculosis, passing away from the disease a year after 'Winter Wonderland' became a hit. Over the years, 'Winter Wonderland' has been covered by myriad artists, including Ella Fitzgerald, Eurythmics, and Snoop Dogg. A year after Kylie's wonder, Ronan Keating was given permission to adapt the lyrics to 'Summer Wonderland' with references to pavlova, cricket, and mozzie spray. Surely for a re-release, Kylie needs this Australasian version!

'Christmas Wrapping' (With Iggy Pop)

Release: November 2015 **Album:** *Kylie Christmas*
Writer: Chris Butler
Producer: Steve Anderson

If anyone thought Kylie duetting with Nick Cave was an odd occurrence, what about her pairing with the 'Godfather of Punk' Iggy Pop? The two most unlikely of music pals croon a warped new wave tune originally recorded by The Waitresses in 1981. Other artists who have covered 'Christmas Wrapping' include Spice Girls, The Saturdays, and the cast of the *Glee* TV series. Pop, a true enigma, might be the closest Kylie gets to singing with hero David Bowie, who would die two months later. A member of influential American punk-styled band The Stooges in the early 1970s, Pop invented the stage dive and had his songs covered by Bowie, Tina Turner, and even Michael Hutchence ('The Passenger' on 1995's *Batman Forever* soundtrack).

'Only You' (With James Corden)

Parlophone: Digital download **Single release:** November 2015 **Album:** *Kylie Christmas*
Writer: Vince Clarke
Producer: Steve Anderson

'Only You' had already been a huge hit twice in the 1980s before Kylie and showbiz luvvy Corden pounced on it. Yazoo's original 'OY' became an instant early '80s electropop classic, with *a cappella* group The Flying Pickets scoring the 1983 Christmas UK #1 with their version. The Minogue/Corden version was chosen as the lead single from the *Kylie Christmas* project, released a week ahead of the album in November 2015. It peaked at #155 in the UK, but served as a launch pad for an album attempting to get the mix of cool Yuletide and kitsch Christmas just right. In place of a proper video, a low-key lyric video was produced.

'I'm Gonna Be Warm This Christmas'

Release: November 2015 **Album:** *Kylie Christmas*
Writers: Hank Hunter, Mark Barkan
Producer: Steve Anderson

It is back to the 1960s for this festive chestnut first crooned by Connie Francis, whose 'cry singing' style influenced female artists like Dolly Parton, Gloria Estefan, and ABBA's Agnetha Fältskog. The opening lyric of the original Francis version 'we met at a ski lodge' was changed for the single's UK release to 'we met on a winter day' after her record company realised that England had no ski lodges. Kylie sticks to the original lyric though. A noted ski bunny, she made the front cover of *Hello!* magazine in 2009 in her ski gear after canoodling Spanish model Andrés Velencoso on the piste. By the time of *Kylie Christmas*, however, she was cuddling up to new après-ski chum, British actor Joshua Sasse, confirming they were a couple as her new album was released. Happy holidays indeed!

'Every Day's Like Christmas'

Parlophone: Digital download **Single release:** December 2015 **Album:** *Kylie Christmas*
Writers: Mikkel Eriksen, Tor Erik Hermansen, Chris Martin
Producers: Stargate, Steve Anderson

Coldplay's Chris Martin wrote this song with Norway's Stargate team, responsible for one of Rihanna's biggest hits, 2011's 'Only Girl (In the World'). The very Coldplay sounding 'Every Day's Like Christmas', the third single from *Kylie Christmas*, was released in December—with an extra special Christmas gift for long-time Kylie lovers (see below)!

Vid Bit!

Director: David Lopez-Edwards

Want to take a sneaky peek at Kylie, new *beau* Joshua Sasse as a Christmas elf wearing 'having a Sassy Christmas' sweater, party pals, dogs, and more enjoying their Yuletide at a chic London bungalow? This might just be as close as we mere mortals ever get to living the dream (pass the cracker, thanks Kyles!). After they split, Kylie removed the video from her YouTube channel.

Remix Fix!

Stock Aitken Waterman—long since separated and not particularly amicably at that—were cajoled back into the studio to remix 'Every Day's Like Christmas'. It was their first, and only, collaboration after twenty years apart and first with Kylie in twenty-five years. 'They wanted the record to sound like we'd just walked out of the studio in 1987,' Pete Waterman told ITV. 'I told the others this is what Kylie wants and they said, "Let's do it, return at the top!"' Although the single release didn't chart, it spurred sales of *Kylie Christmas*, which charted at #12 in the UK (certified gold for sales of over 100,000), #7 in Australia, and #184 in the US.

'Let It Snow'

(See entry in Chapter 17.)

'White December'

Release: November 2015 **Album:** *Kylie Christmas*
Writers: Kylie, Karen Poole, Matt Prime
Producer: Matt Prime

Not to be confused with 'White Christmas', this is a new tune co-penned by Kylie herself. With five co-writes on the *Kylie Christmas* album, this was more creative input than she had had on an album since 2001's mega-selling *Fever*. 'White December' had her teaming up with old pal Poole and producer/songwriter Prime. Taking its cues from Mariah Carey's perennial 'All I Want for Christmas' and Darlene Love's 'Christmas (Baby Please Come Home)' from 1963, Kylie's '60s girl group 'White December' even features some retro-sounding saxophone.

'2000 Miles'

Release: November 2015 **Album:** *Kylie Christmas*
Writer: Chrissie Hynde
Producer: Steve Anderson

Originally a hit in 1983 for The Pretenders, '2000 Miles' was written by singer Hynde in memory of band member James Honeyman-Scott who had died the previous year of a drug overdose at age twenty-five. Although it has since become a radio staple every December, '2000 Miles' only reached #15 on the UK and was released on the B-side of the band's 1984 hit 'Middle of the Road' in the US. Kylie's version does not stray too far from The Pretenders's arrangement, though it soups up the Christmas bells and turns down the jangly guitars.

'Santa Baby'

(See entry in Chapter 10.)

'Christmas Isn't Christmas 'Til You Get Here'

Release: November 2015 **Album:** *Kylie Christmas*
Writers: Kylie, Steve Anderson, Karen Poole
Producer: Steve Anderson

The second Kylie co-write on *Kylie Christmas* lets producer Anderson in on the festive cheer at last. Producing twelve out of the thirteen tracks on the standard album version, this stood as the most tracks for a single producer, or team, on a Kylie album since 1989's *Enjoy Yourself*, solely produced by SAW, if not ever! Kylie performed this '60s girl group homage at the Royal Albert Hall in 2015 during her TV special. Surrounded by dancing Christmas trees and decked out in fur-trimmed red boots and a red sequined dress with 'Kylie Christmas' emblazoned in gold glitter, this was truly the happiest, if not campest, time of the year.

'Have Yourself a Merry Little Christmas'

Release: November 2015 **Album:** *Kylie Christmas*
Writers: Hugh Martin, Ralph Blane
Producer: Steve Anderson

The final track on the standard *Kylie Christmas* album, 'Have Yourself A Merry Little Christmas' is most closely associated with another gay icon, Judy Garland, sung in the 1944 musical *Meet Me In St. Louis*. The song's 'make the Yuletide gay' lyrics took on a new meaning within the LGBT+ community in later decades. Frank Sinatra recorded a version, updating the lyrics which is the version Kylie sings. 'Have Yourself a Merry Little Christmas' was ranked #76 on the Top 100 songs in American cinema in 2004. #1? Garland singing 'Over the Rainbow' from 1939's *The Wizard of Oz*, also previously covered by Kylie.

'Oh Santa'

Release: November 2015 **Album:** *Kylie Christmas*
Writers: Kylie, Ash Howes, Richard Stannard, Steve Anderson
Producers: Ash Howes, Richard Stannard, Steve Anderson

Courtesy of the Biffco team, with Anderson in the mix too, on the first of three deluxe edition bonus tracks Kylie conjures up a finger-snapping big band jazz number. Kylie's lyrics read like her own private 'Santa Baby' wish list—a Bentley, a house in Chelsea (another one?), a little pony, Tony awards, a Jacuzzi, a bubble bath, a back rub with George Clooney, a tiara, a baby llama, dinner with President Obama, a super fixer (because it rhymed with 'an elixir'?), a trip to outer space, oh, and a kiss too. Mrs Claus won't be happy.

'100 Degrees' (With Dannii Minogue)

Parlophone: Digital download **Single release:** December 2015 **Album:** *Kylie Christmas*
'100 Degrees (Still Disco to Me)' (Kylie + Dannii)
Parlophone: 0190295971076 **12″ release:** June 2016
Writers: Kylie, Ash Howes, Richard Stannard, Steve Anderson
Producers: Ash Howes, Richard Stannard, Steve Anderson

After decades of promising, finally the Minogue sisters delivered a duet that Kylie herself helped write. Sisters really were doing it for themselves! Although included as a deluxe edition bonus track, '100D' was promoted as the second single from *Kylie Christmas* complete with video and remixes. An alternate (read: Christmas-free!) version appeared in April 2016 retitled '100 Degrees (Still Disco to Me)'. 'There's not enough party Christmas songs, everyone has Christmas parties, but what music do you put on? This song is perfect for dancing to,' Disco Dannii told the press. 'It's going to be a very sparkly, very Minogue Christmas.' Although the song failed to chart, '100D' became one of the twenty biggest vinyl sellers in the UK that year.

Vid Bit!

Director: David Lopez-Edwards

A charming/disarming 'in the studio' clip of the Minogue gals in baggy white T-shirts ('Kylie Kissmas' and 'Disco Christmas' respectively) scorching through their seasonal sister act.

Remix Fix!

Steve Anderson spun things out on his Classic Disco Mix of '100 Degrees (Still Disco to Me)', while 7th Heaven and Boney also came to the Christmas/après-Christmas disco party.

'Cried Out Christmas'

Release: November 2015 **Album:** *Kylie Christmas*
Writers: Kylie, Karen Poole, Matt Prime
Producer: Matt Prime

The final of the three *Kylie Christmas* bonus tracks is the final Kylie co-write for the album. It also boasts some of the niftiest, not even Christmas-specific, lyrics she has penned—'You're in the East End/And I'm here in Chelsea/The minute you get here/Is the minute you melt me'. She also sultrily encourages her lover (presumably Joshua Sasse) to get a cab while she will take the tube. Who knew Kylie had an Oyster Card for getting around London? As if Amy Winehouse and the Spice Girls had made a sexy, sullen Christmas record together, 'Cried Out Christmas' was another good reason *Kylie Christmas* was repackaged the following year.

'This Wheel's On Fire'

Rhino UK: 0190295941666 **Promo single release:** July 2016 **Soundtrack:** *Absolutely Fabulous: The Movie Soundtrack*
Writers: Bob Dylan, Rick Danko
Producers: Richard 'Biff' Stannard, Ash Howes

This was Kylie's update of the theme song originally used in the BBC's *Absolutely Fabulous* comedy TV series (1992–2012) for the 2016 one-off hit movie sequel. 'This Wheel's On Fire' ranks as the second time Kylie has covered Dylan (quiz time: can you remember the first? Answer below.). 'This Wheels On Fire' became a UK Top 5 hit in trippy hippy 1968 for Julie Driscoll with Brian Auger and the Trinity. Kylie's electro-stomp version was a promotional single and on the movie soundtrack. 'As a huge fan of the *Ab Fab* series and both Jennifer (Saunders) and (co-star) Joanna (Lumley),' Kylie gushed, 'I'm over the moon to be singing the theme song.' (Quiz answer: 'Death Is Not the End' with Nick Cave in 1996.)

'Stay Another Day'

Release: November 2016 **Album:** *Kylie Christmas: Snow Queen Edition*
Writers: Tony Mortimer, Ron Kean, Dominic Hawken
Producer: Steve Anderson

In November 2016, *Kylie Christmas: Snow Queen Edition* was released to supersede the previous year's sixteen-track CD/six-track DVD set. This time round there were twenty-two songs (twenty-three at French discotheques!) but, alas, no DVD. The first of the six/seven new tracks added was a cover of East 17's 'Stay Another Day', the UK's 1994 Christmas #1. Written by band member Mortimer about his brother, Ollie, who committed suicide, this meant the supposedly fluffy, stocking-filling *Kylie Christmas 2.0* now contained two songs written about people who had died. Kylie may have been inspired to record the stirring 'Stay Another Day' in honour of her beloved grandmother, who passed in 2013.

'At Christmas'

Parlophone: Digital download **Warner Music Benelux:** GBAYE1601627
Promo single release: November 2016 **Album:** *Kylie Christmas: Snow Queen Edition*
Writers: Peter Wallevik, Daniel Davidsen, Patrick Joseph Devine
Producers: Peter Wallevik, Daniel Davidsen, Eric J. Dubowsky

It's beginning to look a lot like a Scandi Christmas! Released a few days prior to the release of *Kylie Christmas: Snow Queen Edition* as the revamped album's first single, clearly the writers' brief here was to write something that would be a match for the world's most popular Christmas song, Mariah Carey's 'All I Want For Christmas Is You' which finally hit #1 in the US in 2019. Kylie sang 'At Christmas' live on *The Jonathan Ross Show* in 2016 with a performance that somehow brought together the worlds of Dita Von Teese and 1980s supermodels perfectly.

'Wonderful Christmastime' (With Mika)

Parlophone: Digital download **Single release:** December 2016 **Album:** *Kylie Christmas: Snow Queen Edition*
Writer: Paul McCartney
Producer: Steve Anderson

Although she had a year between Christmas releases, all six/seven of the new tracks were covers, or written for Kylie, but none by Kylie. 'Wonderful Christmastime' was a Top 10 hit for Beatles/Wings member McCartney in 1979 and thereafter a Christmas radio staple. For her version, Kylie yanked in pop pal Mika to help out, released as the second single from *Kylie Christmas: Snow Queen Edition*. Although it made the charts in Belgium, 'Wonderful Christmastime' failed to do much elsewhere, though Kylie and Mika performed it on his Italian variety TV show *Stasera Casa Mika*. Kylie's revamped festive album managed #41 in the UK and #30 in Australia, thereafter becoming a perennial holiday seller.

'I Wish It Could Be Christmas Everyday'

Release: November 2016 **Album:** *Kylie Christmas: Snow Queen Edition*
Writer: Roy Wood
Producer: Steve Anderson

It was not so much a disco Christmas with this track as a glam rock Christmas with a cover from British '70s band Wizzard. Originally a #4 UK that year, in 2012 'I Wish It Could Be Christmas Everyday' was voted #2 best Christmas song by the British public, just behind The Pogues featuring Kirsty MacColl's 'Fairytale of New York'. Kylie had actually sung the song the previous year during her London Albert Hall concert and it got such a rousing response it was obvious 'I Wish It Could Be Christmas Everday' needed to be part of the repackaged collection.

'Christmas Lights'

Release: November 2016 **Album:** *Kylie Christmas: Snow Queen Edition*
Writers: Chris Martin, Guy Berryman, Jonathan Buckland, William Champion
Producer: Steve Anderson

Originally released by Coldplay in December 2010, 'Christmas Lights' became a UK and US Top 30 hit for them. The second of two Martin songs on Kylie's album, 'Christmas Lights' details a marriage breakdown around the 'happy holidays', presumably written about then-wife Gwyneth Paltrow, whom Martin 'conscious uncoupled' with in 2014. Kylie's version of 'Christmas Lights' rebirths a mid-tempo rock song into a twinkly piano ballad that surges into an anthemic singalong emphasising Martin's keen turn with a phrase. In 2019, *The Telegraph* ranked 'Christmas Lights' one of the 100 best Christmas Songs of all time.

'Everybody's Free (To Feel Good)'

Release: November 2016 **Album:** *Kylie Christmas: Snow Queen Edition*
Writers: Nigel Swanston, Tim Cox
Producer: Steve Anderson

Here is the final song (and final cover) on the *Kylie Christmas: Snow Queen Edition* album. A global dance hit in 1991 for Zambian-born Rozalla (aka the 'Queen of Rave'), 'Everybody's Free (To Feel Good)' became an early crossover hit from the underground rave scene. Kylie's version, as perhaps befitting a Christmas album, remakes it into a jolly singalong before switching to anthemic within the space of two minutes. Kylie also appeared on the UK's *X Factor* show that year to belt out 'Everybody's Free (To Feel Good)' alongside finalists Saara Aalto and Matt Terry.

'Night Fever'

Release: November 2016 **Album:** *Kylie Christmas: Snow Queen Edition (France only)*
Writers: Barry Gibb, Robin Gibb, Maurice Gibb
Producer: Stuart Price

While that was the end of Kylie's Christmas cheer for the English-speaking world, it was not quite the end of *Kylie Christmas: Snow Queen Edition*. Inspired by the *Saturday Night Fever* musical due to open in Paris in early 2017, Kylie recorded the Bee Gees '70s disco classic 'Night Fever', added as a 'French exclusive' to the album. Sung at her Christmas gig at London's Albert Hall in 2016, 'Night Fever' was all sequins, glitter, and sparkles—a very Minogue Christmas indeed. In 2020, during her *Disco* era, Kylie finally revealed Price was the producer behind 'Night Fever'.

'Still Feels Like the First Time' (Zoot Woman Featuring Kylie Minogue)

ZWR: ZWR101CD **Release:** June 2017 **Album:** *Absence*
Writers: Kylie, Stuart Price, Adam Blake, Johnny Blake
Producer: Stuart Price

While many fans hankered for a proper reteaming of Kylie with producer whizz Price, it appeared a more and more unlikely event, sadly. After executive producing 2010's *Aphrodite* album, Price returned momentarily on Kylie's covers of 'Bette Davis Eyes' and 'Night Fever', and a year later was briefly in the producer's chair again. This time round it was for a pulsating, somewhat underappreciated, psychedelic synth-pop track from British *avant garde* electronic act Zoot Woman's *Absence* album. With Kylie on whispery vocal duties, 'Still Feels Like the First Time' is esoteric electronica with a retro-futuristic lust for late '60s pop.

'Off With His Skirt'

Hollywood Records: D002552002 **Release:** June 2017 **Soundtrack:** *Galavant: The Complete Collection*
Writers/Producers: Alan Menken and Glenn Slater

This delightful ditty featured in season two of US network ABC's musical comedy series *Galavant* where Kylie appears as a singer in the Enchanted Forest's medieval men only club. Talk about typecasting! It was on the set she met future fiancé Joshua Sasse. He is not just the star of *Galavant*, but the subject matter of the song and, boy, did Sasse look good shirtless. 'Off With His Shirt' prances through some of the campiest, gayest, knowingest lyrics ever sung by Kylie (and that's saying something!). Released in mid-2017 on *Galavant: The Complete Collection*, by this stage, Kylie and Sasse had already called off their engagement. Sniffle.

21

Golden Album (2018)

Golden

BMG/Darenote: 538360762
Originally released: April 2018
Standard Edition

'Dancing'	2:58
'Stop Me from Falling'	3:01
'Golden'	3:07
'A Lifetime to Repair'	3:19
'Sincerely Yours'	3:28
'One Last Kiss'	3:41
'Live a Little'	3:07
'Shelby '68'	3:35
'Radio On'	3:42
'Love'	2:52
'Raining Glitter'	3:33
'Music's Too Sad Without You' (With Jack Savoretti)	4:09
Deluxe Edition	
'Lost Without You'	4:04
'Every Little Part of Me'	2:58
'Rollin''	3:32
'Low Blow'	2:56
Streaming Edition	
'Stop Me from Falling' (featuring Gente de Zona)	3:01

'Chirpy Chirpy Cheep Cheep'

Becker Film Group: January 2018 (Australian cinema release) **20th Century Fox:** April 2018 (Australian DVD/Blu-ray) **Movie:** *Swinging Safari*
Writer: Lally Stott
Producers: Marius De Vries, Stephan Elliott

Is 'Chirpy Chirpy Cheep Cheep' the revenge of 'the singing Budgie' at last? Although *Swinging Safari*, the Aussie movie Kylie starred in and this track came from, earned not-so-swinging reviews, Kylie gamely contributed a cover of the ultimate bubble-gum pop hit—a 1971 UK #1 and Australian #2 for Middle of the Road. Writer/director Stephan Elliott's earlier 1994 drag-in-the-desert *Priscilla* movie, incidentally, was originally written full of Kylie songs after Elliott did a deal with Stock Aitken Waterman, then later de-Kylied by its new financiers. Boo.

'Dancing'

BMG: 538360851 **Single release:** January 2018 **Album:** *Golden*
Writers: Kylie, Steve McEwan, Nathan Chapman
Producer: Sky Adams

New label, new sound—here she goes again! For her label debut on BMG, and first album on her own Darenote imprint with Australia's Liberator (formerly Mushroom), Kylie wandered down that old town road towards Dollywood. There are certainly lashings of Dolly Parton's signature sassy country style smothered all over the first single from her fourteenth album. 'When I go out I wanna go out dancing' might be the most Minogue line Kylie has ever sung—and one she had a hand in writing herself—but also the scariest, as she actually does dance with the Grim Reaper at the end of the video. Not only did 'Dancing' set up the *Golden* album for a #1 album debut in the UK and Australia, it became her fifty-first UK hit (certified silver in 2020), was certified gold in Oz, and appropriately was the final song on Kylie's Golden Tour. Mention must also be made of her sparkling performance of 'Dancing' at 2019's Glastonbury Festival in the aptly-named legends slot—the only song from *Golden* to make the set list. 'I got there in the end,' Kylie told Vogue.com through tears in 2020. 'It's not just Glastonbury, it means so much more to me and really was a kind of triumph actually in my personal history.'

Vid Bit!

Director: Sophie Muller

Kylie playing the guitar? Sorry partner, that's only thanks to some clever editing before there is a spot of lasso-laced line dancing. Kylie revealed Muller's pitch for the 'Dancing' video was 'Dolly Parton meets *Day of the Dead*'. It also featured Kylie's debut as a line dancer. Yee-haw!

Remix Fix!

Kylie scored her fourteenth US Dance Club Song #1 with 'Dancing', and much of that was thanks to Illyus & Barrientos. Other remixers in-line were Anton Powers, Initial Talk, and DIMMI.

'Rollin''

Release: January 2018 **Album:** *Golden*
Writers: Kylie, Amy Wadge, Sky Adams
Producer: Sky Adams

The B-side of 'Dancing' and the third Deluxe Edition bonus track on *Golden* was more country/electro to make Taylor Swift quiver in her cowboy boots. 'I know a lot of people were nervous—"What do you mean country?!"—it's a flavour that I love,' Kylie was at pains to point out. The main inspiration behind *Golden*, Kylie revealed to *Rolling Stone*, was 'Dolly! Dolly! Dolly!' She also watched the movie *Coal Miner's Daughter* about Loretta Lynn for inspiration.

'Stop Me from Falling'

BMG: Digital download **Single release:** March 2018 **Album:** *Golden*
Writers: Kylie, Sky Adams, Steve McEwan, Danny Shah
Producer: Sky Adams

Golden's second single, released a month ahead of the album, reached #52 in the UK. Nursing a broken heart (after her three-year romance with Joshua Sasse turned him into another tabloid 'loverat') Kylie took her diary of heartbreak and headed to Nashville, the birthplace of country music. 'It was, in many ways, a great escape,' she told *Marie Claire* magazine. 'I was quite fragile when I started work on it, but being able to express myself in the studio made quick work of regaining my sense of self.' Evidence of her honky-town heartache is all over *Golden*, her most personal album, perhaps even more so than 1997's *Impossible Princess*. 'Stop Me from Falling' is literally Kylie telling herself not to keep getting involved with pretty, shallow men ('One kiss a dangerous situation/I'm lost in hesitation/My heart's a little shaking').

Vid Bit!

Directors: Colin Solal Cardo (First version), Sophie Muller (second version)

The initial cute-if-underwhelming 'Stop Me from Falling' video was filmed at Café de la Danse, Paris, during her *Kylie Presents: Golden* showcase. A second video, sending up Kylie's predilection for male eye candy, was filmed in Havana by Muller for the version featuring Cuban reggaeton band Genta de Zona.

Remix Fix!

For 'Stop Me from Falling' Joe Stone, PBR Streetgang and disco legend Cerrone made folks fall about on dancefloors, while multi-culti hybrid Gente de Zona version had Kylie singing in English and Spanish (*gracias* again, Andrés!).

'Golden'

Single release: May 2018 **Album:** *Golden*
Writers: Kylie, Liz Rose, Lindsay Rimes, Steve McEwan
Producer: Lindsay Rimes

Befittingly 'Golden' was the album of the same name's third single released—momentously and appropriately—on Kylie's very own fiftieth birthday on 28 May that year. Kylie called her album *Golden* because 'on my previous album promotion I was just asked so much about having an answer for being a woman my age in the industry. I do have to rise above that sometimes ... I wanted to have this phrase on the album saying, "We're not young, we're not old, we're golden."' Composer/producer Rimes had just worked on Kane Brown's US big country #1 'Heaven'.

Vid Bit!

Director: Sophie Muller

Filmed on a roof terrace in Havana with, according to Kylie, 'no lights, no crew ... no make-up!'

Remix Fix!

Weiss shifted 'Golden' into classic piano house territory for clubbing instead of line dancing.

'A Lifetime to Repair'

BMG: Digital download **Single release:** August 2018 **Album:** *Golden*
Writers: Kylie, Sky Adams, Danny Shah, Kiris Houston
Producer: Sky Adams

Released as the fourth single from *Golden*, the anthemic 'A Lifetime to Repair' is again Kylie on lyrical fire as if she has been squirrelling away her best material for the past twenty years. She probably had! From its opening 'Cupid don't love me like he used to do/'Cos I'm broken-hearted way too soon', this is Kylie using her creative outlet as therapy. 'A Lifetime to Repair', with banjo and fiddle, also pays homage to country and western's hallowed history of heartache, heartbreak and hoedowns. In an alternate golden age, 'ALTR' would have been a big clubland tune.

Vid Bit!

No official video for 'ALTR', but a cute lyric video (by Halo Jones) with a thang for scrapbooking.

Remix Fix!

Rising Sun added modern anthemic dance vibes to Kylie's country ode to good ole resilience.

'Sincerely Yours'

BMG: Digital download **Single release:** November 2018 **Album:** *Golden*
Writers: Kylie, Jesse Frasure, Amy Wadge
Producers: Jesse Frasure

The sixth and final single from *Golden* (in Oz only), 'Sincerely Yours' was a slow banger Kylie called a love letter to her fans, but alas there was no video, or remix, to support this Australian only release. In 2019, *The Guardian* declared *Golden* 'a reaffirmation of identity: in her personal life, following her split from fiancé Joshua Sasse in 2017; musically, with her relocation to Nashville to record the album with softer country tinges instead of hard dancefloor trim; and psychologically, with its addressing of age'. Frasure worked also with Kacey Musgraves in 2018.

'One Last Kiss'

Release: April 2018 **Album:** *Golden*
Writers: Kylie, Ash Howes, Richard Stannard, Seton Daunt
Producers: Ash Howes, Richard Stannard

The most unashamedly romantic song on *Golden*, 'One Last Kiss' belongs to the great country music tradition of turning heartbreak/heartache into gold, or in this case golden, hits. It did not start out that way however. A year after *Golden* was released Stannard posted a minute's worth of Kylie's original version writing 'here's where "OLK" began before the direction for the album changed.' A big atmospheric synth-pop track that harks back to 'All the Lovers' it would be criminal if this version of 'OLK' never gets released. The full glorious demo leaked in early 2022.

'Live a Little'

Release: April 2018 **Album:** *Golden*
Writers: Kylie, Sky Adams, Danny Shah
Producer: Sky Adams

London-based Nigerian-German producer/songwriter/rapper Adams had previously worked with Effie, Rizzle Kicks, Rochelle, and Zak Abel and went on to work with Doja Cat. Kylie clearly clicked with Adams because not only was he part of the team for her subsequent album, but during 2020's global lockdown was one of the patient people who guided her on how to use, and make the most of, her home studio. 'Live a Little' is more country power-pop bravado about making a great escape that must have set Kylie in good stead for her next romantic adventure.

'Shelby '68'

Release: April 2018 **Album:** *Golden*
Writers: Kylie, Ash Howes, Richard Stannard, Seton Daunt
Producers: Ash Howes, Richard Stannard, Seton Daunt

Landing somewhere between Taylor Swift and Shania Twain, 'Shelby '68' is Kylie realising she just cannot help making bad choices. Kylie told *Rolling Stone* magazine she 'definitely wanted to be truthful to myself and therefore to my fans ... I haven't written a whole album about heartbreak. Just making sure that whatever I am singing is authentic. So something like "Shelby '68"—that's an invented story, but stems from wanting to write something that somehow links to my family. My dad's been a bit of a Mustang maniac his entire life, basically. I played it for my dad and of course he loved it.' Ron Minogue, her dad, was as an accountant for a car company incidentally.

'Radio On'

Release: April 2018 **Album:** *Golden*
Writers: Kylie, Amy Wadge, Jonathan Green
Producer: Jon Green

There is a long tradition in pop, but especially so in country music, for the radio to feature heavily as a recurrent theme. Now in her fifties, the subject of radio play was something of a tinderbox for Kylie and her team. If ageism in the music business is rife, then ageism on the radio is endemic! Kylie had not had a proper radio 'hit' for around a decade, hence the venture into country music territory to try something new. In 2020, talkaboutpopmusic.com ranked all Kylie's albums to date placing *Golden* at #6 (*Fever* was the obvious, if safe, choice at #1), singling the heartfelt 'Radio On' out as one of its 'beautifully raw moments'.

'Love'

Release: April 2018 **Album:** *Golden*
Writers: Kylie, Sky Adams, Steve McEwan
Producer: Sky Adams

'The last thing I'd want is a breakup album,' Kylie informed *Entertainment Weekly* in the midst of promoting *Golden*. 'It's about *me* and about where I find myself at this point in my life!' So where does 'Love' figure in that? It's Kylie kicking up her heels, literally, and realising love is—yes!—'a disco ball'. And all this is on a supposedly country album! '*Golden* is an organic stylistic detour that finds the Aussie pop goddess smack in the middle of a "Dolly Parton/ Disco" Venn diagram,' *Billboard* decreed incisively. 'Oh yes, there will be sequins.'

'Raining Glitter'

BMG: Digital download **Promo track release:** April 2018 **Album:** *Golden*
Writers: Kylie, Alex Smith, Mark Taylor, Eg White
Producers: Alex Smith, Mark Taylor, Eg White

NME called 'Raining Glitter' 'the album's soaring highlight, a total joy and a reminder of Kylie's enormous likeability. This electro-country hoedown oozes fun.' In many ways, 'Raining Glitter' is not only Kylie's eternal mantra—turning pain into sequins—it is her coda to *X*'s 'No More Rain'. A decade after co-writing 'Cosmic' on *X*, White returned for *Golden*'s first promotional single. After initially concluding White's song was 'off brief', it morphed into a disco-country hybrid with Kylie taking inspiration from The Jacksons's 1980 'Can You Feel It' video where glitter rains down on the world. Little wonder *Attitude* described 'RG' in one word as 'fabulous'.

'Music's Too Sad Without You' (With Jack Savoretti)

BMG: Digital download **Single release:** October 2018 **Album:** *Golden*
Writers: Kylie, Jack Savoretti, Samuel Dixon
Producer: Samuel Dixon

While plenty of real heartache and sadness went into *Golden*, as with any great country record, by the time of the album's release, Kylie debuted her new romance with Paul Solomons, creative directive of British *GQ*. 'Music's Too Sad Without You' was released in October as the final international single from *Golden*. Originally, the bizarre plan was for Kylie and British singer Savoretti to record a version of Boney M's 1979 hit 'Rivers of Babylon' for a soundtrack. 'I wanted to write this song and had in mind Edith Piaf. Hers was a life full of heartbreak and challenges,' Savoretti told *The Evening Standard*, 'so I just wanted to get Kylie to sing a really, really sad song.' The swoonsome 'Music's Too Sad Without You' garnered some airplay, later appearing on Savoretti's #1 UK album, *Singing to Strangers*, in a live version recorded in Venice.

Vid Bit!

Director: Joe Connor

Filmed at Venice's Teatro La Fenice, Kylie vamps it up solo in an empty cinema seat in a deserted theatre as a lonely Savoretti strums his guitar presumably somewhere else in the building and the two never meet. Did this director never see the ending of 'Especially for You'?

'Lost Without You'

Release: April 2018 **Album:** *Golden*
Writers: Kylie, Jonathan Green
Producer: Jon Green, Charlie Russell

Moving into Deluxe Edition terrain with the stirring 'Lost Without You', Kylie recalled that when she 'gently meandered back into the studio, one of my longtime producers said, "if you can think of some sort of country angle or influence" ... for better or worse, I'm always happy to try anything, so I immediately said, "Sure" ... and then there was the suggestion to go to Nashville ... I'd never been, and it just made total sense. All "glitter and tears", just like the lyrics of "Lost Without You"!'

'Every Little Part of Me'

Release: April 2018 **Album:** *Golden*
Writers: Kylie, Amy Wadge, Sky Adams
Producer: Sky Adams

The second bonus track—*Aphrodite*-meets-electro-country—came courtesy of Adams. 'Avicii's "Wake Me Up" opened people's minds to country music in electronic music,' Adams explained. Wadge, who spent a week in Nashville writing tunes with Kylie, is a Welsh singer/songwriter who paid off her mortgage co-writing the Grammy-winning 'Thinking Out Loud' for Ed Sheeran. She co-wrote 'Every Little Part of Me' and three other *Golden* songs (plus one for Kasey Musgraves's Album of the Year Grammy winner, *Golden Hour*, the same year). 'Country tells a story within a song,' she maintained, 'so you don't have to play tricks with the audience.'

'Low Blow'

Release: April 2018 **Album:** *Golden*
Writers: Kylie, Danny Shah, Sky Adams, Steve McEwan
Producer: Sky Adams

The final track from the *Golden* project, 'Low Blow' tells it like is country-style—'Swingin' your lasso at my rodeo/You're pullin' me in with another low blow'. Asked if it had been a difficult experience recording the album after a break-up, Kylie replied, 'I was just a bit broken. I needed to get a few songs out, get the words out of my system.' In an Australian TV interview, Kylie further admitted, 'I had just been through a bit of a rotten time.' Her interviewer told Kylie to 'stop dating incredibly good-looking dickheads.' Talk about a low blow. Sheesh.

'What You Waiting For' (Sigala Featuring Kylie Minogue)

Ministry of Sound: 88985497362 **Release:** September 2018 **Album:** *Brighter Days*
Writers: Bruce Fielder, Gina Kushka, Jason Pebworth, George Astasio, Jonathan Shave
Producer: Sigala

Released in September 2018, *Brighter Day* was the debut album for British DJ and producer Felder, aka Sigala, featuring some big names—Paloma Faith, Craig David, John Newman, The Vamps, and plenty more. Kylie's track, pounding roof-raiser 'What You Waiting For', was one of only six out of sixteen songs on the album that failed to get a single release with six going Top 10 in the UK. That was probably due to record company politics, it can only be assumed. There was a lyric video, but Fielder informed the UK's Official Charts site his favourite track on the album was 'probably the Kylie collaboration'. Understandable, really.

22

Step Back in Time: The Definitive Collection Compilation (2019)

Step Back in Time: The Definitive Collection

BMG/Darenote: BMGCAT385DCD
Originally released: June 2019
Disc One

'Can't Get You Out of My Head'	3:50
'Spinning Around'	3:27
'Love at First Sight'	3:58
'Dancing'	2:58
'In Your Eyes'	3:17
'Slow'	3:13
'All the Lovers'	3:20
'I Believe in You'	3:20
'In My Arms'	3:31
'On a Night Like This'	3:32
'Your Disco Needs You'	3:32
'Please Stay'	4:05
'2 Hearts'	2:53
'Red Blooded Woman'	4:20
'The One'	4:04
'Come into My World'	4:06
'Wow'	3:12
'Get Outta My Way'	3:39
'Timebomb'	2:57
'Kids'	4:20
'Stop Me from Falling'	3:01

'New York City'	3:20
Disc Two	
'Step Back in Time'	3:05
'Better the Devil You Know'	3:52
'Hand on Your Heart'	3:50
'Wouldn't Change a Thing'	3:12
'Shocked' (DNA 7″ Mix)	3:08
'Especially for You'	3:58
'I Should Be So Lucky'	3:22
'Celebration'	3:57
'The Loco-Motion' (7″ Mix)	3:13
'Give Me Just a Little More Time'	3:06
'Never Too Late'	3:20
'Got to Be Certain'	3:20
'Tears on My Pillow'	2:28
'Je ne sais pas pourquoi'	4:02
'What Kind of Fool (Heard All That Before)'	3:44
'What Do I Have to Do' (7″ Mix)	3:34
'Confide in Me'	4:26
'Breathe'	3:40
'Put Yourself in My Place'	4:13
'Where the Wild Roses Grow'	3:57

'New York City'

BMG: Digital download **Single release:** May 2019 **Compilation:** *Step Back in Time: The Definitive Collection*
Writers: Kylie, Daniel Stein, Karen Poole, Myles MacInnes
Producer: DJ Fresh

'New York City' was the single/one new track from *Step Back in Time: The Definitive Collection*. A two-disc affair in its standard version and three for the expanded edition of 'pop precision since 1987', it returned Kylie to the #1 spot on the album charts in the UK and Australia (and #32 in the US). The dancefloor igniting 'NYC', featuring a sample from Mylo's 'Drop the Pressure', was written during the *Golden* sessions, but dropped because it did not fit the country theme. Although 'NYC' unfathomably failed to chart, *Billboard* anointed it an 'irresistibly joyous ode to sowing wild oats in the Big Apple'. It also provided a preview of what Kylie planned next.

Vid Bit!

Director: Blink Inc. (Tour Footage)

Within the first five seconds, there is a mirror ball, a Studio 54 sign, and Kylie in a slinky dress slit up to her waist amid a chant of 'I want the first plane to New York'. Gaystarnews.com confirmed 'it makes all other music videos look like a PTA meeting'.

Remix Fix!

The sparkling DJ Fresh Edit chopped this Big Apple ode to a way too-brief three minutes.

'Step Back in Time' (Mousse T's Remixes)

BMG: Digital download **Single release:** July 2019
Writers/Producers: Stock Aitken Waterman
Remixer: Mousse T

German house producer/remixer Mousse T was brought in to remix 1990's classic 'Step Back in Time' to promote the compilation album of the same name, *Step Back in Time: The Definitive Collection.* A digital release of four Mousse T mixes also came with the original 'SBIT'. Kylie and Mousse T made a perfectly classic shizzling match made in disco heaven, but it fizzled after this.

'Really Don't Like U' (Tove Lo Featuring Kylie Minogue)

Universal Music AB: 00602508064999 **Single release:** September 2019 **Album:** *Sunshine Kitty*
Writers: Ebba Nilsson, Caroline Ailin, Ian Kirkpatrick
Producer: Ian Kirkpatrick

This scintillating pop jam between Kylie and Swedish pop maverick Nilsson, aka Tove Lo, featured on her third album *Sunshine Kitty*. After meeting Kylie at an AIDS benefit in Hong Kong, Tove decided, 'once I felt I had the perfect song to share with her I just hoped she would love it and want to do her magical thing to it. She did and I couldn't be more thrilled and honoured to have someone I love and respect so much on this track.' 'Really Don't Like U' was a Top 40 hit in NZ and scraped into the UK download charts at #74. That said, 'Really Don't Like U' was a sure sign Kylie was done with her country music foray.

Vid Bit!

Directors: Natalie O'Moore and Thomas English

Although deemed a lyric video, both Tove and Kylie appear (Tove in Prague and Kylie in London). Surprisingly, it is Tove who bares all the skin with Kylie uncommonly rugged up.

'LAZY' (The Vaccines and Kylie Minogue)

Sony Classical/Milan: 19439704532 **Release:** September 2019 **Soundtrack:** *A Shaun the Sheep Movie: Farmageddon (Original Motion Picture Soundtrack)*
Writers: Freddie Cowan, Árni Árnason, Justin Hayward-Young, Timothy Lanham, Yoann Intonti, Cole Marsden Greif Neill
Producers: The Vaccines

Lock up your impossible princesses, IndieKylie is back for a brief surf rock jaunt from animated sci-fi comedy *A Shaun the Sheep Movie: Farmageddon*. Kylie and The Vaccines had both appeared at Glastonbury earlier that year. 'We love Kylie and love Aardman (Studios), both [are] national treasures,' Vaccines' singer Justin Hayward-Young bleated. An official lyric video for 'LAZY' was created for the movie, which received an Oscar nomination in 2021 for Best Animated Feature Film (losing to Pixar's jazz flick *Soul* with its Jon Batiste score also winning).

'On Oublie Le Reste' (Jenifer featuring Kylie Minogue)

TF1 Musique: 1 78998 43253 5 **Single release:** October 2019 **Album:** *Nouvelle Page*
Writers: Cathy Dennis, Rob Davis, Alain Corson, Barbara Pravi, Boban Apostolov, Manon Palmer
Producer: Bob Sinclar

French singer/songwriter Jenifer did not so much sample as interpolate Kylie's 'Can't Get You Out of My Head' for 'On Oublie Le Reste' ('We forget the rest'). 'This is a collaboration I had been hoping for, for a long time,' Jenifer told French media. 'It was really done with the heart, it's not a simple marketing story.' A music video heavily influenced by Kylie's early noughties videography sadly failed to feature Kylie lip-syncing the 'la-la-la' refrain. While unjustifiably ignored in English-speaking territories, 'On Oublie Le Reste', produced by French DJ/remixer/producer Sinclar, reached #9 on the French sales chart. Ooh la la la!

'F9 Megamix'

BMG: BMGCAT385TCD **Release:** November 2019 **Compilation:** *Step Back in Time: The Definitive Collection* (Expanded Edition)
Tracks: 'Step Back in Time', 'I Should Be So Lucky', 'What Do I Have to Do', 'Hand on Your Heart', 'Better the Devil You Know', 'Shocked' (DNA Mix), 'Step Back in Time', 'Confide in Me', 'On a Night Like This', 'Your Disco Needs You', 'Spinning Around', 'Love at First Sight', 'Can't Get Blue Monday Out Of My Head', 'The One' (Instrumental), 'Slow' (*a cappella*), 'The One', 'All the Lovers', 'Dancing'
Year: 2019
Writers/Producers: *(See previous individual entries)*

Five months after the initial release of *Step Back in Time: The Definitive Collection* an expanded, three-disc set was released for Christmas including 'Into the Blue', 'Chocolate', 'Did It Again', 'Word Is Out', and 'It's No Secret', plus a Freemasons mix of Kylie classics, reminiscent of PWL's SAW-tastic 1993 *50+1 Non Stop History* mix album. The Minimix ran for 7:16, while the Megamix was a huge 40:33. Why Freemasons & Kylie never collab-ed properly is a mega-mystery.

23

The *Disco* & *Guest List Edition* Albums (2020–2021)

Disco

BMG/Darenote: 4050538633979
Originally released: November 2020
Tracklisting

'Magic'	4:10
'Miss a Thing'	3:56
'Real Groove'	3:14
'Monday Blues'	3:09
'Supernova'	3:17
'Say Something'	3:32
'Last Chance'	3:03
'I Love It'	3:50
'Where Does The DJ Go?'	3:01
'Dancefloor Darling'	3:12
'Unstoppable'	3:34
'Celebrate You'	3:41
Deluxe Edition bonus tracks	
'Till You Love Somebody'	3:02
'Fine Wine'	2:44
'Hey Lonely'	3:28
'Spotlight'	2:42

Disco: Guest List Edition

BMG/Darenote: 4050538701937
Originally released: November 2021
Additional disc added to *Disco* tracklist

'A Second to Midnight' (with Years & Years)	3:27
'Kiss Of Life' (with Jessie Ware)	3:13
'Can't Stop Writing Songs About You' (with Gloria Gaynor)	3:04
'Real Groove' (with Dua Lipa—Studio 2054 Remix)	4:22
'Say Something' (Basement Jaxx Remix)	5:22
'Say Something' (F9 Club Mix)	6:34
'Say Something' (Syn Cole Extended Mix)	4:04
'Magic' (Purple Disco Machine Extended Mix)	5:07
'Real Groove' (with Dua Lipa—Studio 2054 Initial Talk Remix)	3:43
'Dance Floor Darling' (Linslee's Electric Slide Remix)	3:55
Infinite Disco (Audio CD with 'Disco: Guest List Edition'—Deluxe)	
'Magic' (Intro)	1:33
'Come into My World (Interlude)'	0:21
'I Love It'	3:03
'In Your Eyes'	3:05
'Light Years'	2:45
'Supernova'	3:13
'Light Years' (Reprise)	0:33
'I Should Be So Lucky' (Interlude)	0:25
'Dance Floor Darling'	3:17
'All the Lovers (with House Gospel Choir)	3:36
'Say Something' (with House Gospel Choir)	4:00
'Real Groove'	2:54
'Slow'/'Love to Love You Baby'	3:13
'Monday Blues'	3:11
'Where Does the DJ Go?'	2:54
'Love at First Sight'	4:05
'Last Chance'	2:46
'Magic'	4:39

'Say Something'

BMG: Digital download/7″ red vinyl (538642231) **Single release:** July 2020
Album: *Disco*
Writers: Kylie, Ash Howes, Jon Green, Richard Stannard
Producers: Jon Green, Richard 'Biff' Stannard, Duck Blackwell, Kylie

From rhinestones and sawdust to glitter and fairy dust—a new decade brought a new musical direction, although disco has never been too astray from the Minogue gal pals (Dannii's *Club Disco* album being released back in 2007). Kylie previewed her fifteenth studio album *Disco* with 'Say Something', not exactly disco but more 'emotional pop' as she termed it. Saluting Donna Summer's 1982 euphoric 'State of Independence', and 'about the search for and the meaning of love', it was written in September 2019 in Brighton and the first Biffco track in twenty years to be a lead album single. The song's finely honed lyrics said something about Kylie's impressive poetic finesse, with 'Say Something' especially prescient ('we're a million miles apart in a thousand ways') released during a global pandemic. Kylie listed it among her own top five songs alongside 'Slow', 'Love at First Sight', 'Dancing', and—surprise—'The Loco-Motion'. 'Say Something' originally peaked at #82 in the UK and outside Australia's Top 50, but the week of *Disco*'s release hit a new UK peak of #56. *The Guardian* ranked it #15 on their list of Kylie's thirty greatest singles and *Billboard* among their 100 best of 2020.

Vid Bit!

Director: Sophie Muller

Kylie promised 'galactic disco' and did not disappoint. What 'Say Something' lacked in narrative it made up for in '70s iconography, fashionable inspiration from actor/model Marisa Berenson in a striped Halston dress and—ta-dah!—that shiny something extra called tinsel!

Remix Fix!

While Syn Cole and F9 remixes perked up the BPM, Kylie performed a stirring acoustic retake with new vocal (engineered at her home studio) for Mika's I Love Beirut online charity event. A retro-house Basement Jaxx remix turbo-boosted the Super Deluxe Edition of *Disco*.

'Magic'

BMG: Digital download/7″ yellow vinyl (538643871) **Single release:** September 2020 **Album:** *Disco*

Writers: Kylie, Michelle Buzz, Daniel Heløy Davidsen, Peter Wallevik, Teemu Brunila

Producers: PhD

Disco's second single and Kylie's 'perfect intro to the album' was more a melding of a classic '70s vibe pared with a languid '80s R&B groove. Co-writers Davidsen and Wallevik had conjured up 'Get Outta My Way' for Kylie exactly a decade earlier. Recorded at the same time as 'Say Something', 'Magic' 'was a really good starting point for us,' Kylie explained. 'I knew I wanted to make an album that was about the dance floor.' 'Magic' originally peaked at #75 in the UK charts, then went back in at #53 the week of *Disco*'s release, but failed to crack the Australian chart. *Billboard*, however, later ranked it as one of their twenty-five best dance songs of 2020.

Vid Bit!

Director: Sophie Muller

Yes sir, she can boogie! The 'Magic' video found our new Queen of Disco time-warped into NYC's fabled Studio 54 on her intergalactic armchair. Filmed at London's Fabric nightclub, Kylie described it as Mystic Meg crossed with *Lord of the Rings*'s Gandalf and Grace Jones at a disco. Her Paco Rabanne mirror-ball dress was true couture magic.

Remix Fix!

Purple Disco Machine found that magical sweet spot between '70s disco and '80s house!

'I Love It'

BMG: Digital download **Promo track release:** October 2020 **Album:** *Disco*
Writers: Kylie, Richard 'Biff' Stannard, Duck Blackwell
Producers: Richard 'Biff' Stannard, Duck Blackwell, Kylie

The first promotional track from *Disco*, the swirling '70s lovin' 'I Love It'—inspired by Lionel Richie's 'All Night Long (All Night)' from 1983—was released a fortnight ahead of the album (exactly thirty years since 'Step Back in Time' in 1990). Co-writer Biff tweeted he was 'proud of this one'. With two further additions to the Kylie catalogue, Biff now tallied up some twenty recordings over twenty years for Kylie. 'I've worked on every record since *Light Years*,' he told BBC Radio. 'I Love It' had its big loved-up gay moment in early 2022 when used for a 'lip sync for your life' battle on Season 14 of *RuPaul's Drag Race*.

'Cool'

Apple Music/iTunes: Digital download **Release:** October 2020 **EP:** *At Home with Kylie Minogue: The Session*
Writers: Troye Sivan, Alex Hope
Producers: Jon Green, Teemu Brunila

A week before *Disco* dropped, Kylie issued a three-track digital EP, *At Home with Kylie Minogue: The Session,* on Apple Music/iTunes. The trifecta consisted of cosy bedroom renditions of 'Say Something', 'Magic', and a duvet day cover of fellow Aussie Sivan's 'Cool'. A track on the openly gay pop star/movie star's 2015 debut album *Blue Neighbourhood*, Sivan and co-author/fellow Aussie Hope penned the effortlessly 'Cool' about LA. 'I love the way Troye uses '80s influences and soft synth-pop tones in the original,' Kylie clarified, 'and, of course, I'm really happy to be covering a track from such a talented, young Aussie artist!' Sivan understatedly declared Kylie's 'Cool' cover 'the greatest thing that's ever happened'.

'Miss a Thing'

Release: November 2020 **Album:** *Disco*
Writers: Kylie, Ally Ahern, Teemu Brunila, Nico Johann 'Stadi' Hartikainen
Producers: Teemu Brunila, Nico Johann 'Stadi' Hartikainen

With *Disco* mostly written/recorded during a period of self-isolation, Kylie reasoned 'the songs that are pure escapism have even stronger purpose'. Thus, the roller-disco ripe 'Miss a Thing' was 'a heady mix of nostalgic and futuristic disco', according to Miss Thang. While no one could actually attend a disco during lockdown, they did not need to miss a thing because Kylie was providing it for everyone's kitchen, lounge, or bedroom. 'I've reached the conclusion that a disco can be anywhere,' Kylie spluttered, 'but ultimately the best place for a disco is when it involves moving furniture.' *Disco* proved a huge critical and commercial hit (not miss), reaching #1 in the UK (outselling Dua Lipa and Lady Gaga for best first week 2020 tally), #1 in Australia (her seventh), and #26 in the US (her third highest ranking ever there). The super-catchy 'Miss a Thing', meanwhile, seemed a missed single thing.

'Real Groove'

BMG: Digital download/7" green vinyl (538666960) **Single release:** December 2020/April 2021 **Album:** *Disco*
Writers: Kylie, Alida Gaprestad, Teemu Brunila, Nico 'Stadi' Hartikainen
Producers: Teemu Brunila, Nico Johann 'Stadi' Hartikainen

Really groovy third single 'Real Groove' initially took time to perfect until Kylie sourced its 'sweet spot'. *The Independent* noted both the irresistible 'Real Groove' and 'Dance Floor Darling' mix 'shameless vocoder' with Daft Punk-esque undertones. 'It's grown-up disco,' Kylie told *GQ*. Kylie warbled 'Real Groove' alongside a hero-worshipping Dua Lipa during the popette's Studio 2054 global streaming concert, their version creeping into the UK Top 100 in early 2021.

Vid Bit!

Directors: Michael Baumohl, Roger Yager (original 'On the Go—Live in Japan' footage)

After lauded performances on her *Infinite Disco* showcase and Dua Lipa's Studio 2054 stream, Kylie nixed plans for a 'Real Groove' video to fly home instead to Melbourne to become a quarantine queen with her family, but a clever video curating footage from Kylie's 1989 Japanese tour synced perfectly with Initial Talk's retro remix.

Remix Fix!

Those 'dancing queens', as *Billboard* tagged them, gelled so well on the Studio 2054 global stream a KyliexDua retake got its groove on for a NYE single release. The 7″ lime green vinyl 'Real Groove' single featured the KyliexDua remix as its B-side. An EP containing the original version, Dua duet, plus Cheap Cuts and Claus Neonors remixes, was issued in January 2021. That really great Initial Talk remix—straight out of SAW's playbook and really good—dropped two months later and was wisely added to 2021's *Disco: Guest List Edition* reboot.

'Monday Blues'

Release: November 2020 **Album:** *Disco*
Writers: Kylie, Linslee Campbell, Maegan Cottone, Daniel Shah, Sky Adams
Producer: Sky Adams

While 2018's *Golden* was written in the midst of heartache, *Disco* was borne of a Kylie love attack both personal ('one second without you is just too long') and professional ('disco ballin' every weekend'). A retelling of 1978's weekender bender 'Thank God It's Friday' originally lumped with a different chorus, Kylie kept hustling on 'Monday Blues' 'until it ended up like this'. During early 2020, she worked with the Adams, Cottone, Campbell, Shah, and Houston dream team in various formations. Songwriter/vocal producer Cottone, aka Megatron, co-wrote ten tunes for *Disco*, seven of which passed muster. She previously composed material for Little Mix who Kylie battled, and defeated—in a chart battle reminiscent of 2001's Kylie 'Can't Get You Out of My Head' *v.* Victoria Beckham for #1 single—for the UK #1 album debut the same week with *Disco*. That was a big win too as it meant Kylie became the first female in history to score a #1 album (her eighth) in five consecutive decades.

'Supernova'

Release: November 2020 **Album:** *Disco*
Writers: Kylie, Maegan Cottone, Sky Adams
Producer: Sky Adams

'Supernova', which shuttles between Cerrone's 1977 'Supernature', Sarah Brightman's 1978 'Starship Trooper' and Kylie's own 'Light Years' (as per her

Infinite Disco performance), blasts off with Kylie giving us what she called 'space voice' on vocoder. Producer/writer Adams (whose son Jupiter is namechecked in the lyrics) insisted his writing team 'poured our hearts and souls into this'. *Disco* wound up garnering super ecstatic, if not the best, reviews of Kylie's illustrious career. *Rolling Stone* dubbed it 'classic disco euphoria as only Kylie knows how', *Billboard* called it 'a glittery throwback to the glorious dancefloors of Studio 54', *Evening Standard* chimed 'Kylie returns with a bang to save 2020', *New York Post* anointed her 'the dancing queen from Down Under', and *Variety* summed it up concisely as 'our disco needed her'. In a Facebook poll, 'Supernova' was voted Kylie fans' favourite as potential third *Disco* single.

'Last Chance'

Release: November 2020 **Album:** *Disco*
Writers: Kylie, Maegan Cottone, Sky Adams
Producer: Sky Adams

'Last Chance', which *Classic Pop* magazine deemed 'almost ABBA-like', since it owes a melodic affinity to the super Swedes' 1979 'Voulez-Vous' hit, also manages to make a Mary Poppins's lyrical reference to 'supercalifragilistic' dancetastic. With its title wink to Donna Summer's 1978 'Last Dance' classic, 'Last Chance' might also be viewed as a comment on Kylie having a last fling at singles chart glory. 'I've had to recalibrate my understanding of success in that way,' Kylie replied when asked if it was strange not having big hits in the streaming age. 'You're just able to let go and let the song do what it's going to do ... success to me right now is being on playlists, being played on radio and just reaching people.'

'Where Does the DJ Go?'

Release: November 2020 **Album:** *Disco*
Writers: Kylie, Daniel Shah, Sky Adams, Kiris Houston
Producers: Sky Adams, Kiris Houston

Kylie not only co-wrote every *Disco* song she engineered them all, bar 'Magic'. 'Kylie the bedroom producer?' she guffawed. 'That story's got legs, but honestly I can just get recorded what needs recording. But that was very satisfying and a means to an end.' The relentlessly euphoric 'Where Does the DJ Go?' ('No other pop star would be quite so considerate!' *NME* appraised in its four-star review) is about the club after-party. Kylie does not want to stop dancing, ever, referencing Gloria Gaynor's 1979's chestnut 'I Will Survive' and updating her own 'So Now Goodbye' from *Light Years*. Gloria later sent Kylie a sweet tweet honey-tonguing 'bless you for keeping #Disco alive'. Not surprisingly, another of GG's disco-era hits is 'Reach Out I'll Be There'.

'Dance Floor Darling'

Promo track release: April 2021 **Album:** *Disco*
Writers: Kylie, Linslee Campbell, Maegan Cottone, Sky Adams
Producer: Sky Adams

Disco's almost fourth single, which Kylie declared her favourite, was an homage to NYC's fabled Studio 54 discotheque featuring Campbell on talk box. The daring delayed tempo surge recalls both Diana Ross' 'Love Hangover' and Donna Summer's 'Dim All the Lights' (which Kylie demoed back in 1985). Kylie's first live performance of any song from *Disco* was showstopper 'Dance Floor Darling' (followed by a discofied 'Can't Get You Out of My Head') at 2021's 'Global Citizen' TV/multimedia concert event. A new Kylie fragrance, Disco Darling, was due in 2022.

Remix Fix!

Campbell's 'Electric Slide Remix', a funky '80s Cameo/Zapp darling, was a fresh drawcard for *Disco: Guest List Edition* released a year after the original *Disco* album.

'Unstoppable'

Release: November 2020 **Album:** *Disco*
Writers: Kylie, Fiona Bevan, Troy Miller
Producer: Troy Miller

Kylie's unshakeable devotion to dance floor fillers was not limited to '70s disco, but also '80s funk courtesy of Prince and the Jackson clan, as 'Unstoppable' showcased. Calling it 'my Diana Ross moment', Kylie composed 'Unstoppable' with Bevan, whose biggest previous claim to fame was penning 'Little Things' with Ed Sheeran for One Direction in 2012, while Miller is someone Kylie described as 'another writer I only know from the waist up on Zoom'. A month after the album's release Bevan revealed she had only earned £100 for co-writing 'Unstoppable'. A lifeblood for Kylie that proved stoppable due to 2020's global lockdown was touring. Instead, she global-streamed *Infinite Disco* (named after her makeshift home studio) the day after the release of *Disco*. The fifty-minute 'sparkly world of dance floor euphoria' roped in Biff Stannard/Steve Anderson to spin *Disco* trax and love to loved-up Kylie classics.

'Celebrate You'

Release: November 2020 **Album:** *Disco*
Writers: Kylie, Maegan Cottone, Daniel Shah, Sky Adams
Producer: Sky Adams

Classic Pop magazine deemed 'Celebrate You' '*Disco*'s perfect finale'. Twenty-eight years after Kylie covered disco evergreen 'Celebration', she partied hard on her own nu-disco nugget about a character called 'Mary'. The last time Kylie was surrounded by a bunch of Marys on record was 1999's 'In Denial'. Although Kylie insisted Mary 'is anyone and everyone who needs reassurance that we are enough and we're loved', this rousing tune rejoiced like a true celebration of her fans—gay, straight, and otherwise—with its uplifting 'everything I like about myself is better with you' refrain. In November 2021, Kylie designed a T-shirt for breast cancer research with an 'I celebrate you' motive, adding a weighty message to her celebratory album closer.

Remix Fix!

'Celebrate You', like the other eleven tracks on the standard album, finally got their extra moment(s) on the superior *Disco: Extended Mixes* double vinyl released in November 2021 tailored to DJs—and cashed-up lovers. It also got a digital release thanks to fan demand.

'Till You Love Somebody'

Release: November 2020 **Album:** *Disco*
Writers: Kylie, Linslee Campbell, Sky Adams, Teemu Brunilla
Producers: Sky Adams, Linslee Campbell

The first of the four *Disco* Deluxe Edition tracks, and 'Magic' B-side, 'Till You Love Somebody' arguably boasts the album's cutest lyric—''cos I'm a better dancer with you'—plus a riff nicked from Chic's good times back catalogue. In mid-2020, *The Guardian* revealed a secret that up to that point only true Kylie fans were privy to—she is, they proclaimed, 'blessed with the perfect pop voice'. On 'Till You Love Somebody', Kylie lives up to this late-coming revelation eliciting a high note rivalling the 'Your Disco Needs You' crescendo some twenty years earlier.

'Fine Wine'

Release: November 2020 **Album:** *Disco*
Writers: Kylie, Maegan Cottone, Sky Adams
Producer: Sky Adams

As a name brand, Kylie has been successful in the realm of perfume, bedding, candles, and, oh yes, music. She even fought off another Kylie (i.e. Jenner) in a major courtroom win in 2019 to legally retain the title of 'the' Kylie. In 2020, she branched out into beverages, hence 'Fine Wine'—which beep-beeps at Donna Summer and strikes a pose with Madonna—is not so much a tribute to Kylie ageing gracefully, like a fine wine, as a subtle form of product placement. Thanks to the success of her Vin de France rosé, debuting in May 2020, kyliewines became one of the most successful plonk launches ever. Cheers, sweetie!

'Hey Lonely'

Release: November 2020 **Album:** *Disco*
Writers: Kylie, Maegan Cottone, Sky Adams
Producer: Sky Adams

The titles of all sixteen *Disco* Deluxe Edition songs were sneakily announced across a dozen social media and digital platforms including Spotify, Instagram, TikTok, Twitter, Facebook, the SayHey Forum (celebrating its fourth decade), Popjustice, and, in the case of 'Hey Lonely', a good old-fashioned email from kylie.com. Is loved-up 'Hey Lonely' where our gal finally lays bare her future nesting plans with *beau* Paul Solomons—'What you doin' for the rest of your life/'Cos I just wanna give you my love'? In 2019, Solomons was introduced to the extended Minogue clan at a party celebrating her surviving grandmother's 100th birthday with Kylie insisting 'he did very well'. Bye, lonely!

'Spotlight'

Release: November 2020 **Album:** *Disco*
Writers: Kylie, Daniel Shah, Kiris Houston, Sky Adams
Producers: Sky Adams, Kiris Houston

The final spin under Kylie's *Disco* glitter ball, 'Spotlight' is suitably uptown retro-electro, but what also came under the spotlight after the album's release was how highly touted collabs with Alex Gaudino and Mirwais Ahmadzaï failed to materialise. 'I'd love to see that track out there someday,' Kylie brooded about Gaudino's effort, 'it's a hidden gem'. Frequent Madonna collaborator Mirwais later announced his third album, *The Retrofuture*, would contain a Kylie contribution. Speaking of Madonna, 'Spotlight' marked the fifth time she and Kylie shared a song title. The others? 'Jump', 'Burning Up', 'Fever', and 'Santa Baby', of course!

'Stop Crying Your Heart Out' (BBC Radio 2 Allstars)

Decca: Digital download **Single release:** November 2020
Writer: Noel Gallagher
Producers: Mark Taylor, Brian Rawling

In the midst of Kylie's *Disco* flurry, she glitter-bombed BBC Children in Need's congested charity single. This twenty-four-artist cover of Oasis's stadium-singalong 'Stop Crying Your Heart Out' also included Cher, (him again!) Robbie Williams, Lenny Kravitz, and Jack Savoretti. 'It was a privilege to take part in this recording with so many amazing artists,' Kylie affirmed of 'SCYHO', which peaked at #7 in the UK. In June 2002, the week before Oasis's original 'SCYHO' debuted at its #2 UK peak, the song it replaced at #2 was Kylie's 'Love at First Sight'. Heartless!

Vid Bit!

Director: Phil Deacon

A socially-distanced video shot outdoors where Kylie and another celeb participant Nile Rodgers briefly share a frame, as well as a windswept Kylie flaunting the view from what might just have been her soon-to-be-vacated London balcony. All for a good cause, of course.

'Starstruck' (Years & Years—Kylie Minogue Remix)

Polydor: Digital download/CD single 3834984 **Release:** May/June 2021
Writers: Clarence Coffee Jr., Mark Ralph, Nathaniel Ledwidge, Olly Alexander
Producers: DetoNate, Mark Ralph

After Years & Years's original 'Starstruck' struck out at #38 in the UK charts in April 2021, Kylie added star cachet for a remix released a month later (surging it to #31). 'I first got starstruck by Kylie Minogue in 2015 when we supported her show,' Olly Alexander (now sole Y&Y member) recalled, 'then we performed "Better the Devil You Know" at the Royal Albert Hall at Christmas 2016 and then we played right before her iconic Glastonbury performance in 2019. So I asked her if she'd be up for jumping on "Starstruck" and she said yes!' What had been a fine, if pedestrian bop, 'Starstruck' morphed into a striking star vehicle for both Olly and Kylie, superseding Kylie's 'Dancefloor Darling', sent to radio and mooted as the fourth *Disco* single.

Vid Bit!

Director: Fred Rowson

No Kylie in the Years & Years clip as the Olly-as-solo-star clip was completed before their remix was conceived. Better luck next time—and indeed there was a next time and it was better.

Remix Fix!

A limited-edition CD single featuring the Kylie 'Starstruck' revamp, original Y&Y version, a Paul Woolford remix and an acoustic version was issued in early June 2021.

'Marry the Night'

Interscope/Darenote: Digital download **Single release:** June 2021 **Album:** *Born This Way—The Tenth Anniversary* (Lady Gaga)
Writers: Stefani Germanotta, Fernando Garibay
Producers: Richard 'Biff' Stannard, Duck Blackwell

Kylie and Lady Gaga together at last? Almost, lovers and monsters alike! As part of the tenth anniversary edition of Gaga's *Born This Way* album, she commissioned six 'reimagined' versions of her album's original tunes by LGBTQ+ artists/allies including Kylie. 'Marry the Night' was originally the fifth and final single from Gaga's 2011 album and its smallest hit. Kylie's stomping remake of Gaga's 'warrior queen' anthem delivered a steamy hi-NRG feel with obligatory 'Gaga' shout out. The surprise release was also a remarriage of sorts with Kylie collaborator Garibay, last seen in the Kyliesphere in 2015. The collab happened, according to Kylie, when she was asked if she would be interested and 'I'm a megafan of Gaga, so it was a great opportunity.'

'Visiting Hours' (Ed Sheeran)

Asylum/Atlantic: Digital download **Promotional Single release:** August 2021 **Album:** = (Ed Sheeran)
Writers: Ed Sheeran, Amy Wadge, Anthony Clemons, Johnny McDaid, Kim Lang Smith, Michael Pollack, Scott Carter
Producers: Ed Sheeran, Johnny McDaid

In March 2021, at the age of sixty-eight, Kylie's mentor, Oz record label boss and family friend Michael Gudinski, died at home in Melbourne. Kylie was coincidentally in town spending time with her family (having stage-bombed 'the Big G's' 'Sounds Better Together' charity gig the previous weekend). Sheeran wrote the heart-tugging 'Visiting Hours' in Oz in quarantine in memory of Gudinski, previewing it at his memorial (see Appendix II). 'When I was in Australia I sang with Kylie and was hanging with Jimmy Barnes and I said to them, "You guys have to be on the song!"' Sheeran told British radio. Many Kylie lovers were disappointed then that the finished 'Visiting Hours'—released as a promotional single two months ahead of Sheeran's fifth album = (i.e. 'equals')—barely featured a visit from Kylie. 'Visiting Hours' went Top 5 in the UK and Oz, but missed the US top 50.

Vid Bit!

Director: Dan Massie

A 'performance' video with Ed strumming earnestly in a church in front of a choir, but—talk about bad habits!—no set visit from Kylie.

'A Second to Midnight' (Kylie and Years & Years)

BMG/Darenote: Digital download/Y9CDKM03 (CD single) **Single release:** October 2021 **Album:** *Disco: Guest List Edition*
Writers: Kylie, Olly Alexander, Martin Sjølie, Richard 'Biff' Stannard, Duck Blackwell
Producers: Richard 'Biff' Stannard, Duck Blackwell

A year after Kylie stepped back in time for her *Disco* revival the boogie fever continued with its *Guest List Edition*. The reissue came in a variety of collectible formats—a double CD, three LPs, and a colossal five-disc set comprising three CDs/two DVDs (of her dazzling Infinite Disco streamed show). Debuting a month ahead of the revamped album, the timely 'A Second to Midnight' was released the same day Kylie announced she was moving back to Australia (#KEXIT). Kylie's second Years & Years collab within six months was the first of three new tracks, all featuring a guest, hence that VIP album title. This retro disco banger which references 1999 (when Olly was a child!) was a decidedly dancier tune than any of the preceding *Disco* singles. All three new singles/tracks bolstered *Disco: Guest List Edition* to #10 UK and #7 in Oz. Both Kylie/Y&Y collabs appeared on a special edition of Years & Years's 2022 *Night Call* album, which went to #1 in the UK.

Vid Bit!

Director: Sophie Muller

Shot in London's Collins' Music Hall, the *NME* dubbed this video, which manoeuvres some swift drag switches between Kylie and Olly, 'dazzling'. It also gave a faux fur fashion nod to 'What Do I Have to Do' and—la la la—the formation dancing of 'Can't Get You Out of My Head'. Little wonder Olly decreed he 'literally had the best time ever making this with Kylie'. Kylie's response? 'I had so much fun channelling my inner Olly in this video—felt like a king.'

Remix Fix!

Not official, but Sakgra's Extended Remix is the best SAW remake since Initial Talk's retake! A throbbing official remix by British drag icon Jodie Harsh appeared on New Year's Eve 2021.

'Kiss of Life' (Kylie and Jessie Ware)

BMG/Darenote: Digital download **Single release:** October 2021
Album: *Disco: Guest List Edition*
Writers: Kylie, Jessie Ware, James Ford, Danny Parker, Alexandra 'Shungudzo' Govere
Producer: James Ford

British singer/songwriter Ware is a life-long Minogue superfan. 'Kylie was the first gig I ever went to when I was six,' she told this author in 2021. 'Kylie and Jason Donovan were my first cassettes.' After feeling the love on Ware's food podcast, *Table Manners*, J'n'K made beautiful music together with the delicious, cherry-syruped, Chic-esque second *Disco: Guest List Edition* single, released two weeks ahead of the album. 'Kiss of Life', more Jessie inviting Kylie into her nu-disco musical realm than the other way around, was deemed 'sumptuous' by *The New York Times*. In late 2021, the ASCAP songwriting register reportedly added nine further titles composed by Kylie and Jessie ('So Small Minded', 'From the Darkness', 'Just a Man', 'It's All Over Now', 'Remember When', 'There but for a Good Time', 'On the Road', 'Living Life', and 'Respect You'll Never Gain'). Talk about kissed, er, blessed with a life of workaholism!

Vid Bit!

Director: Sophie Muller

Pucker up for the long-overdue return of camp Kylie in blonde wig giving *Devil Wears Prada* realness shot on a 1980s news camera. London's stylish Ave Mario restaurant hosts a 'five-star' fashion/Almodóvar pastiche involving food porn, false limbs, and fake facial hair. It must have been a hoot to film and thanks to the final few seconds (Kylie as restaurant critic) makes sense. Kind of.

'Can't Stop Writing Songs About You' (Kylie and Gloria Gaynor)

Release: November 2021 **Album:** *Disco: Guest List Edition*
Writers: Peter Wallevik, Daniel Davidsen, Iain James, Sinéad Harnett
Producer: PhD

After giving Gloria Gaynor's 1979 anthemic 'I Will Survive' a wink in 'Where Does the DJ Go?', and the pair engaging in a torrid social media love-in, a duet was virtually inevitable between these disco-lovin' divas. 'Can't Stop Writing Songs About You', recorded while Kylie was in Australia and then seventy-eight-year-old 'First Lady of Disco' Gloria in the US, was the final new *Guest List Edition* cut. Prior to the release of their instant earworm Kylie let slip the one song which always gets her on the dancefloor is GG's 'I Will Survive'. 'You have to!'

she exclaimed. 'It would be rude and inconsiderate not to dance to that.' Fun fact: both Kylie and Gloria began working with SAW in 1987.

Vid Bit!

Director: Sophie Muller (rumoured)

Kylie and Gloria were not actually in the same frame at the same time as 'it was recorded remotely and I was in touch with her on Zoom when she was shooting her part,' Kylie told BBC Radio 2, 'but [she is] absolutely legendary—I was like a preschooler.' She later cooed to Australian radio 'the fact [Gloria] knows my name still blows my mind.' As of early March 2022, the 'Can't Stop Writing Songs About You' video remains unseen and unreleased.

Appendix I

Kylie Completists: 'Through the Years'

While there may be more demos and rarities to add to this list, here is a roughly comprehensive guide to date of what 'Kylie completists' need to attain some kind of bliss!

1985

'New Attitude', 'Dim All the Lights', 'Just Once': Demos of Patti LaBelle's 'New Attitude', Quincy Jones/James Ingram's 'Just Once', and Donna Summer's 'Dim All the Lights' recorded with Greg Petherick, the musical director of *Young Talent Time*, the Australian TV show sung for kids by kids, including sister Danielle. During a 2020 lockdown clear-out, Kylie finally unearthed the cassette. Describing her voice as 'tiny', she called it 'a demo tape more for acting—if a production needed someone who could sing I could hand it over ... I'm singing so high and I could have chosen easier songs!'

1986

'Sisters Are Doin' It for Themselves' (with Dannii Minogue): Big-haired duet with (renamed) sister Dannii of Eurythmics/Aretha Franklin 1985 hit, during *Young Talent Time*. Later released as part of a Universal Australia DVD *The Young Talent Team: Young Talent Time—The Collection* in 2003. Even better—available online now!

1987

'Endless Love' (with Jason Donovan): *Young Talent Time* duet of 1981 Lionel Richie/Diana Ross #1 hit

'Twist My Arm'/'No One Is to Blame' (with Dannii Minogue and Jason Donovan): Kylie, Dannii, and Jason team up for *YTT*'s anti-drug concert in Melbourne. Dannii and Kylie perform Pointer Sisters's 1985 hit 'Twist My Arm', before Kylie and then *Neighbours* co-star/real-life boyfriend Donovan duet on Howard Jones's 1986 hit 'No One Is to Blame'.

1988

'Goin' Back to School' (Kylie Mole and Kylie Minogue): Mole (Mary-Anne Fahey) was a character on Australia's *The Comedy Company* TV show

1990

'Suicide Blonde' (INXS): First single from INXS *X* album. Kylie confirmed in 2020 the title came from her talking to then-boyfriend Michael Hutchence about her character in *The Delinquents*. 'Suicide Blonde' hit #2 in Oz, #9 in the US, and #11 in the UK.

1992

'Baby Doll' (Prince): 'My musical crush since my teenage years,' Kylie posted in May 2016 after Prince's death. 'I met Prince after his concert at London's Earl's Court in 1992. I said I would love to work with him and he said, come visit the studio. He asked me where my lyrics were and where I would like my mic set up. Joking with me. I did end up giving him lyrics for a song called "Baby Doll". His driver delivered a cassette to me later that night. It was a demo of Prince singing and playing the song "Baby Doll" he had written using the lyrics. We never recorded it properly. I then had the privilege of visiting Paisley Park. It was a dream come true. Thank you for the music and memories.'

1994

Kylie Minogue (Demos)

'At the End of the Day': Leaked in 2014. Despite a great Kylie vocal and cool trumpet break true B-side material

'Aston Martin': Goofy, groovy baby retro pastiche ('perfect jazz for some romance') that splutters out of gas.

'Automatic Love': Unashamedly more pop-dance/commercial version than the *Kylie Minogue* version.

'Difficult by Design': (See entry in Chapter 10.)

'For All I'm Worth': Starts out as a jazzy piano number before settling down to an average pop-house track.

'Gotta Move On': (See entry in Chapter 10.)

'Living for Your Loving': Another case of great production but a not-so-great song, though we are living for that chorus.

'Love Is on the Line': Catchy, techno-lite track by Kylie/Rapino Bros passed to 'Polish Kylie' Edyta Górniak

'Our Lovin''/'Light I Was Looking For': Kylie gets her funky disco groove on. Later given to Czech artist Dara Rolins.

'When Are You Coming Home': Saint Etienne's other song described as 'too much like (British TV sport show) *Grandstand*'.

1997

Impossible Princess (Demos)

'You're the One': Guitar-driven lovesick IndieKylie BIR collab that leaked then debuted on 2012's Anti Tour.

'Free': (See entry in Chapter 9.)

'Still Your Face Comes Shining Through' (with Nick Cave): Mournful duet with Nick Cave about 'the fine art of peeling grapes' intended for *Impossible Princess* that has leaked.

'Soon': Kylie's lyrics put to music by Nick Cave in a 'roaring ballad' that remains unreleased, as do others of the thirty-plus tracks written for *Impossible Princess*.

'So In Love with Yourself' (Dannii Minogue): Track from Disco Dannii's 1997 *Girl* album with Kylie on background vocals by the Metro team. For Kylie's first songwriting credit, dig out the Janet Jackson-esque 'Love Traffic' from Dannii's debut album *Dannii* (Oz, 1990), repackaged as Love and Kisses (UK, 1991).

'Misfit': Kylie is naked (back to the camera) in this BBC film by Sam Taylor-Wood voicing 'Incipit Lamentatio' as sung by Alessandro Moreschi, the last known recording of a castrato in 1904.

1998

'Should I Stay or Should I Go?': (See entry in Appendix II.)

'Into My Arms': Kylie covers this Nick Cave classic at the Australasian Performing Rights Association (APRA) Music Awards in Sydney.

2000

'Alice in Wonderland': Kylie reads Lewis Carroll's classic to a trippy backdrop produced by Paul Oakenfold for his *Urban Soundtrack* series. The eighty-minute reading was posted online in 2019.

'Always and Forever': Clattering Bond-like theme for ITV soapie *Night and Day* credited to Dave Arch.

2001

'The Sound of Music': Kylie's saucy appearance as the Green (Absinthe) Fairy in the *Moulin Rouge!* movie.

Fever (Demos)

Besides the following, other titles mentioned are 'Finders Keepers' and 'When I Lost You'.

'So High': Meandering melancholy track by Kylie with producers Pascal Gabriel and Paul Statham.

'Feels So Good': Poptastic Kylie/Steve Anderson track given to Atomic Kitten for their UK #1 album in 2001.

'Music Will Always Love You': Sub-par if serviceable pop-dance demo.

'No Better Love': Rather intoxicating, like the lyrics spell out, which leaked in 2014.

'Alone Again': Haunting ballad by Madonna and Rick Nowels sung by Kylie in 2007's *White Diamond* doco.

2002

'Light Years'/'I Feel Love': Superlative leaked studio mashup performed live on KylieFever2002 tour.

2003

City Games (Mighty real or really a fake?)

Prior to the release of *Body Language*, a track listing and writing credits for what was claimed to be Kylie's new album leaked with the title *City Games*. Three of the twelve songs were later released ('Slow', 'City Games', and 'You Make Me Feel').

'E-Z St': Written by Pharrell Williams, Chad Hugo, Stevie Wonder, and produced by Williams.

'In the Dark': Written by Kylie, Emilíana Torrini, Dan Carey, and produced by Torrini/Carey.

'How Can You Say No?': Written by Kylie, Dannii Minogue, Kurtis Mantronik, and produced by Mantronik.

'Second Thoughts': Written and produced by TommyD and Marius de Vries.

'Heavy Handed': Written by Kylie, Cathy Dennis, Kurtis Mantronik, and produced by Mantronik.

'Fly': Written by Kylie, Kurtis Mantronik, Nickolas Ashford, Valerie Simpson, and produced by Mantronik.

'Attention Seeker': Written by Kylie, Richard Stannard, Julian Gallagher, Dave Morgan, and produced by Stannard and Gallagher (Stannard posted a twenty-second snippet online years later).

'That Certain Something': Written by Chris Braide and produced by Emilíana Torrini and Dan Carey.

'Beat U': Written by Kylie Minogue and Pharrell Williams and produced by Williams.

Body Language (Demos)

'On the Up': Pop-disco by Johnny Douglas sampling 1980's 'Spacer' hit by Sheila and B. Devotion.

'I'm Just Here for the Music': Fascinating, funky Danielle Brisebois/Wayne Rodriguez cut released by Paula Abdul in 2009.

'I'm Sorry': Nifty pop-dance track written together with Pascal Gabriel and Paul Statham.

'My Image Unlimited': Proto-electro minimalist number written by former pop singer Javine with Dane Bowers, Andrew Frampton, Mark 'Spike' Stent, and Wayne Wilkins.

'Trippin' Me Up': Kylie co-write with Paul Statham/Gabriel Pascal appears aimed at her ex, James Gooding.

'Color My Life': 'Too upbeat for *Body Language*,' Stannard recalled in 2008, 'very fast electro, very Mantronix.' There is a two-minute in-studio recording of this sexy cut currently on the net. Stannard also mentioned—see above—'Attention Seeker' ('another song we love') and 'Do It' ('again probably too upbeat for *Body Language* but very sexy').

2004

'Copacabana': Kylie, aka 'Lola the showgirl', contributes to *Lyric*, a multimedia project from Motorola, where she creates a short film with photographer Nick Knight and Liz Neal for Barry Manilow's campy 'Copacabana' classic.

Ultimate Kylie (Demos)

Another mentioned, unconfirmed, and unleaked track is 'Ooh', likely to be with Scissor Sisters.

'Loving You': CatchyAF Xenomania nugget could easily have been a single contender.

'(Everything) I Know': Minimalist electro number written by Scissor Sisters that leaked to Kylie's annoyance.

'I'm Fascinated': An official ID listing Kylie and Biffco's Stannard and Gallagher as composers exists in the BMG Rights Catalogue.

'Give Me a Reason': An official ID again lists Kylie, Stannard and Gallagher as composers.

Money Can't Buy

Three-track promotional EP given away in US Target stores if you purchased the *Body Language* album. Tracks from the one-off thirteen-song show in London were 'Can't Get You Out of My Head', 'Slow', and 'Red Blooded Woman' all live. On the night itself, Kylie also mashed up 'Breathe' with enduring naughty night-time hit 'Je T'aime').

2007

X (Demos)

(See chapter 14.)

White Diamond (Demos)

'I do hope the songs we recorded for the *White Diamond* soundtrack are released properly one day—all the Blossom Dearie related material,' Steve Anderson said, 'as I am incredibly proud of that work and it includes some of Kylie's finest ever vocals.'

'White Diamond': (See entry in Chapter 15.)

'Try Your Wings': Recorded by Blossom Dearie in 1958, Kylie crooned this jazz standard on *Jools Holland's Annual Hootenanny* in 2010 and later at a show with Rufus Wainwright.

'You Are There': Touching piano ballad by David Frishberg that leaked.

'I Put a Spell On You': Classic Screamin' Jay Hawkins/Nina Simone staple reportedly recorded by Kylie for her jazz record.

'I'm Hip': Along with 'You Are There', the only briefly heard 'new' song on the *White Diamond* soundtrack was this hipster, again by Frishberg, originally made famous by Blossom Dearie.

'Alone Again': (See entry in *Fever* (Demos) above.)

'Singing in My Sleep': In 2007, Jake Shears announced 'Babydaddy and I wrote a song with Kylie called "Singing in My Sleep", which is really atmospheric and dark'.

'X Allmixedup': On 15 December 2007, this mashup single was released on iTunes in Oz containing four songs from *X*—'2 Hearts', 'The One', 'In My Arms', and 'Like a Drug'.

Darling EP

Promotional EP given out at Harrods for the launch of Kylie's perfume of the same name containing three live tracks—'I Believe in You', 'In Your Eyes', and 'Slow'—plus two *X* album tracks—'Loving Days' and 'Burning Up'.

2008

'The Winner Takes It All': (See entry in Chapter 16.)

'Ruffle My Feathers (Everlasting Love)': (See entry in Chapter 14.)

2009

'You Make Me Feel' (Kish Mauve): UK duo's version of the track co-written by Kylie released on their sole *Black Heart* album.

2010

Aphrodite (Demos)

'Broken Hearted (Love, Love, Love)': Torpid dance-rock lite, though Kylie is as effervescent as always.

'Change Your Mind': Mind-bendingly good version of Deadmau5's 'Brazil (2nd Edit)' refashioned for Alexis Jordan as 'Happiness'.

Pink Sparkle

Five-track EP given away in the UK for the launch of Kylie's new perfume of the same name. Tracks were 'Can't Beat the Feeling', 'Go Hard or Go Home', and live NYC recordings of 'Can't Get You Out of My Head', 'Speakerphone', and 'I Believe in You'.

2011

'Pas Si Loin': Spunky Kylie/Biffco co-write for Christophe Willem's *Prismophonic* platinum French album.

2014

Kiss Me Once (Demos)

'Waiting 4 (For) The Sun': Bombastic ballad assumed to be from Alter Ego, Tommy Trash, and The Runners.

'Voodoo': Bouncy, oddball track reportedly by Kylie, Sky Ferreira, and Bloodshy that leaked in 2016.

'Sugar High': A gooey lyrical metaphor about candy demo ('you whet my appetite!').

'Beat of My Heart': Itchy wistful trip-hop about wanting to 'feel how you feel on the skin' that leaked in portions.

'Kyliewood': Messy EDM tune by Sia (and treated vocals by Brooke Candy?) with unquestionably one of the best titles of all time that leaked in 2021.

'God Only Knows' (Impossible Orchestra): Cover of Beach Boys' hit by original band member/songwriter Brian Wilson and a supergroup called Impossible Orchestra. Created to launch BBC Music, it was promoted as a charity booster for Children In Need. A video, directed by François Rousselet, featured Elton John, Pharrell Williams, Chris Martin, Stevie Wonder, and—at last—Kylie in a bubble!

2016

'Disco Symphony': Duet with pal Robbie Williams, which he insists is 'ready for deployment at the correct time'.

'Boys & Girls': Bouncy will.i.am featuring Pia Mia track sampling Kylie and Garibay 's 'Break This Heartbreak', which reached #21 in the UK (certified silver) and #53 in Australia.

2018

'Love Made Me Do It': Underrated co-write by Kylie for English popstress Cheryl which hit #19 in the UK charts.

Golden (Demos)

'(A) Rose Is a Rose': Co-written with Steve McEwan and Eg White excavated by fans from BMI (British Music Industry) site. 'They should all do freelance work for Scotland Yard,' Kylie spluttered.

'To Be Honest': Registered at BMI as written by Kylie, Nathan Chapman, and Steve McEwan.

'What Do You Know': Registered to BMI as written by Kylie, Steve McEwan, and Peter Mark Hammerton.

'World's Greatest Lover': Registered to BMI as written by Kylie, Steve McEwan, and Lindsay Rimes.

'Don't Ever Forget Me': Registered at ASCAP written by Kylie and Karen Poole.

'Dancing': Original Nashville Edit—much more countrified feel than the released version.

'Islands in the Stream'/'SOS': Live take of 1983 Kenny Rogers/Dolly Parton duet with a little of ABBA's 1975 hit too.

'Drip Drop': Slushy track written by Ben Lee and then seven-year-old niece, Jacinta Reuben, and sung by Kylie about rain, which he posted in 2018 after sitting on Lee's hard drive 'for about 15 years'.

2019

'Matesong': Cute, but corny, and clichéd track written by comedian Eddie Perfect for Tourism Australia ad.

'Every Christmas Day' (Saara Aalto): Written by Kylie with Steve Anderson, Richard Stannard, and Ash Howes and left off *Kylie Christmas*.

2021

'Kylie Minogue': Track by UK rapper Len where he boasts he has 'more hits' than KM. He wishes!

2022

'Our Song': In late 2021, it was rumoured Kylie would feature (alongside Demi Lovato, Anitta, Angèle, Burna Boy, and Wonho) on the official FIFA World Cup Qatar 2022 theme song.

Appendix II

Kylie Concerts

With over three decades' worth of tours, a multitude of Minogueness has wound up on stage over the years. Here is a handy, at-your-fingertips guide to the additional material (barring a few extras here and there on individual stops) sung live by Kylie, which wound up either on CD, DVD, or, if we were lucky, lucky, lucky in dodgy hand-cam/smart phone versions on the internet. Important live TV show appearances or performances by Kylie of songs not otherwise recorded, or noted elsewhere, have also been included.

1987

The Mike Walsh Show

'Blame It on the Boogie': Very '80s rendition on Australia midday TV talk show of The Jacksons '70s disco hit later covered by SAW *alumni* Big Fun in 1989. View it on YouTube now!!

1989

Disco In Dream

Kylie's concert debut in October 1989 was a four-date tour of Japan (her Tokyo show held 40,000 fans) and an eight-song setlist notably including non-single/non-album track 'Made In Heaven' (see entry in Chapter 2). An unofficial Brazilian DVD of *On the Go* was released in 2002 and the full laserdisc version is on YouTube. Best bit: someone says 'Kylie you're a legend!' backstage to which she replies, 'In my own lunchtime!'

The Coca-Cola Hitman Roadshow (UK)

Same show, same set list, same month, same year, but different country, different title!

1990

Enjoy Yourself Tour

'My Girl': Cover of The Temptations' 1964 Motown classic by Kylie's backing vocalists.

'Blame It on the Boogie': Cover of The Jacksons' 1978 disco classic.

'ABC': Cover of The Jackson 5's 1970 pop classic.

'Dance to the Music': Cover of 1967 Sly and the Family Stone soul classic.

John Lennon: The Tribute Concert

Kylie's rendition of The Beatles's 1965 hit 'Help!' (also a 1989 hit for SAW colleagues Bananarama) appeared on 1991's *Lennon: A Tribute* VHS from Pickwick label.

1991

Rhythm of Love Tour/Let's Get to It Tour

'Love Train': Cover of The O'Jays's 1973 disco classic.

1994

Sydney Gay & Lesbian Mardi Gras

Kylie's performance of 'What Do I Have to Do' cemented her love affair with her Aussie gay fans.

Don't Forget Your Toothbrush

Cover of Fontella Bass's 1965 'Rescue Me' soul classic (and her own 'Where Is the Feeling?').

1995

Stonewall Equality '95

Cover of 1954 hit 'Sisters' with gal pal Elton John.

1996

Poetry Olympics (London)

Reading of 'I Should Be So Lucky' at Nick Cave's insistence.

1997

Live performance of 'Some Kind of Bliss' with Manic Street Preachers at their London gig (and allegedly 'Little Baby Nothing', which the band wanted to record in 1992 with Kylie).

Some Kind of Kylie (MTV Special)

'Still Your Face Comes Shining Through': Duet with Nick Cave at London's The Jazz Club.

Crown Casino Opening (Melbourne)

Performance with Ray Charles on 'I Can't Stop Loving You'.

1998

Sydney Gay & Lesbian Mardi Gras

Stepping back in time for another PWL classic: 'Better the Devil You Know'.

Intimate and Live

'Take Me with You': (See entry in Chapter 8.)

'Dancing Queen': (See entry in Chapter 9.)

'Free': (See entry in Appendix I.)

'Should I Stay or Should I Go?': Rocktastic cover of The Clash's 1982 hit. Later recorded again with Jools Holland for his 2014's *Sirens of Songs* album (**East West**: 8256181278).

TFI Friday

Bewigged cover of Eurythmics's '80s electropop classics 'Sweet Dreams', 'Love Is a Stranger', and new song 'Happy to Be Here' with Sinéad O'Connor and Natalie Imbruglia, alongside original Eurythmics member Dave Stewart.

Mushroom 25 Live

Kylie popped out of a birthday cake as a geisha to the tune of 'GBI' (see entry in Chapter 9) before singing 'Happy Birthday' to Mushroom boss Michael Gudinski then an eleven-track medley of her hits.

1999

Fox Studios Australia: The Grand Opening

Cover of Marilyn Monroe's 'Diamonds Are a Girl's Best Friend', from the 1953 MM movie *Gentlemen Prefer Blondes*.

Tour of Duty—Concert for the Troops

'Rockin' Robin': Cover of early Michael Jackson solo hit.

'Jingle Bell Rock': Cover of Christmas classic with The Living End.

'Shout': Cover of '60s classic with John Farnham.

'I Still Call Australian Home/You're the Voice/It's a Long Way to the Top/Take a Long Line': Encore medley of Oz rock classics with all artists present at the East Timor concert.

2000

G-A-Y

Cover of classic Culture Club 1983 'Victims' ballad.

Sydney Olympics Closing Ceremony

Cover of ABBA's 'Dancing Queen' (see entry in Chapter 9).

Paralympics Opening Ceremony

Cover of Australian classic bush ballad 'Waltzing Matilda'.

The Frank Skinner Show

Duet with Skinner of 'It May Be Winter Outside', originally by Barry White and Love Unlimited.

2001

An Audience with Ricky Martin

Cover of 'Livin' La Vida Loca' as a duet with Ricky Martin.

On a Night Like This tour

'Physical': Olivia Newton-John cover (see entry in Chapter 10).

'Can't Get You Out of My Head': A new song that seemed ... passable (we're kidding!).

2002

BRIT Awards

Mashup of 'Can't Get Blue Monday Out of My Head'

KylieFever2002

Snippets, elements, and medleys of covers from artists as diverse as Boy George, Massive Attack, and Beethoven.

2003

BRIT Awards

Duet of Blondie's 1981 'Rapture' hit with Justin Timberlake.

Chloe 50th Anniversary Party (Paris)

Covers of Shirley Bassey's 'Big Spender', Blossom Dearie's 'Peel Me a Grape', Peggy Lee's 'Fever', and Nina Simone's 'My Baby Just Cares for Me'.

21

Kylie added her vocals to the score for this production by the Rambert Dance Company.

2004

MusiCares Person of the Year

Cover of The Police's 1983 hit 'Every Breath You Take'.

2005

Showgirl: The Greatest Hits Tour

'Finally': Cover of CeCe Peniston's 1991 dance classic also featured in the *Priscilla* movie

'Such a Good Feeling': Cover of Brothers In Rhythm's 1991 rave hit.

'Over the Rainbow': (See entry in Chapter 13.)

'Love's in Need of Love Today': Cover of Stevie Wonder 1976 album track.

2006

G-A-Y

Post-cancer impromptu rendition of 'Jump to the Beat' with sister Dannii in London.

Showgirl: The Homecoming Tour

'White Diamond': (See entry in Chapter 15.)

'When You Wish Upon a Star': Cover of classic 1940 ballad used in Walt Disney's *Pinocchio*.

'The Only Way Is Up': Cover of Yazz's 1988 hit.

'Rise of the Cybermen': Excerpt from 2006 episode of *Dr Who* BBC series.

'Doctor Who Theme': Cover of Delia Derbyshire's theme to the BBC series.

2007

Cannes Film Festival

Duets of 'Can't Get You Out of My Head' and 'The Loco-Motion' with Sharon Stone for AIDS charity event.

Jools' Annual Hootenanny 2007

'Come On Strong': Cover of 1964 Sammy Davis Jnr's jazz-pop classic.

'Dance Tonight': Duet with Paul McCartney of his then current hit.

2008

SMAP×SMAP

Duet with Japanese boy band SMAP on 'I Should Be So Lucky', '2 Hearts', and 'Can't Get You Out of My Head'.

KylieX2008

'Mickey': Cover of 1981 Toni Basil hit.

'The Love Boat Theme': Cover of cult TV show theme.

'Got to Be Real': Cover of 1978 Cheryl Lynn disco classic.

'Free': (See entry in Appendix I.)

'Rhythm of the Night: Cover of DeBarge 1985 hit.

2009

Sound Relief

Charity cover of default Australian national anthem, 'I Still Call Australia Home'.

Thank You for the Music: A Celebration of the Music of ABBA

'Super Trouper': Very respectful cover of ABBA's 1980 UK #1 hit with beguiled audience.

'When All Is Said and Done': Duet with piano-tinkling Benny Andersson of ABBA's 1981 tune.

For You, for Me (KylieUSA2009)

'Somewhere': Cover of 1957 Stephen Sondheim classic.

'Fascinated': Cover of 1987 Company B dance classic.

'Ride On Time': Cover of 1988 Black Box Italo-house classic.

'Vogue': Cover of Madonna's 1990 signature song.

MTV Day

'Como Un Lobo': Spanish duet with Miguel Bosé of his 1988 hit (translation 'Like a Wolf').

2010

Glastonbury (Scissor Sisters)

(See entry in Chapter 17.)

Last Song of Summer

Duets with Rufus Wainwright of 'Can't Get You Out of My Head', 'Over the Rainbow', Leonard Cohen's 'Hallelujah', Blossom Dearie's 'Try Your Wings', and 'The Loco-Motion'.

PS22 Chorus

Kids choir duet on 'Can't Get You Out of My Head' and 'Put Your Hands Up (If You Feel Love)'.

Jools' Annual Hootenanny

Cover of Blossom Dearie's 'Try Your Wings'.

2011

Aphrodite: Les Folies Tour

'The Birth of Aphrodite': Instrumental introduction.

'There Must Be an Angel (Playing with My Heart)': Cover of Eurythmics's 1985 hit.

'Fanfarra (Despedida)': Cover of Sergio Mendes's 1992 album track.

'Million Dollar Mermaid': Instrumental interlude.

'Devotion': Cover of Hurts's hit with the duo live (and 'Confide in Me').

2012

Sydney Mardi Gras

Back, back, back for a medley of gay-friendly hits!

Anti Tour

'Mighty Rivers': (See entry in Chapter 17.)

'You're the One': (See entry in Appendix I.)

'That's Why They Write Love Songs': Uplifting Steve Anderson/Kylie collab originally debuted live during KylieX2008 tour.

Commonwealth Games Closing Ceremony (Glasgow)

Kylie medley plus standard 'Auld Lang Syne' as show closer.

Diamond Jubilee Concert

Medley of hits for another celebrating queen.

Proms in the Park

Orchestral versions of her hits for the BBC

Hit Factory Live: Christmas Cracker

'Merry Xmas Everybody': Jolly singalong finale to Slade's festive standard at London's SAW tribute concert.

2013

House of Blues Children's Hospital Los Angeles Benefit

Collab with Deadmau5 on 'All the Lovers' and 'Can't Get You Out of My Head' for charity.

2014

Kiss Me Once Tour

'Need You Tonight': Cover of INXS hit as tribute to ex Michael Hutchence.

The Voice UK

Cover of Kaiser Chiefs's 'I Predict a Riot' with fellow *The Voice UK* judges Tom Jones, will.i.am, and Ricky Wilson. Kylie later covered Primal Scream's 'Rocks' and Eurythmics's 'There Must Be an Angel (Playing with My Heart)'.

The Voice Australia/Italy

Cover of The Script's UK #1 'Hall of Fame'. Duet of 'I Was Gonna Cancel' on *The Voice of Italy* and 'Can't Get You Out of My Head' with singing nun Cristina Scuccia. Kylie and the Aussie *Voice* coaches also covered Havana Brown's 'Warrior'.

Coldplay

Live duets of 'Can't Get You Out of My Head' and 'Where the Wild Roses Grow'.

2015

Summer 2015

'Bette Davis Eyes': (See entry in Chapter 19.)

'99 Red Balloons': Cover of 1983 Nena classic.

A Kylie Christmas

'Jingle Bell Rock': Cover of 1957 Bobby Helms hit.

'The Twelve Days of Christmas': Cover of English Christmas carol.

2016

A Kylie Christmas (the sequel!)

'Silent Night': Cover of perennial Christmas evergreen.

'Glacier': Duet with John Grant of his chilly tune after pairing on 'Confide in Me' at A Kylie Christmas.

2018

Golden Tour

'Blue Velvet': Cover of classic hit for both Tony Bennett and Bobby Vinton.

'The Chain': Mashup of Fleetwood Mac's 1977 track from classic *Rumours* album with 'Can't Get You Out of My Head'.

'Being Boiled': Mashup of Human League's 1978 song with 'Slow'.

'Bad Girls': Mashup of Donna Summer's 1979 disco classic with 'The Loco-Motion'.

BBC2 Live in Hyde Park

'Bette Davis Eyes': (See entry in Chapter 19.)

New York Pride

'9 to 5': Cover of Dolly Parton's classic 1980 movie theme.

The Muppets Take the 02

'Mah Nà Mah Nà/The Rainbow Connection': Kylie joins the famous TV/movie puppet gang live in London for renditions of two of their classic tunes. 'Fan cam' footage exists on YouTube.

2019

Kylie's Secret Night (TV Special)

'Suddenly': Brief cover of Angry Anderson hit associated with *Neighbours*' Scott/Charlene wedding.

Summer 2019/2020 (including Brighton Pride)

'Slow' with David Bowie's 'Fashion' and 'The Loco-Motion' with Summer's 'Bad Girls' reprised.

Glastonbury

Duet with Coldplay's Chris Martin on 'Can't Get You Out of My Head' and duet with Nick Cave on 'Where the Wild Roses Grow'.

2020

BBC Radio 2

'September': Cover of Earth, Wind & Fire's disco calendar gal, mashing in 'Spinning Around'.

Infinite Disco

'Love to Love You Baby': Donna Summer's 1975 orgasmic debut mashed with 'Slow'.

Studio 2054

'Electricity': Vague duet of Silk City hit after Kylie stole the show with 'Real Groove' during Dua Lipa's global streaming concert.

Christmas with Delta

'When You Wish Upon a Star': 'Virtual' duet with Delta Goodrem of the 1940 classic usually associated with Disney (see also 2006).

2021

Michael Gudinski State Memorial

'All the Lovers/The Loco-Motion': Heartfelt duets with Ed Sheeran at the Melbourne state funeral for her Oz mentor/boss/buddy.

Global Citizen Live

'Dance Floor Darling/Can't Get You Out of My Head': Twenty-four-hour multimedia music collective initiative to 'defend the planet/defeat poverty'. Kylie's brief set, with a disco-fied 'Can't Get You Out of My Head', was pre-recorded a day earlier in London for some shrewd, planet-friendly PR ahead of the *Disco* repackage

Appendix III

Kylie's Brit Hit List! 'All the Lovers'

Singles

Release date	Title	Peak Position
16.01.1988	'I Should Be So Lucky'	1
14.05.1988	'Got to Be Certain'	2
06.08.1988	'The Loco-Motion'	2
22.10.1988	'Je ne sais pas pourquoi'	2
10.12.1988	'Especially for You' (with Jason Donovan)	1
06.05.1989	'Hand on Your Heart'	1
05.08.1989	'Wouldn't Change a Thing'	2
04.11.1989	'Never Too Late'	4
20.01.1990	'Tears on My Pillow'	1
12.05.1990	'Better the Devil You Know'	2
03.11.1990	'Step Back in Time'	4
02.02.1991	'What Do I Have to Do'	6
01.06.1991	'Shocked'	6
07.09.1991	'Word Is Out'	16
02.11.1991	'If You Were with Me Now' (with Keith Washington)	4
30.11.1991	'Keep On Pumpin' It' (Vision Masters Feat. Tony King and Kylie Minogue)	49
25.01.1992	'Give Me Just a Little More Time'	2
25.04.1992	'Finer Feelings'	11
22.08.1992	'What Kind of Fool'	14
28.11.1992	'Celebration'	20
10.09.1994	'Confide in Me'	2
26.11.1994	'Put Yourself in My Place'	11

22.07.1995	'Where Is the Feeling?'	16
14.10.1995	'Where the Wild Roses Grow' (with Nick Cave)	11
20.09.1997	'Some Kind of Bliss'	22
06.12.1997	'Did It Again'	14
21.03.1998	'Breathe'	14
31.10.1998	'GBI' (Towa Tei Feat Kylie)	63
01.07.2000	'Spinning Around'	1
23.09.2000	'On a Night Like This'	2
21.10.2000	'Kids' (with Robbie Williams)	2
23.12.2000	'Please Stay'	10
29.09.2001	'Can't Get You Out of My Head'	1
02.03.2002	'In Your Eyes'	3
22.06.2002	'Love at First Sight'	2
23.11.2002	'Come into My World'	8
15.11.2003	'Slow'	1
13.03.2004	'Red Blooded Woman'	5
10.07.2004	'Chocolate'	6
18.12.2004	'I Believe in You'	2
09.04.2005	'Giving You Up'	6
17.11.2007	'2 Hearts'	4
29.12.2007	'Wow'	5
26.04.2008	'In My Arms'	10
09.09.2008	'The One'	36
26.06.2010	'All the Lovers'	3
18.09.2010	'Get Outta My Way'	12
20.11.2010	'Better Than Today'	32
22.01.2011	'Higher (with Taio Cruz)'	8
18.06.2011	'Put Your Hands Up (If You Feel Love)'	93
02.06.2012	'Timebomb'	31
10.11.2012	'Flower'	96
22.03.2014	'Into the Blue'	12
24.05.2014	'I Was Gonna Cancel'	59
21.06.2014	'Crystallize'	60
01.02.2018	'Dancing'	38
19.04/2018	'Stop Me from Falling'	52
31.07.2020	'Say Something'	56
02.10.2020	'Magic'	53
01.01.2021	'Santa Baby'	31
08.01.2021	'Real Groove' (KyliexDua Lipa)	95
28.05.2021	'Starstruck' (Kylie Minogue Remix) – Years & Years	31

Albums

16.07.1988	*Kylie*	1
21.10.1989	*Enjoy Yourself*	1
24.11.1990	*Rhythm of Love*	9
26.10.1991	*Let's Get to It*	15
05.09.1992	*Greatest Hits*	1
01.10.1994	*Kylie Minogue*	4
04.04.1998	*Impossible Princess*	10
15.08.1998	*Mixes*	63
07.10.2000	*Light Years*	2
28.10.2000	*Hits+*	41
13.10.2001	*Fever*	1
30.11.2002	*Greatest Hits 87–92*	20
29.11.2003	*Body Language*	6
04.12.2004	*Ultimate Kylie*	4
20.01.2007	*Showgirl: Homecoming Live*	7
08.12.2007	*X*	4
17.01.2009	*Boombox*	28
17.07.2010	*Aphrodite*	1
20.07.2011	*The Albums 2000–2010*	37
10.12.2011	*Aphrodite Les Folies – Live in London*	72
16.06.2012	*The Best Of*	11
10.11.2012	*The Abbey Road Sessions*	2
29.03.2014	*Kiss Me Once*	2
21.02.2015	*Kylie (Repackaged)*	85
21.02.2015	*Enjoy Yourself (Repackaged)*	94
21.02.2015	*Rhythm of Love (Repackaged)*	96
04.04.2015	*Kiss Me Once Live at the SSE Hydro*	26
26.11.2015	*Kylie Christmas*	12
19.04.2018	*Golden*	1
04.10.2018	*Kylie Minogue (Repackaged)*	67
11.07.2019	*Step Back in Time: The Definitive Collection*	1
19.12.2019	*Kylie – Golden – Live In Concert*	23
13.11.2020	*Disco*	1
19.11.2021	*Disco: Guest List Edition*	10

Source: Officialcharts.com

Bibliography
'Got to Be Certain'

Books

Andrews, M., *We Need To Talk: My Life as a Doggone Celebrity Journalist* (UK: Amazon 2012)
Andrews, M., Isaac, C., & Nichols, D., *Pop Life: Inside Smash Hits Australia 1984–2007* (Australia: Affirm Press 2011)
Baker, W., & Minogue, K., *La La La* (UK: Hodder & Stoughton 2002)
Cole, I., *ABBA: Song By Song* (UK: Fonthill Media 2020)
Cooper, K., & Smay, D., *Lost in the Grooves: Scram's Capricious Guide to the Music You Missed* (US: Routledge 2005)
Flynn, P., *Good as You: From Prejudice to Pride—30 Years of Gay Britain* (UK: Random House 2017)
Goodall, N., *Being Davina* (UK: Kings Road Publishing 2007)
Halstead, C., & Cadman, C., *Michael Jackson: The Solo Years* (UK: NGP 2003)
Harding, Dr. P., *Pop Music Production: Manufactured Pop and Boy Bands of the 1990s* (UK: Routledge 2019)
Medina, N., *The Straight Road to Kylie* (UK: Simon Pulse 2007)
Shears, J., *Boys Keep Swinging: A Memoir* (UK: Omnibus Press 2018)
Stanley, B., *Yeah Yeah Yeah: The Story of Modern Pop* (UK: Faber & Faber 2013)
Stanley-Clarke, J., *Kylie – Naked: A Biography* (UK: Andrews 2012)
Todd, M., *Straight Jacket: How to be Gay and Happy* (UK: Bantam 2013)

Interviews

William Baker, Gerry DeVeaux, Jason Donovan, Gloria Gaynor, Calvin Harris, Dannii Minogue, Kylie Minogue, Graham Norton, Jake Shears, Casey Spooner, Jessie Ware, Pete Waterman.

Magazines and Newsletters

Classic Pop Presents: The Hit Factory A Stock Aitken Waterman Special Edition (UK: Anthem 2020), *Roadblock* (SAW/PWL fanzine), *The Kylie Times (issuu.com)*

Sleeve Notes, Audio Tracks, and Documentaries

Aphrodite: Track by Track, Impossible Princess: Track by Track, Mystify: Michael Hutchence, SoundCloud, White Diamond: A Personal Portrait of Kylie Minogue

TV, Radio, News Media, and Record Labels

Attitude, Australian Playboy, Billboard, BBC Music Magazine, Cherry Red Records, *Classic Pop* magazine, *Cleo* magazine, CNBC, *Daily Express, Dazed* magazine, DigitalSpy, Discogs, *DNA* magazine, *Elle* magazine, *Entertainment Weekly, GQ, Good Housekeeping, Instinct, Irish Independent, Jonathan Ross Show, Kath & Kim, Kylie's Secret Night, Loverboy* magazine, *Marie Claire, Metro, Modern Drummer* magazine, MTV, Mushroom Group, Musicstax.com, *Music Week, News Of The World, NME, Number One* magazine, Official Charts, *Paper magazine, Paris Match, Radio Times, Redhanded, Rolling Stone, RuPaul's Drag Race, 60 Minutes, Smash Hits, Songwriter Magazine, Sound On Sound magazine, Spin, Melbourne Sun-Herald, The Advocate, The Guardian, The Independent, The Mirror, The Morning Bulletin, The New Yorker, The New York Times, Times of India, The Observer, The One Show, The Telegraph, The Times/The Sunday Times, The Los Angeles Times, TIME magazine, Time Out, Top Of The Pops, TV Week, Vice*

Websites, Blogs, and Podcasts

Albumconfessions.com, BBC.com, blogcritics.org, BMI, Discogs, dontstopthepop.blogspot, easysonglicensing, entertainment-focus.com, eqmusicblog, idolator.com, imdb.com, intothepopvoid.com, Joseph Kahn (Twitter), kylie.com, kylie.org.uk, kylie.sosugary.com, kylie Minogue Universe (Facebook), Kylie – The World Still Turns (Facebook), kylieminogue.fandom.com, Kyliepedia (Kylie Wiki), Kylieworld, lessharma.com, hotpress.com, louderthanwar.com, loveispop.com, madonna.com, mail.kylie.org.uk, mixkylie.co.uk, muumuse, myfizzypop, news.com.au, Perth Now, philharding.co.uk, Pop Justice, PopMatters, pwl-empire.com, randomjpop.blogspot, retropopmagazine.com, sayhey.co.uk, shots.net, songwriteruniverse.com, stockaitkenlovethis.itgo.com, talkaboutpopmusic.com, talkhouse.com, The Diminutive Collection podcast, The Huffington Post, The National Student, The Quietus, thewrap.com, Ultimate SAW Facebook Group, vevo.com, vfxblog.com,. Whosampled.com, Wigglepedia, Wikipedia, YouTube